REPEATING OURSELVES

REPEATING OURSELVES

AMERICAN MINIMAL MUSIC
AS CULTURAL PRACTICE

Robert Fink

UNIVERSITY OF CALIFORNIA PRESS

BERKELEY   LOS ANGELES   LONDON

University of California Press
Berkeley and Los Angeles, California

University of California Press, Ltd.
London, England

Fink, Robert.
 Repeating ourselves : American minimal music as
cultural practice / Robert Fink.
  p. cm.
 Includes bibiographical references (p.) and index.
 ISBN 0-520-24036-7 (cloth : alk. paper) —
ISBN 0-520-24550-4 (pbk : alk. paper)
  1. Minimal music — History and criticism.
 2. Music — Social aspects. I. Title.
 ML197.F54 2005
 781.3 — dc22   2005006616

14 13 12 11 10 09 08 07 06 05
10 9 8 7 6 5 4 3 2 1

The publisher gratefully acknowledges the generous
contribution to this book provided by the Lloyd Hibberd
Publication Endowment Fund of the American
Musicological Society.

Contents

Preface

By custom and precedent, the cover of this book should have been a smooth, uniform gray, white, or black broken only by contrasting lettering, preferably lowercase, in an unobtrusive sans serif type. If an image on the cover were needed, it ought to have been a carefully lit art object of reductive purity — perhaps a dark pinstripe painting by Frank Stella, one of Dan Flavin's cool fluorescent-bulb installations, or an assembly of metallic boxes by Donald Judd.[1] The word *minimalism* tends to elicit a generic "tasteful" response from designers and typographers; its once dangerous asceticism has, as Edward Strickland lamented in his own gray-jacketed monograph, become a graphic cliché.[2]

Cliché or not, the formalized emptiness that defines most book jacket images of the "minimal" does tell us something: it is quite easy to judge a monograph on minimal art or music by its neat gray cover. The works discussed inside will be considered completely autonomous abstractions; they will be valued for being rigorous and difficult; messy or imprecise connections between the world of art and the larger culture will be cleaned up, or better, suppressed altogether; the general ambience will be the tasteful, understated elegance of the Museum of Modern Art.

Judged by *its* cover, the musicological study you hold in your hand promises, in comparison, to be somewhat vulgar and uncontrolled. (Unless you are looking at a library hard cover, where durable and defensive minimalism is the norm.) Juxtaposing the garish, repetitive imagery of mass consumer society with signs of musical repetition, I have chosen to figure musical minimalism not against the neutral ground of the museum wall, but against the riotous backdrop of the supermarket cereal aisle and the color television set. My central argument is that the most recognizably "minimal" contemporary music is actually maximally *repetitive* music, and that as a cultural practice, this excess of repetition is inseparable from the colorful repetitive excess of postindustrial, mass-mediated consumer society.

What we now recognize as a "consumer society" first took shape in post–World War II America, and it has been under attack since it was first theorized in the late 1950s. Denouncing wasteful overproduction of consumer goods (John Kenneth Galbraith's *The Affluent Society*) and the pervasive yet sinister advertising practices that mobilized demand for them (Vance Packard's *The Hidden Persuaders*), academics and journalists began laying the foundation for a countercultural critique of consumption as meaningless repetition. Minimalist art and music have usually been considered part of that counterculture. Even if 1960s minimal artists tended to avoid political statements, their art stood ascetically aloof from the world of consumption and its clotted signs. Minimalists, unlike Pop artists, have tended to align themselves with labor, not capital, and with overt imagery of production, not consumption. Richard Serra's stint as a junkyard crane operator, Donald Judd's machined boxes, even Andy Warhol's Factory — all point to the preference for work over shopping that led Robert Morris in 1961 to exhibit (for sale, of course) a crude plywood box containing a tape recording of the hammering that had gone into its construction.[3]

The repeated, rhythmic pounding of a hammer on a nail is certainly within the sonic parameters set the previous year by La Monte Young's foundational text of repetitive musical minimalism, *arabic number (any integer) to Henry Flynt*. Young had dedicated his *Composition 1960 #10* ("Draw a straight line and follow it") to Morris, and in 1961 he recorded a performance of *arabic number* in which he rhythmically pounded 1,698 times on a piano with both forearms as loud as he could. As a work that dramatically foregrounds the labor of composition/performance and just as theatrically resists commodification (Young's recording, though widely bootlegged, has never been authorized for commercial release), *arabic number* actually harmonizes quite well with the austere high modernist ideology of a previous generation of art-music composers. One can easily imagine Young retorting, when audiences broke into cursing and spontaneous protest-singing during an abrasive 1960 protominimalist happening (he was dragging a gong along the floor while Terry Riley repeatedly scraped a wastebasket against the wall), "Who cares if you listen?"[4]

Thus it is not surprising that students of experimental and repetitive music, while disagreeing violently with Milton Babbitt on issues of structure and information density, tend to agree implicitly with his larger assumption that the composer is a (production) specialist whose abstract sound-products demonstrate total disengagement with conventional and commercial culture.[5] As portrayed by its devotees, musical minimalism is indeed simpler, more consonant, more rhythmic, more sensual, even more popular than integral serialism — while remaining just as "purified" of contamination from the compromised world of signs beyond the acoustic. This book will argue at length a contrary position: that as a cultural practice, repetitive music implicates creators, performers, and auditors in repetitive commercial culture like advertising and television; in the consumption of low-caste repetitive functional musics like Muzak, Vivaldi concertos, and disco; and in production "methods" like Shinichi Suzuki's strange repetitive hybrid of Zen pedagogy and the violin factory floor.

My thesis may seem iconoclastic, even destructive, but I disclaim quite explicitly any brief against the music under examination. Rather, I seek to honor minimalist repetitive music for what it truly is: the most protean, popular, and culturally significant music to arise within the last half century of what Richard Crawford has called the "cultivated" tradition of American music. (Minimalism is the perfect example of a musical style that is cultivated without being "classical.")[6] In any case, a monochromatic image has been notably ineffective in protecting repetitive music from commercial appropriation. Strickland, confusing cause and effect, admits: "The later history of Minimalism marks the transition of twentieth-century art from its waning as an autonomous and implicit critique of mass culture to its demystification and acceptance as but another commodity . . . in a society geared progressively on all levels to the unremitting consumption of sensations."[7] To this *cri de coeur* one can reply only that the mystification was always in the critical image, not the art and music. This study will engage directly with the commodity form, unremitting consumption, and pure sensation as a foundation for artistic practice, and will apologize for none of it — for what is the alternative? Minimalism understood as an empty gesture of negation, in a cultural vacuum so absolute that whatever "implicit critique" of society it encodes can never be named, much less specified and evaluated.

Nor is anybody outside the world of contemporary art music likely to be intimidated by a hands-off attitude from formalist musicology. Mainstream culture has tended to deal summarily and satirically with minimalism's pretensions to objectivity and abstraction, taking the style at its "meaningless" word: witness the reliably recurring *New Yorker* cartoons of confused museum patrons staring blankly at bricks, trash, a janitor's broom in the corner, a blank wall, *et cetera seriatim*. The situation is harder to dramatize with sound, of course, but the music and figure of Philip Glass have become a byword in popular art for the culturally null. Witness his cameo during the first season of the Trey Parker–Matt Stone animated series *South Park*. A mordant subplot in the show's first holiday special is the systematic evisceration of South Park's school Christmas pageant by the forces of rampant political correctness. One by one, the usual religious and cultural signifiers are ruled unusable because they might conceivably offend: no nativity scene (Jews), no Christmas trees (environmentalists), no flashing holiday lights (epileptics), and, most damagingly to the pageant, no songs about Jesus, Santa, Frosty, or any of the familiar seasonal figures. What's left after this literal *reductio ad absurdem*?

> *Announcer:* And now, South Park Elementary presents The Happy Non-offensive, Non-denominational Christmas Play, with music and lyrics by New York minimalist composer Philip Glass.
> *The kids are in green leotards dancing about strangely.*
> *Philip:* As I turn and look into the sun, the rays burn my eyes. [Happy, happy, happy, everybody's happy.] How like a turtle the sun looks . . .
> *Sheila:* What the hell is this?!?
> *Music:* [Happy.]
> *Sheila:* This is horrible!
> *Priest:* This is the most god-awful piece of crap I've ever seen.[8]

Philip Glass can be absolved of any responsibility for the lyrical content of the South Park "holiday experience," but the episode's climactic musical passage is accurately Glass-like, if not precisely "(happy)": pulsating synthesizer chords that alternate between a minor tonic and its flatted sixth; faster, rumbling bass arpeggios; finally, a chanting, otherworldly bass choir—the whole a careful evocation of *Koyaanisqatsi* crossed with *Einstein on the Beach*. The creators of *South Park* have consistently shown both the talent and the inclination for dark musical parody. (For what other purpose is Isaac Hayes's "Chef" character?) But the most biting aspect of the South Park minimalist moment is extramusical, not the way Glass's music sounds but what it stands for.

Which is nothing. Nothing at all.

Can this public relations disaster really be the result of decades of formalist critical reductionism? Glass loses both ways: in the world of *South Park*, his "abstract" music, chosen because it ought to be completely inoffensive, since it has absolutely no connection to actual culture, immediately drives the cartoon audience into a show-stopping frenzy of mutual recrimination and escalating violence. Worse than the infamous early-twentieth-century explosion provoked by Stravinsky's *Rite of Spring* — or even the aftershock triggered at Carnegie Hall in 1973 by a performance of Steve Reich's *Four Organs*[9] — this cartoon riot has nothing to do with the mystified essence of "difficult music." Of course, audience members don't particularly like the little bit they hear, but what drives them to blows is not abrasiveness of sound. It is the void, the absence of cultural meaning, that repetitive music reflects back at them. It appears that, at the turn of the twenty-first century, "minimalism" is just another name for nothing left to lose.

With the help of a talking turd (don't ask), the denizens of South Park ultimately rediscover a comedic simulacrum of "the true meaning of Christmas." I do not mean to contend in these pages that repetitive minimal music has one "true meaning," or that my text, musicologically unique, could stabilize that singular meaning for readers and listeners. But I will argue, passionately and at length, that minimalism in music has *a* meaning, has at least the theoretical possibility of meaning, and that careful exploration of its various cultural contexts in the 1950s, 1960s, and 1970s will begin to define the range of signifying practices within which the style can function. The result cannot be a devaluation of minimal music, for it seems self-evident to me that any meaning is preferable to no meaning at all.

I propose to colorize the minimalist monochrome.

Because everything sounds worse in gray and white.

▬▬

This book took a long, long time to write. Some theoretical underpinnings go as far back as my doctoral dissertation, completed with the generous support of what was at that time not yet called the Alvin H. Johnson AMS 50 Dissertation-Year Fellowship. Much of the crucial research and drafting work took place in 1998–99 at the Stanford Humanities Center under the stewardship of Keith Baker, Susan Dunn, and Susan Sebbard; I am deeply indebted to my fellow fellows and our compulsory lunches, especially Mark Seltzer, Bryna Goodman, Brian Reed (whom I particularly thank for his thoughts on video art and television), and Keith Chapin. Some critical ideas on minimalism and the Baroque revival were first tried out in a seminar at Stanford; thanks to Stephen Hinton and Heather Hadlock for hospitality, and to the members of that seminar for perception and patience. I was also a regular and grateful user of material at the Stanford Archive for Recorded Sound.

Previous versions of what are now the first three chapters were delivered as talks at Cornell and Princeton; I am grateful to the graduate students at both those august institutions for the invitations as well as their careful attention and colloquy. Well before that, outlandish ideas were circulating through seminars and colloquia at the Eastman School of Music; thanks for feedback and mentoring to my close colleagues in Rochester, Jurgen Thym, Ralph Locke, Ellen Koskoff, Gretchen Wheelock; and to the many graduate students with whom intense conversations at Danny's on the corner were a formative influence. The extraordinary graduate students at the University of California, Los Angeles, have also taken their collective part in this project through seminars, colloquia, and hallway conversations lubricated by a copious flow of Diet Coke; of many such I would mention those with Maria Cizmic, Charles Hiroshi Garrett, Griffin Woodworth, Andrew Berish, Dale Chapman, Yara Sellin, Lester Feder, and particularly Cecilia Sun, who also provided indispensable research support and gave generously of her own findings and insights into experimental music as the years went by.

Many musicological colleagues have provided moral, convivial, and intellectual support as this manuscript struggled into being: Andrew Dell'Antonio, Robynn Stilwell, Nadine Hubbs, Rebecca Leydon, Byron Adams, Ruth Charloff, Judith Peraino, and Luisa Vilar-Payá. Kristi Brown-Montesano has been a loyal friend and interlocutor for well over a decade. Philip Brett, in whose reading group at Berkeley I met many of the above-mentioned, is in many ways a spiritual ancestor of this work, which he always encouraged with both words and example. It is bitter indeed that he did not live to see it in finished form; *requiescat in pacem*.

The genesis of this book was so extended that it has benefited from the ministrations of no fewer than three editors at the University of California Press. I thank Doris Kretschmer for her interest, Lynne Withey for her (ahem) patience, and, most of all, Mary Francis for her advocacy, therapy, gentle encouragement, and expert editorial management. Griffin Woodworth, Glenn Pillsbury, and Lisa Musca provided key editorial support on my side, and with their opposite numbers at the press, Colette

DeDonato and Kalicia Pivirotto, dealt elegantly with a complex and tricky world of late-twentieth-century permissions, examples, and illustrations. I also thank Annahid Kassabian, Michael Cherlin, Rose Subotnick, and especially Richard Leppert for taking time to do close readings of the manuscript. Obviously I bear the responsibility for any errors — but there are doubtless far fewer than there might have been thanks to this powerhouse editorial collective.

My work bears the intellectual traces of my teachers, most obviously Richard Taruskin and Joseph Kerman, distinguished senior scholars who have seen it evolve from some fuzzy yet urgent intuitions about the way music might be thought to "go" into a very different kind of historical and cultural study. To Professor Kerman, I owe immense gratitude for the space and breadth of his musicological vision — it was he who demanded that my dissertation, which was supposed to be a relatively modest study of Rossini and Verdi, include both Beethoven and minimalism. He upped the ante on me quite successfully, it turns out — and if there is any felicity in my prose, much of the credit goes to his careful pruning of an exuberant (!) young writer's worst habits. On the other hand, it was in a seminar run by Professor Taruskin that the initial kernel of this book's analytical thesis was planted; he has consistently taken a lively interest in how its shoots developed, ever wary of conventional conclusions, sloppy argumentation, or editorial grandstanding. He may not recognize some of the more exotic blooms, but none of my intellectual work would have taken root in quite the same way without his help and encouragement.

My colleagues at the University of California, Los Angeles, have been the best anyone could wish: this manuscript is deeply marked with the traces of their collective intellectual ferment. Elizabeth Upton, Elisabeth Le Guin, Ray Knapp, and Tamara Levitz have been friends, coworkers, and group inspiration: they represent my ideal readers. I fear that Mitchell Morris doesn't quite realize the effect he has had on this and all my work (even the parts I didn't show him or anybody else); he is my oldest and closest musicological sibling, and I truly would not be writing this or any other book without his pioneering presence at Berkeley and beyond. Robert Walser has been a mentor, editor, Chair, inspiration, sparring partner, and good friend; in addition to indefatigable shepherding of my career and work, he was responsible as Chair for securing the several crucial leaves and course reductions that made the final writing pushes possible. I hope that he finds the result worthy.

Pride of musicological place must go to Susan McClary, whose intellectual influence shines from every paragraph of this study. It is no exaggeration to say that I would not have produced this or any other scholarly work without her pioneering critical thought; actually working beside and with her at UCLA on a daily basis is even more inspiring. I also want to acknowledge some quite specific and fundamental propositions about music, temporality, and desire gratefully borrowed; I hope their idiosyncratic use here provides payback with (at least some degree of) interest. This book's long gestation period spanned a sea change in musicological ideology, and it seems absolutely incumbent on me to remind the reader that in 1990, when I began this work in earnest, Susan McClary was not only a powerful musicological example — she was *the only* musicological example of the kind of scholar I sought someday to be. Someday, is, as these things turn out, just about . . . *now.* I hope she will be pleased at what I wrote — and she has wrought.

Pride of place overall must go to Kimberly Fox, my life companion on this long intellectual journey. She met me when I was a stressed-out graduate student casting about for a dissertation topic and has thus drunk the relationship cup labeled "married to a writer" right to the dregs. Words cannot express the depth and complexity of my debt to her as a person and a thinker. (To acknowledge just the most obvious debt, the title of this book is hers.) All I know is that she is surely as relieved as I am that this is the last sentence of the first book I ever wrote.

INTRODUCTION

The Culture of Repetition

Is a sacrifice necessary? Hurry up with it, because — if we are still within earshot — the World, by repeating itself, is dissolving into Noise and Violence.

Jacques Attali, *Noise: The Political Economy of Music* (1977)

I woke up this morning thinking that I might not want to listen to repetitive music ever again — the endless looping of images yesterday was enough for me for quite some time.

Message posted to the .microsound e-list on September 12, 2001

It is late on a Friday night in the industrial consumer society at the turn of the twenty-first century. The culture of repetition is in full swing.

In a converted warehouse near the urban core, hundreds of dancers are moving in rhythm to highly repetitive electronic music; many of them are under the influence of controlled substances, most notably 3,4-methylenedioxymethamphetamine (MDMA), known to them as E, X, or Ecstasy. The DJ, who has been building erotic tension for 45 minutes by carefully interweaving current hard trance with classic disco tracks from the 1970s, pulls a prized 12-inch record from his crate: the 17-minute dance remix of Donna Summer and Giorgio Moroder's "Love to Love You Baby." He spins the record to the halfway point and begins to inter-

1

cut Summers's elaborately structured moans into the driving groove that issues from his other turntable; as the crowd realizes what he is doing, they begin to scream and moan along with the record. Everyone reaches climax together as the bass drum kicks in . . .

A solitary late-night shopper wheels her cart down the soup aisle of a nearby supermarket; she finds the repeating pattern of the colored labels vaguely relaxing as she glides by. (Clinical monitoring of her eye-blink rate would show that she has entered the first stage of hypnoid trance.) She wonders, as she does every time she traverses this aisle, why there are so many different brands of soup and who buys them all. She remembers, suddenly, that she has been wanting for a long time to try some chunky chicken noodle. The music drifting down from speakers embedded in the ceiling hardly registers on her consciousness . . .

A writer sits in his suburban study watching a videotape of network television. He has almost 100 sets of tapes, 24 hours of every channel available from his local cable provider on a given day almost two months ago. He is watching them all, trying to make sense of the torrential flow of information pouring from the nation's TV sets. He has seen dozens of sitcoms, hundreds of reruns, literally *thousands* of commercials, and he has thousands more to go. He is exhausted — and a little terrified. Downtown, a junior advertising executive sits in a conference room with a computer printout. He is engaged in a strangely similar task, tallying against the agency's media plan the thousands of television and radio buys they executed last week for a major soft-drink account. The plan, carefully calibrated to maximize both audience reach and frequency, plots bursts of advertising in various mass-media vehicles (the vertical axis) against time (the horizontal axis); it looks rather like the output of a MIDI sequencer in piano-roll notation . . .

A college student sets out to read 150 pages of an overdue sociology assignment. Settling down at her desk with pencil, highlighter, and a one-liter bottle of Diet Coke, she decides the only thing lacking for her invariable study ritual is some sonic ambience. Thumbing through her collection, and passing over the many pop and rock CDs, she picks her favorite relaxing-and-study music, a bargain reissue of a 1958 recording of Vivaldi violin concertos that includes the famous *Four Seasons*. She figures that if she mixes up the 20-odd movements on the 65-minute CD with random and repeat play, she should have enough familiar music in the background to keep her focused for several hours. Absently tapping her pencil in time with the soft music, she begins to read . . .

Down the hall, the girl's mother silently enters the darkened bedroom of her six-year-old son. The headphones have slipped off, so she gently puts them back before flipping the cassette tape over. The music begins again (it is a Vivaldi concerto from the same set that her daughter is half-listening to next door), and she thinks, not for the first time, how strange it is that the Suzuki teacher demands they listen to the same few tracks over and over, even when sleeping. Their first, equally strange, group lesson was the previous afternoon: she was amused and a little intimidated by the repetition and discipline, her little boy sawing away in a line of 12 other children at an exercise that sounded like "peanut-butter sandwich" over and over — his teacher said, laughing, "Let's do it *ichi-man,*" which she later found out meant, in Japanese, *10,000* repetitions! — and then bowing ceremonially at the end of the lesson. It's not music, it's just playing the same thing over and over; repetitious like factory work, she thinks, or like beginning meditation, like the idea of "just sitting" that cropped up in a little book her yoga teacher gave her, called *Zen Mind, Beginner's Mind.* Turning out the light, she says a short mantra that it works. After all, taking up classical music can help improve performance in school, especially for boys, and it's never too soon to start thinking about college for this last one . . .

In a university electronic music studio, a sophomore composition major is fiddling with a keyboard and computer sequencing software. She has been listening obsessively to Steve Reich's 1976 *Music for Eighteen Musicians* and, trying to get the same effect, has created several slow, overlapping analog-string melodies and some faster figures for a sampled marimba. (The dot-dash piano-roll notation she is staring at looks oddly like the ad executive's media plan.) She clicks the mouse a few times, putting virtual repeat signs around all the loops, and starts playback. Cool. *Very* cool. Of course she'll never show this to her composition teacher — he'd just frown and sentence her to 10 more hours of Schoenberg. And, to tell the truth, if he asked her why anybody should care about two idiotic minimal loops repeating over and over and slowly going out of phase, she'd have no answer.

Except that it sounds like, *feels* like . . .

Her life.

The fundamental claim of this book is that the single-minded focus on repetition and process that has come to define what we think of as "minimal music" can be interpreted as both the sonic analogue and, at times, a sonorous constituent of a characteristic repetitive experience of self in mass-media consumer society. Repetition, regimentation, and process are, of course, basic to any form of human organization more complex than hunter-gatherer bands. But the rationalized techno-world that began to take final shape in industrialized societies during the long post-war boom of the 1950s and 1960s created for the first time the theoretical possibility of a strange feedback loop, whose many paradoxical complexities I want to fold into the single notion of a "culture of repetition." A culture of repetition arises when the extremely high level of repetitive structuring necessary to sustain capitalist modernity becomes salient in its own right, experienced directly as constituent of subjectivity; it is in this sense that we are constantly "repeating ourselves," fashioning and regulating our lived selves through manifold experiences of repetition. "Pure" control of/by repetition has become a familiar yet unacknowledged aesthetic effect of late modernity, sometimes experienced as pleasurable and erotic, but more often as painfully excessive, alienating, and (thus) sublime.

Often very repetitive musical experiences literally structure a given culture — as at the discotheque, in the Suzuki violin class, on classic FM radio, or at the experimental music concert — and thus analyzing the complicated way various kinds of repetitive musicking function within *very* broadly construed cultural contexts will be one of the basic aims of my study.[1] (We'll need to consider along the way such seemingly extra-musical issues as the precise number of orgasms simulated by Donna Summer in her 1975 hit "Love to Love You Baby," the unintended consequences for listening practices of the 1948 "battle of the speeds" fought by Columbia and RCA-Victor, and the doctrinal debate between Rinzai and Soto Zen lineages on the most effective path to enlightenment.) But understanding repetitive music as a cultural practice must also include the possibility that repetitive minimal music itself, taken as an autonomous, not overtly representational cultural practice, might have a hermeneutic aspect: a set of "hidden" meanings that might point at much larger contemporary cultures of repetition, might trope off them, even signify on them in some ambivalent and not easily reducible way.

Eros and Thanatos: Music, Subjectivity, and the Culture(s) of Repetition

The few critical studies to date that attempt a hermeneutic of minimalism have limited themselves, it seems to me, by a pair of reductive assumptions. First, following (at whatever critical distance) the later Freud, they assume that the tendency to repeat is essential to human psychology, a kind of built-in homeostatic mechanism for reducing tension. Freud, biological essentialist to the core, postulated that all organic life strove toward the inorganic, a tendency he identified with Thanatos, the phantasmagorical "death drive." Critics of repetitive music have not forgotten that Freud invented the death instinct to explain a particular war neurosis, the *compulsion to repeat* traumatic events that seemed to seize shell-shocked veterans, in direct defiance of what had seemed an unvarying principle, that organisms always act to avoid unpleasure. With Freud, modern interpreters seek the cultural significance of musical repetition "beyond the pleasure principle": repetition in music is thought to negate teleological desire, and thus repetitive music is allied with any and all psychic forces antithetical to Eros, to the goal-directed patterns of tension and release that define the ego-creating "life instinct."

It follows, second, that many psychoanalytic readings simply assume repetition-structures in music are unequivocal markers of regression — if not all the way back to the inorganic, than certainly back before the human subject, back to the nondialectical psychic states (infancy, schizophrenia) that precede ego differentiation. Theodor Adorno set the tone in *Philosophy of Modern Music* when he attacked Stravinsky's frozen ostinatos as musical "catatonia"; Wim Mertens, whose 1980 monograph still stands as the single extended culture-critical treatment of American minimalism, provides an explicit Frankfurt School echo, turning suddenly at the end of a long and detailed survey to denounce repetitive music as regressive and infantile. He himself appears in the grip of a repetition compulsion, reproducing a sonorous psychoanalytic diagnosis out of prewar Adorno as if by rote: "In repetitive music, repetition in the service of the death instinct prevails. Repetition is not repetition of identical elements, so it is not reproduction, but the repetition of the identical in another guise. In traditional music, repetition is a device for creating recognizability, reproduction for the sake of the representing ego. In repetitive music, repetition does not refer to eros and the ego, but to the libido and to the death instinct."[2]

Mertens is, of course, aware that within experimental musical circles repetition is prized precisely for its ability to dissolve traditional formal dialectics, unleashing strange and unpredictable surges of intensity; as Fluxus composer Dick Higgins once noted, implicit within extreme boredom is extreme danger, and thus extreme excitement.[3] Critics less politically worried by minimalism have followed Mertens in linking those nondialectical fluctuations of intensity to Lacanian tendencies in French thought, turning for an interpretive matrix to the antiteleological *jouissance* of French feminism and the anti-Oedipal "libidinal philosophy" practiced by Jean-François Lyotard and Gilles Deleuze. Here repetitive music is valued precisely for its refusal to route musical pleasure through the symbolic order, for its self-negating regression to a pre-subjective space that Lacanian psychoanalysis calls "the Real." In a memorable turn of phrase, David Schwarz has argued that the repetitions of John Adams's *Nixon in China,* by cutting us off from memory and anticipation — that is, from Eros — cut us off from the self, "trapping us in a narrow acoustic corridor of the Real." By Naomi Cumming's account, the motoric string ostinatos in Reich's *Different Trains* are not just train sounds. They are sonorous pieces of what Julia Kristeva called the "prearticulate," of the Real as refuge from the Holocaust and its "horror of identification."[4]

These psychoanalytical approaches can be elegant, suggestive, and highly ramified; they also demand attention because no one has, as yet, proposed a viable hermeneutic alternative. Lacanian theory has done a service — it has empowered at least a few scholars to "read" minimalist musical repetition as a cultural practice — but its assumptions can lock a critic into a rigid explanatory matrix where repetition is an abstract, purely psychic construct, and its singular meaning is always some form of self-annihilating regression unto death (or birth). One goal of this study is to wean the reader from attachment to such psychoanalytic rigor by linking repetitive music, flexibly and at multiple epistemological levels, to specific historical formations of material culture presented in their thickest, most irreducibly contingent aspects. It will be neither possible nor desirable to read musical repetition as the single aesthetic effect of any one cultural cause. "Culture of repetition" is a neat name for a deliberately shaggy portmanteau concept, useful precisely insofar as it refuses to assert a unitary psychological model or a single chain of cause and effect; rather than assume that one innate subjective drive to repeat always, everywhere, and in the same way weaves culture, why not explore the many different ways that our repetitive subjectivity is constituted, over and over, within the multiple, complex webs of material culture we weave? Reified categories handed down through the Frankfurt School and its epigones will be of little use here. For instance, it is simply not true, as Mertens claims, that teleological desire and subjectivity, the domain of Eros, are irrelevant to this new, supposedly "nondialectical" musical style.[5] In the pages that follow, we'll trace the presence in minimalist music of both Eros and Thanatos, of dialectical entrainment to desire as well as libidinal liberation from it, never forgetting that these lofty psychoanalytic terms are just metaphors for the bodily effects of material social constructions.

The nearest precedent in methodology and scope for the current study is undoubtedly the fourth chapter, "Repeating," of *Noise*, Jacques Attali's influential 1977 treatise on the political economy of music. An alert reader will have recalled that Attali used transformations in the production and consumption of music to predict the advent of "repetitive society," a radical and general transformation of lived experience in postindustrial capitalism:

> Repetition is established through the supplanting, by mass production, of every present-day mode of commodity production. Mass production, a final form, signifies the repetition of all consumption, individual or collective, the replacement of the restaurant by precooked meals, of custom-made clothes by ready-to-wear, of the individual house built from personal designs by tract houses based on stereotyped designs, of the politician by the anonymous bureaucrat, of skilled labor by standardized tasks, of the spectacle by recordings of it.[6]

Clearly Attali is not trapped in psychoanalytic categories; his interpretive field takes in the key twentieth-century material developments in media, technology, and the consumer society. But psychoanalytic obsession with repetition as Thanatos, as drive to death, provides his analysis with its grim subtext. The sound object, infinitely reproducible as commodity and endlessly repeatable as experience, is nothing less, it turns out, than a harbinger of mass cultural suicide. Stamped en masse from a model at basically no cost, pumped up with ersatz exchange-value by crude manipulation of demand, stockpiled uselessly by consumers who thereby mortgage the very time they would need to consume them, mass-produced musical recordings enact the collapse of all systems of value and the cancerous proliferation of meaningless, pleasureless sign exchange. "Death," intones Attali, "is present in the very structure of the repetitive economy: *the stockpiling of use-time in the commodity object is fundamentally a herald of death.*"[7]

Attali deals with repetitive music per se only once in his dark meditation on the repetitive society: minimalism, as it gives rise to the autonomy-negating relationships inside the Philip Glass Ensemble, makes a brief cameo appearance as pseudodemocratic "background noise for a repetitive and perfectly mastered anonymity."[8] In her afterword, Susan McClary tries to revise *Noise* so that Downtown minimalist composers like Laurie Anderson and Philip Glass, both linked by noisy immediacy and outsider status to the punk and New Wave explosions just over Attali's critical horizon, can participate in the "collective play" that he awaited under the utopian rubric Composing.[9] But I suspect that Attali would likely disagree with his musicological interlocutor, preferring to read the pervasive repetition of minimalism as a nightmarish simulacrum of the fully repetitive society, the nonstop refrain of an all-embracing round dance of death. *Noise* is intentionally (and problematically) vague about what styles might ensue once the musical means of production are liberated, but a fully notated, high-tech, nonimprovisatory music performed by professionals, disseminated on recordings, even (in recent years) stockpiled in bulky and expensive box sets is certainly *not* on the menu.[10]

Itinerary: Among the Cultures of Repetition

Attali's broad grasp of socioeconomic realities is unmatched, as is his materialist understanding of how technological advances in production and reproduction engender pervasive repetition in consumer society — but he is too in love with Thanatos to see how complex and multivariate our experience of that repetition might be. The absolute dystopia of Attali's repetitive society is a powerful polemical construct, but an inflexible hermeneutic tool. Accordingly, in the interpretive excursions that follow, I will take up in turn various cultures of repetition, seeking flexible, ad hoc contexts for diverse moments of musical repetition. Some of these will indeed have little to recommend them; but we'll also visit repetition cultures of liberation, self-gratification, even subliminal resistance to authority.

Repeating Ourselves can be divided, on the largest scale, into two not-quite balanced halves, correlated loosely with the two ways that repetition and subjectivity have traditionally been understood to interact, giving rise to formations that I will refer to, in metaphoric Freudian shorthand, as the *culture of Eros* and the *culture of Thanatos*. In the culture of Eros, repetition is a technique of *desire creation,* a more-or-less elaborately structured repetitive entrainment of human subjects toward culturally adaptive goals and behaviors. In Chapter 1 we confront repetition as desire creation in its most unabashed form, the genre of popular music that the Reverend Jesse Jackson once denounced from the pulpit as "disco sex rock." Under the rubric "Do It ('til You're Satisfied)," we'll uncover through close musical analysis the presence of a complex syntax of goal-direction in disco, taking as our text one of the most famously urgent dance floor meditations on sexual desire and, in early 1976, the occasion for one of the first extended dance mixes ever released, Donna Summer and Giorgio Moroder's notorious 17-minute version of "Love to Love You Baby." Moving from disco to what critics of the time liked to call "the higher disco," a correlate analysis of similar linear-harmonic structures in Steve Reich's exactly contemporaneous *Music for Eighteen Musicians* will uncover a similar syntax. Disco and minimalism appear as two linked instances of a new theoretical possibility in late-twentieth-century Western music: not the absence of desire, but the recombination of new experiences of desire and new experiments in musical form across a bewildering spectrum of teleological mutation. Process music's *recombinant teleology* supports a revisionist (and perhaps transgressive) interpretive conclusion: its repetition is not the negation of desire, but a powerful and totalizing metastasis. Minimalism is no more celibate than disco; processed desire turns out to be the biggest thrill of all.

The two chapters that follow make an attempt to excavate the material cultural framework for these new musical thrills. It was clear to most observers that 1970s disco was equal parts sexual desire and consumer display, perhaps even sexual desire *as* consumer display; Chapters 2 and 3 will move back to the 1950s to uncover the mercantile roots of repetitive desire creation in the higher disco. We'll be tracking down the most elusive species of hermeneutic game imaginable, attempting to argue that the pulse-pattern minimalism of Riley, Reich, and Glass uses the incessant pulsed repetition of mass-media advertising campaigns as what Lawrence Kramer would call a *structural trope*, a musical "procedure, capable of various practical realizations, that also functions as a typical expressive act within a certain cultural/historical framework."[11] It may be disconcerting to realize that within the cultural-historical framework of postindustrial consumer society, executing a media plan to deploy the thousands of advertising messages deemed necessary to sell automobiles and underarm deodorant qualifies as a "typical expressive act." It will no doubt be just as deeply dispiriting for partisans of musical minimalism to see the structural tropes of advertising used as a plate-glass hermeneutic window into the "blank" music they have consistently portrayed as resistant to commercialization by virtue of its very opacity.

Though the first wave of 1960s repetitive music has always been positioned as a particularly countercultural kind of noncommercial music (thus the pervasive anxiety of early partisans in the face of its subsequent success), it actually has more in common with Thomas Frank's mor-

dantly expressed alternate view of the 1960s counterculture as "a colorful installment in the twentieth-century drama of consumer subjectivity."[12] Chapter 2 will link minimalism's recombinations of teleology to
the post–World War II debates over formations of subjectivity and desire
in what was being understood for the first time as a newly "affluent"
consumer society. Economists and sociologists outlined what appears in
retrospect as a crisis of consumption: as rising productivity threatened to
flood industrialized economies with a glut of goods, attention shifted to
theories of desire, and desire *creation,* that could rationalize a society
dependent for the first time on the systematic mass production of desire
for objects — in other words, a society dependent on advertising. Advertising executives, proclaiming that "what makes this country great is the
creation of wants and desires,"[13] began to harness repetitive marketing
strategies to transform the rather incoherent field of people's lived desire
for objects into a fully rationalized system — a system that, as sociologist
Jean Baudrillard points out, only at this postwar moment achieved the
discipline and functionality of the preexisting system of mass-produced
consumer objects. The subjective experience of desire within this system
of objects was radically transformed through repetitive process. Consumer *telos* thus underwent in the 1960s the same recombination as did
tonal desire in repetitive music. The isomorphism will become clear when
we compare the representation of this experience within contemporary
literature with the unmarked yet identical phenomenology of minimalist
process music. (We'll read closely for structural tropes in George Perec's
remarkable experimental novel-of-consumption, *Things: A Story of the
Sixties.*) Thus forearmed, we can trace the phenomenology of consumer
desire deep into the rhythmic and tonal structures of a pivotal text of
musical minimalism, Steve Reich's 1973 *Music for Mallet Instruments,
Voices, and Organ.*

As Chapter 3 will make clear, the point is *not* to trash an influential
compositional style, but to use close reading of its characteristic forms to
illuminate both the music and a revisionist claim of materialist historical
causality. Whatever their ideological relation to Fluxus experimentalism,
Hindu mysticism, Ghanaian drumming, or any other countercultural
scene you care to name, the repetition-structures of American minimal
music broke into the Western cultural mainstream around 1965, the precise moment that the complete transformation of American network television by commercial advertising established the medium's distinctively
atomized, repetitive programming sequence. Minimalism, whatever
judgment of taste one might pronounce upon it, whatever local cultures

of repetition it might abet, thus takes on a unique cultural significance: it is the single instance within contemporary art music of what Raymond Williams called "flow," the most relentless, all-pervasive structural trope of twentieth-century global media culture. The sheer scope and intensity of this media torrent index an aesthetic effect that we might call the *media sublime*. Minimal music turns out to structure its repetitious desiring-production in much the same polyphonic way as a spot advertising campaign spreads out across diversified media vehicles (we'll look quite carefully at just how such campaigns are conceptualized and realized); its effect on the listener is the sublime perception of all those campaigns and all that desire creation perpetually coruscating across the huge expanse of mass-media flow. Once again, in an aesthetic effect absolutely characteristic of consumer society, the sheer excess of processed desire turns out to be the biggest thrill of all.

The painful thrill of the media sublime has more than a little self-abnegating death drive in it; but the second large section of this study is devoted to the recuperation of Thanatos, to a sympathetic look at the use within industrial culture of ambient repetition as a form of homeostatic *mood regulation*. If the major issue in the first half of the book is the repetitive disciplining of desire — and thus the major focus socioeconomic — the overriding concern of the final two chapters is the use of repetition to discipline and control attention. Here technology comes to the fore, specifically as it facilitated a postwar culture of *repetitive listening*. The fortuitous combination of two technologies that had been invented to fight it out — Columbia's microgroove LP and RCA-Victor's super-fast 45 rpm record changer — created by about 1950 an entirely new and unintended possibility for repetitive musicking. One might place a single disc of "Music for Relaxation" on the changer and listen to it over and over — or, better yet, stack a half-dozen records, sit back, relax, and let the changer homogenize them for you into a home-made evening of musical flow. Like television — and actually a little before the broadcasting world caught on to its power — long-playing records could provide controlled ambience, dispensing hours of what the industry was happy to market (discreetly) as a seductive flow of "continuous and uninterrupted pleasure." (The technical language of repetitive listening echoes that of television; as instructional booklets continue to inform users, CD players that hold more than one disc are designed to allow the "programming" of multiple recordings into a smooth "sequence.")

One of the most popular types of recording to pile on the spindle featured instrumental music of the eighteenth century. Baroque music had, until this time, been a rather esoteric taste, but the advent of the LP and the record changer ushered in a revival, not so much of the Baroque per se, but of the kind of brisk, impersonal, generally upbeat concerto movements produced in large numbers by composers like Albinoni, Geminiani, Locatelli, and, of course, Vivaldi — a style of music so perfect for repetitive listening that it was quickly disparaged by musicological critics with the generic label *barococo*. Chapter 4 is built around one of the most powerful denunciations of the Baroque revival ever to see print, H. C. Robbins Landon's calling down of "A Pox on Manfredini" in the June 1961 issue of *High Fidelity*. Attacking in the harshest possible terms, he fashioned a sweeping indictment of barococo as corrosive solvent of traditional musical, cultural, class, and even sex-role distinctions. His hysterical overreaction betrays a profound unease at the effect on musical traditions of Attali's "repetitive society": the technologically mediated modernity exemplified by mass-produced box sets of concerti grossi consumed repetitively and subliminally on the record changer.

Robbins Landon denounced the new use of eighteenth-century concerted music as sonic "wallpaper," a term that prefigures 1980s attacks on minimalism; in both cases the real danger is a soi-disant classical music that submits to inarticulate flow, that allows its structures to dissolve under the antistructural bath of repetitive listening. It will be simple to uncover the sociojournalistic trope that casts minimalism as the "new Baroque," the repetitively patterned wallpaper music of its day; what may be less obvious is how the critical portrayal of composers like Vivaldi *during* the barococo revival had already cast them as unwitting purveyors of minimalist process music, an overdose of which on the record changer would make for a strikingly reductive, even hypnotic experience. (Adjectives like *stripped-down, flat,* and *minimal* start showing up in 1950s record liner notes — in descriptions of interchangeably motoric concertos by Telemann and Vivaldi — well before they crop up in art-magazine reviews of gallery events featuring Young, Reich, and Glass.)

Musicologists professed not to be surprised — just a little depressed — that the obscure eighteenth-century suites and concerti they had gone to such trouble to exhume sometimes ended up providing ambience at fashionable cocktail parties; after all, most of this music was in fact originally designed to function as background music. But barococo on the 1960s record changer was hardly just the technologically enhanced return of *Tafelmusik*. The most characteristic venue for Vivaldi was not the party where he was ignored, but the study or office, where he was indeed listened to, but in a new way. Barococo minimalism is music not for pleasure (Eros), but music for mental discipline, for mood regulation, for the homeostatic equalization of tension encapsulated in the very idea of "easy listening." The repetitive listening habits of the barococo revival were early harbingers of the way most music is consumed now, which in turn is a constituent of the way most people *are* now.

Annahid Kassabian has hypothesized that we live in a world of ubiquitous music, of repetitive, slowly changing tints and ambiences of sound used to regulate mood and construct loose nodal associations of subjectivities. Minimalism pioneered the deliberate creation of this kind of musical ambience in the 1960s, but it was not the first music to address itself successfully to the ubiquitous subject — in other words, like television, to influence everyone and be fully attended to by no one. Barococo concerto sets on the living-room record changer hold that controversial distinction. Satie's infamous *musique d'ameublement* was no more than a visionary failed attempt at "easy listening," as the composer, prodding his too-respectful audience to talk over his deliberately banal and repetitive musical wallpaper, must quickly have realized. What was needed, it turns out, was not furniture music, but just the right piece — from Philco, Decca, or RCA — of musical furniture.

Baroque concerto movements were not only fodder for repetitive listening; they also formed the raw material out of which Shinichi Suzuki, inventor of the *Saino-Kyoiku,* or Talent Education Method, of violin instruction, constructed perhaps the most systematic exercise in repetitive performance as cultural mood regulation ever attempted. In the final chapter of *Repeating Ourselves,* we'll investigate the way this gentle, unworldly pedagogue set out quite literally to repeat the world's children into better, more compassionate versions of their young selves. One of the most seductive cultural hypotheses about minimalism is that it is the revivifying result of the direct encounter of post-Cage experimental composers like Young, Riley, Reich, and Glass, under the sign of 1960s counterculture, with Eastern philosophies and cultures, followed by wholesale transfer of those philosophies into a dying Eurocentric musical discourse.[14] Minimalism has certainly had a whiff of incense and patchouli about it from the beginning; nor is it useful to deny the obvious analogies between time-honored technologies of Vedic mood regulation like drones and mantras and what critic Tom Johnson, trying to make the point nominatively, dubbed the "New York Hypnotic School."[15]

But most such accounts are suffused with a gentle Orientalist longing, as Eastern culture quiets the vain striving of the modern Western compositional soul through its repetition-drenched otherness. Typically, whether the framework is Zen, Confucianism, or the Rig Veda, non-Western musics are characterized—with little regard to the complexities even superficial ethnographic research would uncover—as pure, unspoiled cultures of Thanatos, traditions of disciplined mood regulation as unitary and unchanging as their various musical forms are imagined to be. Even though minimalist composers rightly reject the "exotic" borrowing of musical instruments and textures, goes the argument, they have enriched Western musical culture through their openness to the radical structural difference of Eastern music, its use of "static nondevelopmental forms," and their willingness to imagine those forms as the basis of a new, Western musical *Thanatopia*.[16] My suspicion of this self-congratulatory historiographic trope should be obvious, but I have chosen to recoil from it in what might seem an idiosyncratic direction. Rather than attempt to attack the existence, accuracy, or motivation of Western appropriations of Eastern music, I hope to let the Oriental subaltern speak. We'll consider, and identify as an unsung minimalist art music, the Suzuki Method, one of the most singular and successful appropriations of Western art music into Eastern culture and philosophy ever attempted.

This intense, cross-cultural culture of musical repetition was formed when a young Japanese violin teacher, steeped in both the formal study of Zen and a pedagogical method derived from Buddhist techniques of character formation, attempted to teach his young pupils to play the Mozart he had grown to love on recordings as naturally as they learned their mother tongue at home. Suzuki's Method fused distinctly Japanese repetitive mood-regulation techniques from Zen Buddhist philosophy (teaching as repetitive drill; *katachi de hairu,* or "entering in through basic forms") with the American-style industrial repetition of his father's violin factory and the new technological possibilities for immersive repetitive listening provided by long-playing records and cassette tapes. The pedagogical spectacle that ensued took 1960s America by storm: the parents who had gotten into the habit of piling Vivaldi concertos on the home stereo were now watching, slack-jawed, as those same concertos were played in brisk, inhuman unison by platoons of perfectly turned-out children, some no more than four years old, in military formation on gymnasium floors.

We'll consider Suzuki's pedagogical Method as a unique hermeneutic window into the possible relation of Eastern philosophy and 1960s musical culture—can we really talk about "Zen-like minimalism" in music, and what happens when it crops up within Western musical practices?

Contemporary American accounts of Suzuki and his Method show the traces of profound cultural anxiety; evidently the Western subject did not recognize itself — or the musical practices long thought to underpin that self — when mirrored back through the *ongaku-do,* Suzuki's explicitly spiritual "way of music." The material metaphors that Western journalists reached for — machines, robots, factories, mass production — show Americans misreading Suzuki's Zen-inspired repetition according to their own deep-seated ambivalence over the fate of individual subjectivity in a repetitive and industrialized society.

Suzuki explicitly denied any desire to manufacture musical automatons, returning time and again to a fundamental Buddhist truth: that repetition leads not to the abnegation of the minimal self, but to an expansive mental state where, to quote the title of one of his most famous books, "love is deep." The road to deep compassion passes through the powerful cross-cultural idea of repetitive performance as "practice." In Western musical culture repetitive practice is indeed an industrial concept, a legacy of the nineteenth-century need to rationalize and systematize the mass production of musicality. But in the Soto Zen tradition from which Suzuki's *Saino-Kyoiku* sprung, repetitive practice was valued for its own sake; the endless repetition of what Soto practitioners called "just sitting" *(shikan tazu)* was not a means to some other end, but the goal itself: "These forms are not the means of obtaining the right state of mind. To take this posture is itself to have the right state of mind."[17] Thus Suzuki's Method transmuted one of the least inspiring aspects of Western musical culture, its use of repetitive practice in soul-destroying industrial models of pedagogy and performance, into an avant-garde redemption of musical repetition as a self-justifying act.

Suzuki himself, a lover of Fritz Kreisler's Beethoven and Mischa Elman's recording of Schubert's "Ave Maria," would undoubtedly have been confused by minimalist process music; but his tonalization exercises, short minimalist musical fragments designed to be repeated tens, even hundreds, of thousands of times, epitomize "Zen-like minimalism" in music. As an experiment, Suzuki himself once decided to repeat the most basic of his tonalizations, a single long tone, 100,000 times. (The year was 1957, and it took him 25 days.) Had he done this in a Soho loft, he would now be hailed as an avant-garde originator of musical minimalism; since hundreds of thousands of Suzuki students now do less strenuous versions of that experiment across the world every day, it seems that, taken as a form of musical minimalism, the Suzuki Method is the most powerful culture of repetition, and the most pervasive and successful form of experimental musical practice, ever to come out of the fusion of Occident and Orient.

We in the West would do well to remember that the fusion was not on our terms, but theirs.

Minimalism Rescued from Its Devotees

I would like to finish this Introduction by acknowledging that my investigation into musical minimalism as a cultural practice is bound to appear extremely idiosyncratic in several fundamental ways to those familiar with the extant literature. Some of the motivation for these idiosyncrasies is doubtless to be found in the personality of the author, and its justification found in the overall success or failure of his work as it proceeds from here; but there are a few important methodological choices that, to avoid confusion, I feel it necessary to justify with some degree of formality before we begin.

First, the very act of interpreting minimalist process music as a cultural practice contravenes musicological and critical orthodoxy. This is not simply a matter of twentieth-century musicology's built-in bias toward formalism. Minimalism sits squarely within the "New Sensibility" of the mid-1960s, and Susan Sontag was speaking for many when she observed that the key aesthetic stance tying together the diverse cultural productions — avant-garde Happenings, process art, pop music, New Wave cinema, etc. — that outlined that sensibility was an unremitting hostility toward the interpretation of art. In her 1965 manifesto "Against Interpretation," Sontag imagined cultural hermeneutics (the task of the present study, alas) as subjecting the pristine works of New Sensibility to a kind of environmental degradation, "like the fumes of the automobile and of heavy industry which befoul the urban atmosphere."[18] Some quite extreme contemporary art strategies were understandable as part of an ongoing rear-guard action against interpretive pollution: art could flee into pure decoration, parody, even nonart. The defensive posture Sontag most admired has more than a tang of the minimalist aesthetic: "Ideally, it is possible to elude the interpreters in another way, by making works of art whose surface is so unified and clean, whose momentum is so rapid, whose address is so direct that the work can be . . . just what it is."[19]

If the minimal work of art is to be "just what it is," there is little profit in worrying about what it might mean. Minimalist composers, like their compatriots in the visual arts, have tended to take extreme anti-interpretive stances for granted. Steve Reich, who studied analytic philosophy in college, was particularly fond, at least in early years, of pronouncements that echo the prohibition encoded in the magnificent final axiom — *Whereof one cannot speak thereof one must be silent* — of Ludwig Wittgenstein's *Tractatus Logico-Philosophicus:* "Music Dance Theatre Video and Film are arts in time. Artists in those fields who keep this in mind seem to go further than those mainly concerned with psychology or personality."[20] Most twentieth-century compositional theory has tended to this stern formalism; what is striking about the discourse around minimalist music is how many supposedly independent critical voices are also silent on that about which they assume they cannot speak.

One reason, of course, is that much of the critical discourse around a experimental genre like minimalism has been that of insiders: overwhelmingly until the 1980s, and still significantly thereafter, those who wrote about minimalism also wrote minimalism, and the result has been criticism of a quite remarkable deadpan literalism: "[Music for a Large Ensemble] is a very colorful work, bright in its opening, a little darker in the second section, brighter again as it moves into the third. The first section's timbral blending of women's voices with cellos and basses is very effective within the texture. The mallet instruments, clear and solid at the beginning, gradually blend into the background as trumpets and soprano saxophones surge forward. One could watch and feel the rhythmic patterns lock into place as the players relaxed into the performance. It is a bright, joyous, and exciting work."[21]

Joan La Barbara clearly felt it her duty to report that Reich's work was . . . just what it was, in as much blankly descriptive detail as her editors would allow; clearly she is a supporter of minimalism, as her final simulacrum of a critical judgment attests. But it is not clear why we should care. Self-consciously "minimalist" criticism of minimalism — and examples could be multiplied from the pens of Tom Johnson, William Duckworth, K. Robert Schwarz, and others — limits itself to careful, systematic description of the surface details of musical structures followed by testimony as to their sensuous effects on the critic. Sontag argues — and I would agree — that there is immense cultural value in providing "a really accurate, sharp, loving description" of an artwork; and minimalist insiders have excelled at the kind of "transparent" criticism she championed: "*Transparence* is the highest, most liberating value in art — and in criticism — today. Transparence means experiencing the luminousness of the thing in itself, of things being what they are."[22] Especially in the early days of experimental minimalism, providing a transparent critical reflection of this strange, exotic luminosity was a worthy, even heroic, task:

given the complete disregard of repetitive music by the critical and academic establishment, the gleam of that reflection was often the only light anyone outside a small coterie could see.

But a generation has passed, and there is less need to carry a torch for minimalism. The critical landscape around this music has become cluttered with aging technical descriptions and restatements of compositional manifestos. At least in the neighborhood of contemporary music, the New Sensibility is growing old, and it may be time for Sontag's critical pendulum to swing back. Unfortunately the belated intervention of academic music theory has only exacerbated matters: after decades of ignoring minimalism because it had so obviously upset their modernist compositional heroes, some music theorists began to realize in the 1980s that this music in fact resonated perfectly with the extreme formalism in musical analysis that held sway within their discipline. Pioneering studies by Richard Cohn and Paul Epstein were undertaken at no little risk of apostasy from the high modernist church; but in each case the analytical methodologies that had served to parse Schubert and Schoenberg, tweaked somewhat so as to pay attention less to harmonic stasis and more to rhythmic complexities, seemed to work just as well on Steve Reich and Philip Glass.[23] Jonathan Bernard has been the only American theorist to push past "the music itself," seeking to analyze the structures of minimal music in the context of minimalist and process aesthetics in painting and sculpture. This is indeed a species of musical hermeneutics, but with a strangely tautological aspect: the ascetic formalism of minimalist music simply bounces back off the formalist asceticism of 1960s visual art, highly polished mirrors reflecting each other's cultural emptiness in infinite analytical regress. Pure musical formalism is breached (for which we must be grateful), but the larger formalism, that of the autonomous work of art with no relation to material culture or history, remains inviolate.[24]

A true cultural hermeneutic of minimal music must do more than describe or analyze minimalism: it must attempt to make its emptied-out formal language *signify*. Success will come, in all likelihood, against the collective will of its creators and partisans. In fact, the one reliable source of hermeneutic intuitions about minimalist music is the taunting and jeering of its myriad enemies within the critical community. Minimalism's attackers have tended to show little sympathy for the New Sensibility and feel no compulsion toward a transparent, nonideological criticism. They are unimpressed by the way minimal music *is just what it is* — because they don't feel that *what it is* adds up to very much. Faced with the uncomfortable sociological truth that such a simple-minded music has been vastly more popular than, by their estimation, it should be, they are almost forced to hypothesize about its cultural significance. If minimalism makes no sense on its own terms, perhaps it can be understood as a kind of social pathology, as an aural sign that American audiences are primitive and uneducated (Pierre Boulez); that kids nowadays just want to get stoned (Donal Henahan and Harold Schonberg in the *New York Times*); that traditional Western cultural values have eroded in the liberal wake of the 1960s (Samuel Lipman); that minimalist repetition is dangerously seductive propaganda, akin to Hitler's speeches and advertising (Elliott Carter); even that the commodity-fetishism of modern capitalism has fatally trapped the autonomous self in minimalist narcissism (Christopher Lasch).

Rather than abuse these critics, I want to use them, to gather clues about minimalism as a powerful cultural practice from those who would prefer to see it as a pathological cultural symptom. A truly idiosyncratic feature of the following study is the way it takes such critical putdowns with a kind of inspired literalism, applying hermeneutic jiujitsu to flip and then open up dismissive analogies normally used to close off critical discourse. In the process, the implied value judgments are summarily suspended. Thus, a series of five disreputable diagnoses — metaphorical propositions of the form "Minimalism is just . . ." — provides the chapters of this book with an alternate structure, one that's set in the Table of Contents as subliminal commentary in editorial brackets:

Minimalism is just . . . the higher disco (Chapter 1)

Minimalism is just . . . like a soap commercial (Chapter 2)

Minimalism is just . . . what television should be (Chapter 3)

Minimalism is just . . . wallpaper music (Chapter 4)

Minimalism is just . . . sitting (Chapter 5)

The final idiosyncrasy follows, to some extent, from the decision to follow those who take minimalism as an illness, and that illness as a metaphor: I am going to define "minimal music," the subject of inquiry, in a deliberately antinomian way. The idea that there is a coherent genre of music called "minimalism" is a belated journalistic construction that I am not anxious to reify further.[25] It has become standard parlance because it is terminologically vague enough to encompass the quite different musical strategies followed by a loose coterie of musicians who, conveniently enough for the cultural historian, all knew each other and lived near one another — if not always in amicable proximity — in downtown New York City during the late 1960s and early 1970s. Other names — drone music, hypnotic music, repetitive music, pulse music, modular music — would have cut deeper, and in different ways, through the historical record; in what follows I will not discard entirely the label "minimalist," but the body of music I want to discuss hardly follows the conventional boundaries that term outlines.

In a study of minimal music and late-twentieth-century cultures of repetition, we are primarily concerned, of course, with minimalism *as* repetition, particularly as repetition with a regular pulse, a pulse that underlies the complex evolution of musical patterns to alter listener perceptions of time and *telos* in systematic, culturally influential ways. In terms of experimental music of the 1960s and beyond, this repertoire includes at its center what I will refer to as *pulse-pattern minimalism:* the music of Terry Riley in his post–*In C* vein, Steve Reich, Philip Glass, and their immediate followers. It does *not* include most of the drone minimalism of La Monte Young, excepting early works like *arabic number (any integer) to Henry Flynt,* one of the rare Young works structured by rhythmically regular repetition; nor does it include any composers who followed Young down the reductive path of sustained microtonal drones. Thus I am not invested in the historical revisionism that animates Edward Strickland's heavily researched study on the origins of minimalism; I have no brief in this book to refocus critical attention away from the "famous" minimalists — the pulse-pattern composers — back to the unsullied avant-garde attitude of "original" drone minimalists like Young (the invidious terms are insider-critic Tom Johnson's).[26] If we are interested in minimalism as a cultural practice, we will be drawn not to its purest, most uncompromising instances, but precisely to where minimalism is most "famous," where the cultural practice is widest and most significant. (This is not to deny that microtonal drone music is also readable as cultural practice — but the practice would be a very different one.)

Having disentangled from minimalism its core of repetitive music, we can add to it some key instances of repetitive *musicking.* Latent in the structure of this study, but worth stating openly, is the assumption that certain ways of performing, recording, disseminating, and consuming music can be considered to be forms of musical minimalism — insofar as "minimalism" is the name we give to musicking implicated in contemporary cultures of repetition — even if the music involved has little to do with the experimental avant-garde. Disco and electronic dance music are "minimalist" in this way. It is not so much that any given dance track or record *itself* is like an autonomous, self-contained "piece" of minimalism; rather, it is the entire cultural matrix within which these tracks are chosen, combined, and listened to that defines a repetitive musical practice. Perhaps even more outlandish is my implicit claim in the final two chapters that, in postwar America, a certain subset of eighteenth-century instrumental music, epitomized by the concertos of Antonio Vivaldi, was transformed through advances in reproductive technology into the first widely available minimalist trance music. Obviously any given Manfredini concerto is not "really" minimalist or repetitive, except in a loose metaphorical sense when compared with, for instance, the dense complexities of the elder Bach. But stacking dozens of such workaday concertos on the record changer, turning down the volume, and half-following them in an atmosphere of studious concentration — that is *minimalism as a form of repetitive musicking*. (Christopher Small's definition of musicking includes *all* types of listening to music.) And learning a Vivaldi concerto by playing through its melodic patterns 10,000 times and then submerging your musical ego by performing it in unison along with 500 other students is, conversely, *repetitive musicking as a form of minimalism*.

One final thought: If the subject of this book is, at the most basic level, the implications within our culture of a widespread taste for repetitive musicking, then, as Small would be quick to point out, what is really at stake is a taste for certain kinds of repetitive relationships. "Musicking," he writes, "is about relationships, not so much about those which actually exist in our lives as about those we desire to exist and long to experience."[27] It is my belief that most commentators have shied away from a cultural reading of minimalist repetition because they cannot believe that we *really* desire the types of deadly, inhuman relationships *(I want my MTV?)* such musicking would seem to encode. To be sure, not all repetition cultures set up human relationships that are death-obsessed and oppressive, as the diametrically opposed, vigorously life-affirming examples of disco and Zen make clear. But perhaps the act of musicking is more complex than even Small gives it credit for; need every act of music making express the desire to actualize and idealize the often problematic relationships encoded in its structures? As will become clear in the explorations that follow, repetitive musicking rarely expresses a longing for authentic relationships that don't exist, and in this way has at least the virtue of honesty that more traditionally avant-garde musicking often lacks. More often repetitive music provides an acknowledgment, a warning, a defense — or even just an aesthetic thrill — in the face of the myriad repetitive relationships that, in late-capitalist consumer society, we all must face over and over (and over and over . . .).

We repeated ourselves into this culture.

We may be able to repeat ourselves out.

PART I

THE CULTURE OF EROS

Repetition as Desire Creation

ONE

DO IT ('TIL YOU'RE SATISFIED)

Repetitive Musics and Recombinant Desires

When I first heard Donna Summer, I just laughed. I said,
"That's exactly what we're doing!" How could you miss it?
Philip Glass, 1997

. . .

ONE TWO THREE FOUR . . .
Oooo, love to love you, baby . . .
ONE TWO THREE FOUR FIVE SIX . . .
Oooo, love to love you, baby . . .
ONE TWO THREE FOUR FIVE SIX SEVEN EIGHT . . .

During the spring, summer, and fall of 1976, a radically new type of musical experience — strictly patterned, tonally static, beat-driven — insinuated
its way into the mainstream of Western music culture. Opportunities to
respond with the whole body to extremely long, extremely loud stretches
of repetitious music had been available at the Downtown margins since
the late 1960s — either live in the galleries and loft spaces of the experimental avant-garde, or blasting from unlabeled 12-inch records over the
sweaty dance floors of what were just beginning to be called "discos." But
in that Bicentennial year the new repetition-driven sound went Uptown,
into the concert halls of the classical Establishment and onto the top-40
radio play lists of the pop conglomerates.

It was the year of minimalism and disco. *How could you miss it?*

In February 1976, after months of heavy club play, Donna Summer and Giorgio Moroder's 17-minute "Love to Love You Baby," arguably the first extended dance remix in disco history, peaked at number 2 on the Billboard Hot 100.[1] In March, Steve Reich (whose growing fame and Deutsche Grammophon contract were already irking longtime supporters like the *Village Voice*'s Tom Johnson)[2] finished his most extended concert piece to date, *Music for Eighteen Musicians;* he premiered it to a packed house and standing ovations at New York's Town Hall on April 24. In that same week, Philip Glass and Robert Wilson unveiled *Einstein on the Beach* to a rapt preview audience in Greenwich Village. (The number 1 Billboard single during that week: "Disco Lady" by Johnnie Taylor.) *Einstein* toured Europe to mounting acclaim over the summer, as dance-oriented singles began to take over the pop charts back home. In October Glass and Wilson received an offer to produce the American premiere of *Einstein* at New York's Metropolitan Opera House; they brought all 5½ hours to the Met for two historic sold-out performances in late November.

And then Glass went back to driving a cab, $90,000 in debt; DGG declined to release Reich's *Music for Eighteen Musicians;* and Summer ended up in a California hospital with a bleeding ulcer. But the breakthroughs of 1976 were clearly the beginning of mainstream crossover success for both minimalism and disco. (The Billboard Top 10 later that fall included at one time or another "A Fifth of Beethoven," "Disco Duck," "You Should Be Dancing," "[Shake, Shake, Shake] Shake Your Booty," and, prophetically enough, "Play That Funky Music, White Boy.") By the end of the decade, *Music for Eighteen Musicians* had sold over 100,000 copies on ECM and been named one of the 10 best pop albums of 1978. Glass had recorded *Einstein* and become a major star, with commissions from European opera houses and an exclusive contract with CBS Records. Meanwhile the team of Summer and Moroder had ridden the rising tide of disco to chart domination enjoyed only by the likes of Elvis and the Beatles: three number-one hit singles in a single year (1979), and an unequalled three number-one double albums in a row.

By 1979, in fact, pursuit of repetition-driven ecstasy was bringing minimalism and disco's practitioners into proximity. Mike Oldfield, whose portentous 1973 *Tubular Bells* had shamelessly pastiched early minimalism, worked up a funky, Latin-tinged "disco remix" of a track from Glass's 1977 *North Star* for his 1979 *Platinum* album.[3] Glass himself was playing occasional keyboards for Polyrock, a New York postdisco band. He and his sound engineer Kurt Munkasci produced Polyrock's 1980 debut album, which "combined minimalist repetition with electro-pop" to make "extremely single-minded dance music."[4] For a while the two worlds were close enough that a versatile and talented soul like Arthur Russell could slip back and forth easily. Russell (who richly deserves a study of his own) was a habitué of the Kitchen and a cellist who performed with Allen Ginsburg and the avant-garde Mabou Mines theater group (where he played music written for him by Glass); later he was a composer of art songs and extended meditative works like *Tower of Meaning* (1983). But in 1979 Arthur Russell was also Dinosaur, who wrote and produced "Kiss Me Again," the first disco single released on the Sire label. As Loose Joints ("Is It All over My Face," 1980) and Dinosaur L ("Go Bang," 1982), Russell was responsible for two of the more influential underground dance hits of the early 1980s, pioneering a stripped-down fusion of club music and experimentalism lovingly dubbed "avant-disco" by its gay fans.[5]

PLAY THAT FUNKY REPETITIVE MUSIC, WHITE BOYS

This historical convergence did not go unremarked; in fact, dance music provided the new context within which critics tried to decode minimalism's import. General circulation stories about minimal music from the 1960s tended to explain it as another wacky tangent of the post-Cage-and-Beatles hippie-drug counterculture; in the middle of the 1970s, minimalism was gravely taken at face value, and the merits of extreme reductionism in art hotly debated pro and con. But by the late 1970s and early 1980s, minimalism's new technical range and virtuosity — and its new popularity with audiences — made the comparisons to ABC art and white canvases feel stale. The pulsating example of contemporary disco, at the precise pinnacle of its popularity, provided a new trope: minimalism was no longer about being simple, or simpleminded — it was about writing classical music with a beat: "Steve Reich and Philip Glass [were] both once referred to as 'New York minimalists,' since they use the simplest of musical materials, combined and recombined in intricate ways. Their work has also been called 'the higher disco,' since it can have a similar visceral effect on its listeners."[6]

Thus Richard Sennett in *Harper's*, retrospectively, in 1984. Minimalism not only resembled disco; its pounding repetition could be made to prefigure disco, as *Rolling Stone* had argued back in 1979: "[Philip Glass's] techniques have long been dismissed by both pop and classical worlds as abstruse, yet concepts he developed more than a decade ago can be heard in everything from the jet-propelled paganism of disco to the industrial clanking of technorock." (Glass himself seemed happy to take credit; he told the *Stone* that "The music I hear on the radio seems to be getting more and more similar to what I do.")[7] Even the *New York Times,* whose senior classical music critics had fought the rising style bitterly through the 1970s, now lauded its crossover potential: "[Glass's] ensemble has helped to place new experimental music on a continuum ranging from academic modernism to progressive rock and jazz, and influenced many of the popular music trends of the 1970's — from New Wave rock to the constant repetition of disco. 'It's the most commercial sound around,' rock star David Bowie remarked several years ago about the ensemble, 'a fact only Philip and I know.'"[8]

More austere experimentalists recoiled from the "minimalism as dance music" trope — and its focus on the pop sound of Philip Glass. (La Monte Young, plaintively, in *Time:* "My direction is much less commercial. It's not the kind of thing you can sell at the disco.")[9] But perhaps the most striking confirmation of the trope's power and ubiquity comes from the world of experimental dance. In a pivotal 1980 *New Yorker* piece, dance critic Arlene Croce surveyed a group of avant-garde choreographers — Andy de Groat, Lucinda Childs, Meredith Monk, David Gordon — which she dubbed the "school of Glass" because they favored minimalist music as accompaniment to their ritualized repetitious movements. Croce's description of Glass's music certainly makes it sound funky ("there is a very heavy beat tying dance and music together"; "Glass's hammering beat seems to drive the dancers ever onward"), but she lets one of the dancers make the inevitable pop-music comparison for her: "The diminished scale of modern and post-modern choreography — the fact that it can't project over opera house distances — will always limit its appeal. This is why what Gordon calls 'art disco' — amplified, big-beat walking music — is getting popular with dancers."[10]

"Avant-disco" in the clubs, "art disco" in the lofts, "the higher disco" in the concert hall — the critical shorthand of 1980 challenges us to examine in depth the similarities between the repetitive big beats of 1970s minimalism and 1970s dance music. We may well discover that Steve Reich and Donna Summer represent two routes to a single post-modern listening experience, two examples of sonic art that forges new mass-mediated relations between musical time, directionality, and desire. In fact, the trajectory of this argument will lead us well past the family resemblance to Eurodisco that made Glass laugh and think of *Einstein* when he heard (I am guessing here, but it's not that far a stretch) the chugging synthesizer arpeggios that underpin Summer's 1977 "I Feel

Love."[11] Even a historical and critical survey as brief as the one above should make the analytical argument of the following pages, built around an in-depth comparison of form and process in Reich's *Music for Eighteen Musicians* and Summer-Moroder's "Love to Love You Baby," seem less outré. These two slabs of mid-1970s repetition — one venerated as the austere masterpiece of minimalism, the other notorious as the car-nivalesque site of 22 simulated orgasms — actually do much the same cul-tural work, in much the same way.[12] I agree with Glass: *How could you miss it?*

Get Up, Get Down

Well, you could get hung up on the divide between high and low. Before we plunge in, a cautionary word about the cultural politics of the project. For minimalism and disco to meet on equal terms necessarily implies a (salutary) leveling out of traditional hierarchies of musical value.[13] Their linkage in critical reception by no means guarantees this. In fact, it often implies the opposite, a putting of minimalism "in its place," a reassertion of cultural hierarchy in the face of a mongrel music that attempts to have it both ways, usurping (it is claimed) the cultural privilege of "high art" while reaping the easy rewards of mass culture. Thus critic Samuel Lipman, dogged neoconservative supporter of Great Books and Great Music, famously dismissed minimalism in 1979 as just "a pop music for intellectuals."[14] He would undoubtedly have seen the quotes collected above, however laudatory in tone, as more dire evidence for his thesis. Even sympathetic observers have sometimes worried about minimalism's embrace of the pleasure principle in terms that resonate strikingly with attacks on dance music culture: "To a certain extent, Glass's music is anti-intellectual. It is emotion-first, feel-good music that depends, at least for part of its effect, on high amplification and a glittery, glassy surface."[15]

It does not seem likely that anyone who has read this far is expecting a laborious work of dance-floor-to-concert-hall recanonization, but this might be a good moment to state my radical disinterest in validating either minimalism or disco by cross-(sub)cultural comparison. Since I am arguing that minimal music and disco are two aspects of the same cul-tural phenomenon, I am by definition eschewing any attempt to use a perceived value gradient between the two styles to do cultural work. Obviously I have no desire to trash minimalism by comparing it to disco; nor do I want to rob disco of its subcultural authority by assimilating it to the dominant (white, male, European) discourse of classical music.[16]

But I have even less interest in rescuing disco by "classicizing" and "intellectualizing" it; or in making minimalism more hip and "transgressive" by associating it with the marginalized denizens of club culture.

To what purpose the comparison, then? Finding the common practice of minimalism and disco is a step toward defining (in a very old-fashioned way) a possible late 1970s musical Zeitgeist: the "Empire of the Beat," where communal consumption and solipsistic desire, rigid control and apocalyptic excess are simultaneously, dialectically in tension. Subcultural theory has long explained disco culture as a distorted reflection of the most extreme fantasies of consumer (mass) culture as appropriated and critiqued by those at its margins.[17] Disco music, then, can be seen as immanent critique, transposing the world constructed by mass consumer capitalism into a sonic environment that is equally loud, overwhelming, repetitious, exciting, exhilarating, exhausting, relentless, and (sometimes) terrifying. So, too, can minimal music, even though minimalism might seem to relate to this "disco zeitgeist" only by negation. (Andy Warhol was a regular at Studio 54, but Donald Judd and Agnes Martin were not.) Barbara Rose set the tone for generations of art critics when she set up Minimal and Pop as opposite responses to postwar American mass culture: "If Pop Art is the reflection of our environment, perhaps [Minimalism] is its antidote, even if it is a hard one to swallow."[18] Comparing the beat-driven repetition of Steve Reich and Donna Summer is likely to make one suspicious of such neat binarisms. Minimal music may well be an "antidote" to the endless repetition of signs in the consumption-driven mass-media environment — but, like disco, it turned out to be quite easy to swallow, because it works on homeopathic, not allopathic, principles. (As disco-porn diva Andrea True cried during the summer of 1976: "More, *more, MORE!* — How do you like it, how do you like it?")[19]

The discussion that follows, though rooted in this mass-cultural context, veers much more sharply toward the phenomenological in its particulars. I will be using disco and minimalism as simultaneous analytical foils: *Reading disco through minimalism* will keep us grounded as the carnival of sexual s(t)imulation explodes. Minimalism's deadpan attention to the "pure object" will allow the analyst to focus dispassionate attention on the structure and process at work in "Love to Love You Baby." This, in turn, will let us acknowledge Donna Summer's virtuoso control of musical erotics without falling into the morass of race-and-gender inflected essentialism that had contemporary journalists (cued by Summer herself) groping for comparisons with Josephine Baker and

Marilyn Monroe. On the other hand, *reading minimalism through disco* will help banish the lingering puritan and ascetic strains in the reception of joyously physical works like *Music for Eighteen Musicians*. Disco can help us uncover in detail the libidinal realities of the rhythmic repetition and process it shares so obviously with minimalism.

CAN'T STOP THE MUSIC:
TELEOLOGY, REPETITION, DESIRE, *JOUISSANCE?*

> One evening in the summer of 1960 I visited Karlheinz Stockhausen with the intention of explaining to him that fixed form has to be maintained because it is based on the form of sex, one-direction-crescendo (can you imagine a many-direction-crescendo? We have but one heart), climax, catharsis — human nature — Ying Yang — Nature of Nature — proton and electron.
>
> As if he had expected me to say something like this (and I never got around to really say it to him), he began to explain that we must get rid of fixed musical form because it is like sex. It has no freedom. It is as old as the theory of tragedy of Aristotle, of Faust, etc. Then Stockhausen explained the possibility of a free and calm love.
>
> **Nam June Paik, "Essay" (1961)**

Unfortunately that libidinal reality takes on a rather paradoxical aspect as it is described and interpreted in the critical literature.[20] Clear to everyone is that both disco and minimalism use a vastly extended timescale and large amounts of "hypnotic" repetition to reconfigure a fundamental phenomenological aspect of the Western listening experience: the sense that the music has a coherent *teleology.*

This feeling that the work as a whole "is going somewhere" (and that it makes you, the listener, want to go there too) has long been considered *the* virtue of Western music. From Arthur Schopenhauer, who thought that music's abstract tonal striving, its mirroring of the pure Will-to-Exist, made it the highest of the arts; to Heinrich Schenker, whose entire theory of musical form is built on a mystico-organicist faith in the *Tonwille,* the "innate desire" of voice-leading spans to work out their destiny over time; to Charles Rosen and his more matter-of-fact, but no less dynamicist, definition of "the Classical Style" ("the music no longer unfolds, but is literally impelled from within") — coherent, perceptible teleology has been seen as an essential feature of high art music since the early nineteenth century.[21] And though one cannot quote a similarly monolithic party line about the importance of teleology in popular music, the simple vernacular of popular song carpentry — *vamp, hook, drive, build, release* — shows how deeply rock and pop are invested in directed motion toward a goal, a trait writ cartoonishly large in concert at those arena-rock moments of "ejaculatory release . . . celebrated theatrically with the eruption of flash pots and the vigorous wagging of guitars and mike stands."[22]

The End of the Renaissance

Given the central position of teleology within Western musical aesthetics, it is not surprising that critics saw its abandonment by the post–World War II avant-garde as an epoch-making paradigm shift. Leonard Meyer was one of the first to recognize the profound implications of Cage's chance music: "The music of the avant-garde directs us toward no points of culmination — establishes no goals toward which to move. It arouses no expectations, except presumably that it will stop. It is neither surprising, nor, once you get used to its sounds, is it particularly startling. It is simply *there*."[23] Meyer dubbed this kind of art "anti-teleological" and saw it as the harbinger of nothing less than a new, posthumanist metaphysic: "Underlying this new aesthetic is a conception of man and the universe, which is almost the opposite of the view that has dominated Western thought since its beginnings. . . . Man is no longer to be the measure of all things, the center of the universe. . . . His goals and purposes, his egocentric notions of past, present, and future; all these are called into question. For these artists, writers, and composers, *the Renaissance is over*."[24]

For Meyer the difference between the teleological and the anti-teleological is necessarily absolute, since the two aesthetics represent two fundamentally opposed views of man and the cosmos. The epistemological rigor was unimpeachable in 1963, mobilized to explain one specific, extreme case: the radical aleatoricism of John Cage and his immediate followers. But it set a Manichean precedent that was to prove extraordinarily deleterious to nuanced understanding of minimalism/disco.

By the 1970s the post-Cagean avant-garde was a much more multifarious phenomenon, but Michael Nyman's classic *Experimental Music: Cage and Beyond* (1974), as its title suggests, still defined the new musical space outwards from the radical indeterminacy of the New York School (Cage, Christian Wolff, Morton Feldman, Earle Brown). But Nyman's "beyond" now took in a lot of territory, including, for the first time, minimal music, which he shoehorned in under the provisional rubric of "The New Determinism."[25]

Nyman believed as strongly in the absolute division between an experimental avant-garde and what he calls "modernist" compositional ideology as did Meyer. In his version experimental music replaces the teleology of the "time-object" with the antiteleology of the "process": "Experimental composers are by and large not concerned with prescribing a defined *time-object* whose materials, structuring and relationships are calculated and arranged in advance, but are more excited by the prospect of outlining . . . a *process* of generating action (sounding or otherwise). . . . (Non- or omni-directional) *succession* is the ruling procedure as against the (directional) *progression* of other forms of post-Renaissance art music."[26]

Nyman, himself both a minimalist and experimentalist, broadened the scope of Meyer's argument, declaring that "processes may range from a minimum of organization to a minimum of arbitrariness." Thus the simple repetition of the New Determinism is a viable species of musical process, and "a situation [of] uniformity and minimal change — for example, the music of Steve Reich" is as radical a break with "classical" teleological music as anything cooked up by Cage.[27]

Nyman surely felt on somewhat solid ground here — after all, the first real manifesto of musical minimalism was, in fact, a description of musical processes (Steve Reich's 1968 "Music as a Gradual Process"). Had Nyman been called to account in 1974, he could have adduced Glass's freshly minted program note for *Music in Twelve Parts,* as stark a statement of the antiteleological position as has ever been penned: "The music is placed outside the usual time-scale substituting a non-narrative and extended time-sense. . . . [The listener] can perhaps discover another mode of listening — one in which neither memory nor anticipation (the usual psychological devices of programmatic music whether Baroque, Classical, Romantic, or Modernistic) have a place."[28]

That quotation features prominently in the chapter devoted to Glass in Wim Mertens's 1980 monograph *American Minimal Music.* Mertens's work — still the only full-fledged piece of cultural criticism devoted to minimalism — is clearly indebted to Nyman's survey. He takes over from Nyman (who wrote a preface to the 1983 English edition of his book) the historiographic position that minimalism is a subspecies or descendent of Cagean experimentalism, and thus must categorically negate teleology.

The binarism has become so reified in Mertens that he simply defines *repetitive music* (his term for minimal music) as the opposite of *dialectical music,* the music of "memory and anticipation."[29]

Disco *Jouissance?*

Note the strong influence of Adorno; it should come as no surprise that Mertens ultimately dismisses the "antidialectical" aspect of the minimalist experience as politically retrograde and psychologically regressive: "Repetitive music can lead to psychological regression. The so-called *religious* experience of repetitive music is in fact a camouflaged erotic experience. . . . The drug-like experience and the imaginary satisfaction it brings about are even more obvious in disco music and space-rock, the popular derivatives of repetitive music. This music at least leaves no room for doubt about its intentions."[30]

Here is a first musicological attempt to read minimalism through disco. Though Mertens's heavy-handed neo-Freudianism leads him to the wrong answer, he does use the graphic hedonism of disco to raise the right question — a question that must be the key to any general investigation of what one might call, after Susan Sontag, the "erotics"[31] of repetitive music. What *is* the libidinal implication of eliminating teleology from the musical experience?

In the late 1970s, as disco and minimalism surged in popularity, this question was very much in the air. Not just in the pages of obscure musicological journals — readers of *Rolling Stone* were treated to constant dissertations on the subject. In April 1979 John Rockwell laid out the leading hypothesis in a flamboyant review of *Music for Eighteen Musicians* and *Einstein on the Beach* that is worth quoting at length:

> The paradigm of Western music, classical or popular, is the sexual act, and the conclusion of the sexual act for most Westerners (or at least Western males of the slam-bam variety) is the orgasm. Climax is central to our music, since music is the art closest to the emotions and to sexuality. But not all kinds of music proceed so purposefully, just as some sorts of Oriental sex are more concerned with the meditative aspects of sensation than with pumping to a climax.
>
> All of which may seem a needlessly salacious way of leading into the two albums discussed here. But, in fact, these works by Steve Reich and Philip Glass are the newest and best representatives of what has been called "trance music," and trance music is nothing less than the adaptation of non-Western notions of musical stasis to a highly organized, rhythmic, structured Western sensibility.

The result isn't just a new kind of classical music. . . . Trance music has also become genuine fusion music that can appeal effortlessly to fans of progressive rock, jazz, and even disco. And it does so not by borrowing the surface style of a foreign idiom, but by remaining true to itself.[32]

Rockwell's logic is simple: Teleological music's "climax mechanism" is akin to the (Western, male) orgasm; teleology is thus the drive to orgasm; banishing teleology must mean banishing orgasm. Minimal music is antiteleological and is thus akin to tantric ("Oriental") sex, where the ability to put the (male) body into orgasm-defying stasis even as it engages in what for most humans is the most goal-directed activity imaginable is the sign of profound yogic accomplishment.[33]

This position precisely anticipates a line of hermeneutic argument later taken by Susan McClary. But McClary, laying the foundations for a feminist musicology, is interested in thinking across genders, not time zones. Like Rockwell, she identifies the thrusting, often openly violent principle of musical teleology with the male drive to orgasm; she then contrasts this experience with one created by a woman composer using minimalist process more attuned to female constructions of desire: an experience of "shared and sustained pleasure," of "constant erotic energy," of "ecstasy."[34] Critic Richard Dyer had already constructed a gay defense of disco along the very same lines back in 1979, when dance music was as unfashionable among macho left-wing intellectuals as minimalism among musicologists: "Rock's eroticism is thrusting, grinding — it is not whole-body, but phallic. Hence it takes from black music the insistent beat and makes it even more driving; rock's repeated phrases trap you in their relentless push, rather than releasing you in an open-ended succession of repetitions as disco does."[35]

A consensus emerges: Rockwell, McClary, and Dyer each identify the teleology of traditional mainstream music (Beethoven, "hard" rock) with straight white masculinity, a general (and oppressive) "cultural tendency to organize sexuality in terms of the phallus."[36] Each sees minimalism/disco as radically different — a music whose freedom from *telos* opens up a space where the (non-Western, woman-identified, gay-lesbian) sexual Other can dance in freedom, constructing dissident, subaltern pleasures that are, in Dyer's blunt formulation, "not defined in terms of cock."[37]

The musical construction of a radically new, nonteleological space of pleasure is taken for granted in late-1970s writing on minimalism and disco — even when the critic is deeply suspicious of the cultural consequences. Stephen Holden's McLuhanite riff on disco in the August 1979

High Fidelity ("Disco: The Medium Is the Message") holds fast to binary thinking as absolute as Leonard Meyer's in 1963: "The pop song, like most other Western European musical structures was a rough (and in radio's case, a shortened) parody of the sexual act, but it still retained its traditional linear form. Disco's elongated chant dispensed with melodic line in favor of a hook-break structure whose aim was to suspend the dancer in a vertical, timeless pulse embellished with sound effects. The result was a very literal, in-depth sexual parody, not a superficial one."[38]

But Holden goes on to describe the world of disco sexuality in terms of infantilism ("Abba . . . recalls the benign regimentation of a perfect grade school"), consumerism (Chic's producers are "hanging aural décor behind the voices"), and submission to technocratic authority ("the techno-world evoked by Donna Summer and her producers is a sexual amusement park in which the synthesizer is an erotic toy and the sexual ideal a mechanically quantifiable orgasm"). His 1978 *Rolling Stone* review of Summer and Moroder's *Once upon a Time* credits "Love to Love You Baby" with "a nearly total fragmentation of narrative musical structure [that] signaled disco's break from short radio forms to longer, more organic structures" and praises Moroder's solo synthesizer work for evoking "a deep, empty space beyond the erotic." Yet Holden's description of the album itself is laced with the terminology of perversion — "frantic stimulation," "pornography's fantasy of sexual insatiability," "nightmarish intensity," "obsessive interior monologue," "schizophrenia," "sadistic" — and the critique of disco as mechanical regression is, if anything, more stinging: "[Moroder and Bellotte's] work with Summer suggests a climate in which eroticism has been debased, exploited and placed under such close technological scrutiny that its value can only be redeemed by fantasy."[39]

Mertens's *American Minimal Music* takes a much more highly theorized path to the same negative conclusions. Explicitly referencing Adorno and Marcuse, Mertens painstakingly defends an outdated Marxist ideological framework within which minimalism's libidinal freedom from dialectics is, like the fantasy world of the disco, perverse and infantile — merely another "repressive desublimation" in the service of late capitalism: "Processes of production without negativity are utopian and historically unrealistic, like the absolute libido in repetitive music."[40] Ironically Mertens was probably the first to make explicit the link between the nonteleological repetition of minimalism and the anti-Marxist, antidialectical drift (so antithetical to his Frankfurt School mentors) of French poststructuralism.

Mertens ultimately concludes that minimal music mirrors in sound the dangerously seductive "libidinal philosophy" of Deleuze/Guattari and Lyotard, exalting moment-to-moment intensity over narrative, repetition over dialectics, unbounded and goalless desiring-production over Oedipal stories of castration and lack.[41] In the most extreme formulations of libidinal philosophy, subjectivity itself disappears: the discrete "self" (e.g., the closed musical work) is replaced by momentary, shifting assemblages of body parts (e.g., musical processes) that channel an essentially free-flowing libidinal energy through the endless cycling of what Deleuze and Guattari famously dubbed "desiring-machines." Once reconfigured in this way, the human organism — and its music — is simply not subsumable into the oppressive ranks of late capitalism (or state capitalism, for that matter). Libidinal philosophy (like disco?) offers liberation through "pure" desire, not dialectical struggle.

We are closing in on a very specific, highly theoretical moment of libidinal discourse: the evocation (laudatory or minatory) of a pleasure that is goalless and avoids the phallus; a pleasure that is the domain of subjectivities — non-Western, gay, female — defined in opposition to the norms of Western patriarchal culture; a pleasure that offers a respite from the pressures of the Ego; a pleasure that is "pure" desiring-production without Oedipal struggle. Mertens was right to reference French poststructuralism, for it is there, specifically in the works of Lacanian feminists like Luce Irigaray and Julia Kristeva, that the phenomenon has been most persuasively theorized. Rock music and Beethoven, musics of phallocentric narrative teleology, are musical texts of *plaisir;* minimalism and disco, musics of endless repetition and sustained erotic pleasure, must then be the musical texts of *jouissance.*[42]

Reading disco/minimalism as nonteleological *jouissance* would explain so much: If we were to identify the pleasures of beat-driven repetitive music as *jouissance,* we would be linking them to a pleasure that is radically Other, that is by definition linked to an uniquely female sexuality, and thus to patterns more diffuse, fluid, cyclic, and holistic than the straight-line teleology of the phallus.[43] It would be a pleasure already theorized as the province of marginalized groups like the ones who created disco and found liberation there. Disco *jouissance* could also explain the extremely polarized reception of minimalist dance music we traversed above. *Jouissance* is inarticulate — that is, outside of the narrative symbolic discourse of the Father — and calls up both passionate longing and intense anxiety in the patriarchal Ego. Repetitive music's refusal of narrative articulation seems to have the same effect: lack of teleology can make critics hear serene purity ("the meditative aspects of sensation") —

or monstrous, excessive perversion ("pornography's fantasy of sexual insatiability").

If minimalism and disco really deliver pure *jouissance* (what McClary calls "the ecstasy of the clockwork") to their listeners, then a reading of musical repetition in terms of post-Lacanian psychoanalytic theory should fall neatly into place. Traditional teleological music is the music of *desire*, of the pleasurable delaying and circling around a syntactically determined goal that Jacques Lacan identifies with the order of the Symbolic and the Law of the Father — and musicology can identify with the Law of (teleological) Tonality. Antiteleological music, the music of *jouissance*, is the music of the *drive*, whose "ultimate aim is simply to reproduce itself as drive, to return to its circular path, to continue its path to and from the goal. The real source of enjoyment is the repetitive movement of this closed circuit." As Renata Salecl points out, Lacan identifies *jouissance* with the endless repetition of the drive, and thus with "knowledge in the Real . . . which resists inclusion into the narrative frame."[44] The mechanical and mindless insistence of the drive points to the essential horror/pleasure of the Real: that we are part of a physical world *outside of* the Symbolic order that is random and meaningless, without plan, just going on and on. (John Cage was the poet laureate of the Real.) Mediating between desire and drive is the *objet petit a*, which —

Ah . . . but don't worry, girlfriend. We're not going there just yet.

The Teleology of the Dance Floor

The overwhelming trend within advanced critical reception of both disco and minimalism notwithstanding, I am not at all sure that it is useful to conceptualize repetitive music as absolutely nonteleological and its constructions of desire as the musical equivalent of *jouissance*. Let me be clear here: the desiring-constructions in question are indeed new, and if there is a "teleology of the dance floor," it works quite differently than the kinds of goal-direction found in a movement of a Beethoven symphony. (Just *how* differently we will investigate below.)

Another disclaimer: if you wish to take the above descriptions of disco/minimalist *jouissance* as a prescriptive template for listening (or dancing), well and good. Furthermore, there is no reason to think — *pace* Mertens — that choosing the "blissed-out," *jouissance* response to repetitive music must be either politically or psychologically reactionary. (The history of early 1990s San Francisco and U.K. rave shows how a communal ethos of drug-and-beat-induced self-immolation could quite easily cross-fertilize with New-Age spirituality and ecotopian "planetary consciousness" to create an authentic, if fuzzy-headed, post-Marxist counterculture.)[45]

For the cultural theorist, though, the Lacanian route can be a dangerous temptation: disco-as-*jouissance* provides both a satisfyingly radical take on the music, and a hermeneutic window that opens onto one of the most high-status theoretical discourses in postmodern academia. But try to use the trope seriously, and you will soon find out that *jouissance* is a rather blunt hermeneutic instrument. The axiom that disco/minimalism engenders an absolutely nonteleological ecstasy fails the cultural analyst in at least three ways: it is spectacularly destructive of analytical method; it has little to do with the way dance music is produced and consumed; and it ignores huge swaths of popular reception.

First, analytical method: In the work of Lacanian cultural theorists like Slavoj Žižek, *jouissance* is an epistemological black hole — radically Other. Since *jouissance* is by definition an experience of being outside of the Symbolic order, being outside of phallogocentric discourse ("knowledge in the Real") — one can't really talk about it, much less do analysis of it. (Lacan eventually took to drawing gnomic diagrams.) When *jouissance* is translated into a critical category — Roland Barthes's "text of *jouissance*," for instance — it is usually seen as an aesthetic effect of the high-modernist avant-garde, arising in the moments when a text frustrates a reader's drive for narrative *plaisir* and becomes impenetrable, resistant to discursive syntax.[46]

Thus *jouissance*, the pleasure outside of discourse, effectively checkmates any attempt to understand music as a discourse of pleasure. It forecloses in advance any musical erotics, any discussion of how tonal and rhythmic syntax construct desire, in favor of the more romantically extreme claim that repetitive music has no discursive structure at all, that it is radically open, excessive, and Other. This may well be a valid interpretive strategy for John Cage — and it is, after all, Cage whom Barthes and Lyotard would identify as the progenitor of the musical text of *jouissance* — but it seems a little extreme for dealing with disco.

Analytical criticism that treats Donna Summer like Morton Feldman — that accepts the rigid separation of *telos* and anti*telos*, assigns disco to the more "avant-garde" side, and then tries to argue its experiential pleasures are nondiscursive *jouissance* — can be strangely desiccated and clueless. What else explains how Carolyn Krasnow, whose historical and cultural observations on disco are so acute, gets its phenomenology so badly wrong?

Disco producers layered many different parts — some played by studio musicians, others produced synthetically — over the beat. *The result was an interaction between parts that was cyclical rather than linear, refusing the closure that is central to most European-derived music,* including much seventies rock. . . . Tunes open with percussive riffs that are then built up with additional layers. As the songs prepare to close, the layers are removed one by one until the songs return to their original basic riff. *This sort of privileging of the beat by refusing to contain it harmonically is what makes disco so distinct from the increasingly teleological, decreasingly dance-oriented rock of the seventies. . . . The details of the piece do not create a narrative.*[47]

Krasnow's 1992 description is superficially correct: disco tunes do privilege a steady beat, and they do not feature the kind of emphatic tonal closure we demand from a Beethoven symphony or the B side of *Abbey Road.* She is also quite right to point out that disco tracks (and minimalist compositions, for that matter) often structure large spans of musical time by adding and subtracting textural layers. But trapped by antiteleological absolutism, she can provide no answer for the obvious next question: what is the purpose of all that building up and breaking down? Evidently nothing — for if "the details of the piece do not create a narrative," then it is not clear why one should bother changing them at all.

In fact, as any producer or club patron will testify, the build-up and breakdown of the basic groove *is* the narrative of electronic dance music. Thus a second objection to disco-as-*jouissance* arises: it has nothing to do with the way actual dance musicians think. One can only imagine the looks on the faces of disco's pioneer producers when told that their music is interesting to theorists because it eschews narrative and teleology. *They* know that the successful track, set, or mix is interesting to dancers precisely because it has a carefully shaped teleological "build": "[In the early 1970s] Tom Moulton was a fashion model on hiatus from the music business when he visited Fire Island's Botel [dance club] during a photo shoot. 'I got a charge out of it, all these white people dancing to black music.' Painstakingly, he spent 80 hours making a 90-minute dance tape using sound-on-sound and vari-speed to create a nonstop build. At 2:30 on a Saturday morning, Moulton was awakened by a call from the Sandpiper that was unintelligible except for the screaming of dancers. To a tape!"[48]

Moulton is generally credited as the inventor of the club remix (his early productions include "Disco Inferno" and Andrea True's "More, More, More"), and he was quite clear in interviews about the goal-directed narrative that underpins an extended dance track: "You start here [he points down], and go *allll* the way up."[49] DJs often talk about the teleology of the dance floor in terms of a narrative journey ("[People] have their shirts off, their hands in the air, and are so into what I'm playing that they're ready to go on a journey. I'm always there ready to take them"; "I liked taking them on a magic carpet ride; I was all over the place as far as moods go") or reminisce like superstar Frankie Knuckles about their most powerful *coups de club-théâtre:* "At the height of the night, I would switch all the lights out. The windows of the Warehouse were painted black, the crowd would be high on the music and on drugs. I'd pump up the bass, then play this record, which was the soundtrack of an express train. People would scream — it was a mixture of ecstasy and fear — it sounded like a train was racing through the club."[50]

Despite reams of antiteleological rhetoric, testimony of similar climax-effects in minimal music is easy to find. Though Glass himself asserted in 1974 that his five-hour *Music in Twelve Parts* is music where " 'nothing happens' in the usual sense,"[51] at least one critical listener has described *something* happening, something that makes a Philip Glass concert sound as exhausting as an outstanding night at the Warehouse: "Part IV is extraordinary: after a brief introduction, it becomes a lengthy examination of a single, unsettled chord that sweats, strains, and ultimately screams for resolution until the musicians suddenly break into the joyous, rushing catharsis of Part V."[52]

Similar descriptions could be multiplied ad libitum, and not just of Glass's music. An 1971 encounter with the austere sound of early Steve Reich left Michael Nyman impressed in teleological terms that directly contradict his later assertions about the New Determinism: "In *Phase Patterns* (for four electric organs) the music is so stripped of the inessential that when, after 15 minutes or so of a single chord-rhythm, a second, related chord appears, the effect is startling, almost a self-indulgence. In terms of sheer pent-up energy *Phase Patterns* has no parallels in Western music."[53] Alan Rich found *Music for Eighteen Musicians* "extremely hypnotic" (as we might expect), but he also reported a quite different sensation as the piece developed, "something that, when heard in the proper spirit can churn up the gut — *very* slowly, but with terrifying control."[54]

Reich shares his "terrifying control" with dance music producers and DJs. It is *syntactic* control, a transformed, complex musical erotics of repetitive tension and repetitive release, and as such completely inaccessible to a hermeneutics of musical *jouissance*. Let's baldly state the obvious: people *do* experience tension and release — and something akin to

climax — over and over on the dance floor, and in a less physically extro-
verted way when listening to repetitive music. This brings on the third
and final objection to disco *jouissance*: the popular reaction to a pioneering disco track like "Love to Love You Baby" had little to do with
"floating erotic energy" or "knowledge in the Real." It was about orgasms. *Multiple* orgasms.

Twenty-two multiple orgasms, to be exact.

The precise number was, we must presume, interpolated during late
December 1975 by some anonymous research intern at *Time* from the frequency and intensity of the heavy breathing in Donna Summer's 17-
minute virtuoso performance.[55] With the imprimatur of a national news-
magazine, this statistical factoid went on to become the bellwether of a
yearlong sexual carnival in the press, of which only the barest outline can
be surveyed here. Neil Bogart's Casablanca Records paid radio stations to
air the full-length track at midnight, with the slogan "seventeen minutes
of love with Donna Summer" (Bogart leeringly told fans to "take Donna
home and make love to her"); record buyers duly reported that the
extended dance mix provided an inspirational template that had restored
their sex lives; the Reverend Jesse Jackson's PUSH threatened to boycott
"X-rated disco sex-rock"; finally, persistent rumors of sexual excess and
perversion began to surface, from the whimsical (her ass was so perfect
that the German artist Klaus Fuchs had paid her to let him paint it) to the
deeply twisted (Summer was really a transgendered man).[56]

Evidently "Love to Love You Baby" impressed hearers not as an abandonment *of* the climax, but as an abandonment *to* an almost superhuman multiplicity of climaxes. An advocate for disco *jouissance* might
argue that 22 orgasms in 17 minutes is in effect one long orgasm, a continuous high plateau of pleasure — but even making that argument
implies a level of phenomenological detail conspicuously absent from the
critical literature to date. The question of what happens when the teleological cycle of tension-release is repeated so many times that the iterations blur into one another is exactly the kind of issue that a musical
erotics seeks to raise. What if "Love to Love You Baby" and *Music for
Eighteen Musicians* set the libido free not by eliminating teleology, but by
mutating and then metastasizing it?

Recombinant Teleology

It is not at all clear why we should remain attached to the essentialist
binary opposition "teleological/nonteleological," when the equally essen-

tialist binarisms of sexuality and gender with which it is so often coordinated have been so repeatedly deconstructed. Stealing an apposite term from Judith Butler, we can begin by hypothesizing that *teleology is performative.* By this I do not simply mean that the experience of goal-directedness in music is dependent on the vagaries of performance (though this is obviously true). A more radical antiessentialism asks that music perform its teleology as nimbly as the Butlerian subject performs (with) traditional sexual and gender roles. A disco tune (or an avant-garde process piece) should have the right to "pass" as goal-directed (for a while); to assume and then cast off whatever pieces of the old, supposedly totalized structure of teleology please it, whenever and wherever it chooses; to maintain a distanced and perhaps even ironic stance toward "traditional" teleological dictates even as it plays with their undeniably pleasurable aspects.

Or, more to the taxonomic point, perhaps we should be discussing the multiplicity of what one might dub, paraphrasing Weimar sexologist Magnus Hirschfeld, *teleologische Zwischenstufen* — "intermediate teleological types." What Leonard Meyer saw as a stark divide between the teleological and the "antiteleological" (redolent now of old barbed-wire borders between gay and straight, masculine and feminine) we will remap as a wide field of intermediate possibilities, of para- and semiteleology — even, in the case of disco, of polymorphous-perverse teleology. Instead of parsing musical styles as either teleological or not, we can contrast musics that perform *classical teleology* — Beethoven, Brahms, Berg, the Beatles — with the various *recombinant teleologies* displayed by repetitive concert and dance music. (I borrow the terminology of gene splicing to emphasize the radical metamorphosis — through technology — of codes that were once thought "natural" and immutable.)

The strong version of this hypothesis would claim that there is in fact no nonteleological experience of music in Western culture, only new recombinations of teleology not yet recognized as transformations of goal-directedness. I believe the position could be argued, but there is no need for its extremity here. Let us accept a weaker, but still broadly revisionist claim: there are some truly nonteleological musical styles (John Cage, La Monte Young, Brian Eno), but any music with a regular pulse, a clear tonal center, and some degree of process is more likely to be an example of recombinant teleology.

The taxonomy of recombinant teleologies is theoretically infinite — and certainly not limited to the particular mutations that characterize 1970s repetitive music — but the fundamental breaks that separate the mass of possible recombinations from the classical paradigm of teleology are, provisionally, reducible to two.

First, recombinant teleologies abandon the "human scale" of classical musical teleology. Most goal-directed music in the Western tradition maintains a basic phenomenological congruence with the way we perceive quotidian bodily rhythms. The timescale of the individual (or cumulative) arcs of tension and release in classically teleological music is closely related to the timescale within which basic drives like hunger and sexual desire manifest themselves to consciousness. Thus the constant analogies to intercourse as an experiential metaphor: to put it crudely, we can imagine having sex to *Bolero,* The Righteous Brothers' "Unchained Melody," or even (transgressively) a movement of Beethoven's Ninth Symphony, because the time of the pieces themselves, and the spacing of climaxes within that time, provide a template that, as an event sequence in time, allows for correlation with the temporal scale of human sexual intercourse. (Or with a nice, brisk game of tennis, to borrow a wry counterexample from Pieter van den Toorn.[57] We can concede him the point, for now; what is important here is not the unique congruence of sex and tonal drive, but a more general coincidence of scale.)

Recombinant teleologies tend to disregard this anthropic principle. They create musical universes in which tension and release are pursued on a scale that far outstrips the ability of the individual human subject to imagine a congruent bodily response. (Thus Philip Glass: "One of the main things about my music is that it doesn't exist in colloquial time.")[58] Sometimes the technique is simple temporal extension: the five hours of *Einstein,* the seven hours of Young's *Well-Tuned Piano,* Terry Riley's "all-night flights" on *Poppy Nogood and His Phantom Band,* an entire weekend of nonstop Ecstasy-fueled techno in a warehouse in Manchester. Or the absolute length of a work's *telos* might remain within classical bounds while the quantum of teleological change is reduced, so that build-ups and breakdowns take place with an "inhuman" slowness and regularity. Reich's gradual process works this way; even *Drumming,* his longest continuous work, averages in performance no longer than a typical Romantic symphony. But Reich's music changes so *"very* slowly, but with terrifying control"* (Rich) that the 16 minutes of *Four Organs,* or the 21 minutes of *Piano Phase,* listened to at the microscopic level the process demands, can leave one exhausted and overwhelmed.

Such sublime excess of teleology can explain the reception of minimalism/disco as perverse, excessive sex. The response is not to musical pleasure in the absence of teleology *(jouissance),* but to an expanse of teleology that the music does not articulate within time frames listeners can recognize as "normal" or "human." Perhaps this is why disco and minimalism are constantly imagined as the music of machines, androids, and cyborgs. Stephen Holden painted Summer and Moroder as the demiurges of a campy "techno-world" pounding away toward "a mechanically quantifiable orgasm"; Tom Johnson's description of Glass's *Music in Twelve Parts* — "it just keeps chugging away toward some ultimate high" — can stand in for literally hundreds of similar robotic takes on minimalism. Repetitive music, if it is sex, is bionic, *superhuman* sex: "[With its] comic-book erotic/astral configurations, limited only by the studio and synthesizer technologies that produce and reproduce it, [Eurodisco's] camp eroticism pulls humor out of the gap between pornography's fantasy of sexual insatiability and actual human sexual capacity."[59]

On the other hand, recombinant musical teleology can spread itself so thin, or coalesce so infinitesimally, that listeners simply fail to register it as such — thus leading critics to ascribe the arousal they feel to *jouissance*, to teleology's absence. Even determined proactive listening is often not equal to the stamina and concentration needed to follow an entire tension-release arc as it stretches out past the phenomenological horizon of awareness. Carried along unaware, one only clicks in at the moment of dramatic release; or one begins doggedly to follow a process and then loses track because its progression is simply *too* slow and regular. The actual experience of repetitive music is often a series of fragmented tensionings and releases with (let's be honest) periods of directionless ecstasy — or wool-gathering — in between. The shape of the piece no longer coincides with the shape of the teleological mechanism as we experience it.

In the case of a classical sonata form, this experience would be classified as a failure of "structural hearing." (Thus Adorno's famous plaint that the man on the street listens to a Beethoven symphony as if it were a potpourri of famous themes from a Beethoven symphony. When the listener's mind wanders during the "boring parts," what is he missing if not the *telos* that ties themes together?)[60] But in the late twentieth century, splitting off the tension-release mechanism from the "rest" of the musical fabric is often a conscious compositional choice, marking a second — and perhaps more fundamental — break with classical teleology. In the Beethovenian, classical paradigm of teleology, the complex arc of a single tension-release curve coincides exactly with the shape of the piece; it may interact dialectically with older formal symmetries (exposition repeats, recapitulations), but ultimately *telos* determines form. Recombinant teleologies abandon the cherished "one piece, one orgasm" model of teleology that began with Beethoven, reached its purest expression in Wagner's *Tristan,* and remains a fundamental rule of thumb in compositional studios to this day. (Why keep the piece going after its goal is reached? And what is all that stuff doing at the beginning if it is not helping set up the ultimate resolution?)

Detach teleology from form, and an entire panoply of new arrangements opens up: One might create tension-release arcs that organize only *some* of the musical space, beginning in the middle, petering out before the end of a piece. Or a composer could present *incomplete* tension-release cycles: just an "unmotivated" climax (perhaps itself repeated cyclically), or, more interestingly, long build-ups with no clear moment of release. Why not a piece that is all climaxes — or, conversely, nothing but rising tension? One can imagine a complete teleological mechanism fragmented and dispersed through a larger span of featureless musical time — in effect, a repetitive-style piece with the "woolgathering" built right in. (In between the widely spaced "turning points" of the narrative structure — time usually filled in traditional tonal music by hierarchically organized prolongations — one might imagine plateaus of simple repetition, aleatoric noise, or even free improvisation.)[61]

Or — and this is the particular recombination that will interest us for the rest of this study — a complete tension-release arc might be much smaller than the piece, perhaps as small as the four-bar rhythmic cycle (three bars of groove plus a final "turnaround" bar that leads back to the beginning again) that is the primary building block of disco, house, and techno, or the four-to-six-fold repetitions of measure-long modules in a typical minimalist process piece. Hundreds of these might be added together to make a piece that is cyclically teleological at every moment but has no *necessary* long-range goal. Often the cycles will pile up into what sound like higher-level goal-directed sequences — the systematic addition and subtraction of beats, a gradual rhythmic phase shift, build-up and breakdown of grooves, even the artificial rise and fall of a sampled loop's pitch through sliding band filters — but these very rarely determine the overall form of the work. This kind of "systematic build through the repetition of incrementally modulated cycles" can create energy-accumulating pitch plateaus that only sometimes lead to more traditional moments of teleological release.[62] As often — and especially in popular music — the moments of release are left for the DJ or the listener to provide.

As predicted, we are focusing in on an *intermediate* teleological type. If one's model of musical teleology is the perfect simulacrum of phallic desire encoded by a Mahler symphony movement, then the endless mechanical accretion of cycles-within-cycles-within-cycles that characterizes repetitive music must seem like *jouissance,* its pure negation. (Or, if the cycles themselves happen to form tight tension-release arcs, like an endless, deliberate parody of *plaisir,* as McClary reads the cyclic progressions in Glass's *The Photographer.*)[63] Perhaps, with Beethoven still in the back of our musical imaginations, we might unbend enough to recognize in minimalism and disco a "de-natured" teleology. This would be a great epistemological point gained: we would at least acknowledge the *possibility* of constructions of desire in repetitive music, however tantalizingly tantric or disturbingly insatiable.

Minimalism and disco challenge us to go further. Recognizing a recombinant musical teleology is the first step to discovering postmodern recombinations of desire itself. It is possible for music to sound entirely different than Beethoven or Little Richard and still do cultural work by performing the construction of desire. The music sounds so different because *desire* is so different now — as different in experience as late-twentieth-century American mass-consumer culture is from nineteenth-century bourgeois Vienna, or from the decaying feudalism of the Mississippi Delta in 1929. Reading disco as nonteleological *jouissance* has pushed critics toward deep Lacanian speculations that hold out enticingly abstract and utopian promises; reading disco as recombinant musical teleology will allow us to explore material cultural issues that are messier, but ultimately just as rewarding. How does disco/minimalism's syntax construct (new) desires? What kinds of new desiring production in the wider culture might the music be modeling? And, ultimately, what sociological structures might produce that new production? To answer these larger questions is the task of later chapters. It is to analytical specifics — to the erotics of repetitive music — that we now turn.

DANCE PARTY FOR EIGHTEEN MUSICIANS
(READING MINIMALISM THROUGH DISCO)

Reading disco as minimalism is my final goal, but to make the comparison stick we need first to explore a contemporaneous stretch of musical minimalism and establish how repetitive art music organizes its recombinant teleology. The initial order of business is to determine at what scale to make the comparison: *how much* dance music does *Music for Eighteen Musicians* represent?

On one level, the hour-long *Music for Eighteen Musicians* is structured like the extended dance remixes of pop album tracks that have for decades been appearing as whole sides of 12-inch LP singles. Although not all contemporary extended remixes work this way, the classic way to expand a three-minute track to fill the 10–15 minutes of an LP side has always been to play the cut itself, vocals and all, at the beginning of the side, cross-fade into a set of percussion-driven instrumental and textural "variations" on its basic groove, and then fade back into a recapitulation of the original album track. This is exactly how the 17-minute version of "Love to Love You Baby" was constructed (see below); the resulting structure bears a clear resemblance to that of bebop jazz (head-solos-head) and, more suggestively, to the highly symmetrical formal procedures (exposition-development-recapitulation) of the classical sonata.

Music for Eighteen Musicians also begins with a "song": the approximately three-minute presentation of the basic chord cycle of the piece that Reich called "Pulse." The Pulse section returns to round off the work; in the interim Reich constructs an extended percussion-driven set of "variations." Each variation extends a single chord of the basic cycle through additive-subtractive process and layering, so the middle of Reich's work, like the middle of a dance remix, is a series of long textural builds and breakdowns over a (for the most part) harmonically static, rhythmically dynamic groove. (It's worth noting that Music for Eighteen Musicians has actually been treated like a dance remix of a previously existing track; when the piece was anthologized by Wired magazine and Rhino Records as part of their Music Futurists collection,[64] they used what they clearly saw as the "radio edit," reproducing only the opening three-minute Pulse section and none of the process music.)

On the other hand, Music for Eighteen Musicians lasts about 60 minutes, or the length of a good dance floor workout; it may ultimately be more useful to consider Reich's piece as the equivalent not of a single track, but of a long set of tracks mixed by an expert club DJ. Since each section of the piece (except the opening and closing Pulse) uses additive and subtractive process to create a textural arch form, each section has a "build" at the beginning and a "breakdown" at the end, just as most disco 12-inch remixes have a symmetrical buildup and breakdown so they can be mixed in sequence. By 1976 Reich had developed multiple interlocking musical methods of building and then breaking down a basic rhythmic groove. The most obvious and familiar, pioneered in Drumming (1971), he called "gradual replacement of rests with notes": over a steady pulsation, complex and irregular rhythmic riffs are assembled and disassembled, note by note, often in two or more parts sequentially (Example 1).

Example 1 Steve Reich, *Music for Eighteen Musicians* (1976), opening of Section II.

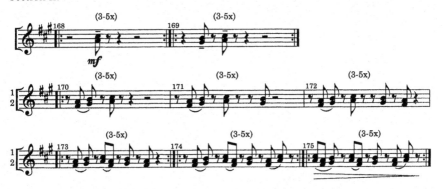

In *Music for Eighteen Musicians* Reich comprehensively explored the possibilities afforded by this simple musical process and combined it with two newer ways of raising and lowering the level of musical energy. About half the sections make prominent use of registral expansion and contraction to create a clear arch form: once the rhythmic patterns are assembled, Reich transposes them upwards (and the bass downwards) through the pitch material of the chord being sustained — and then returns them to their original registral position. At the same time rhythmic expansion and contraction are systematically employed, so that a one-measure riff, once assembled, will be repeated two or even four times over an oscillating irregular bass line that extends itself through symmetrical additive and subtractive process (Example 2). The phenomenological impression of each section is of a painstaking, inexorable flow and ebb of tension ("something that, when heard in the proper spirit can churn up the gut — *very* slowly, but with terrifying control"), as the rhythmic pattern either assembles itself or begins to mount up through an arpeggiated tonal *Zug;* lines up in longer and longer groupings over a bass whose expansion makes it ever more insistent; collapses back in register and duration to its starting point; and then dwindles away into an undifferentiated pulsing.

Furthermore — and this where we begin to move away from simple description into the erotics of repetitive music and a first encounter with a recombinant teleology — Reich marshals his sections (mixes his tracks) into a series of larger-scale teleological spans. I am not claiming that *Music for Eighteen Musicians,* like a Beethoven symphony movement, exhibits a single, coherent teleological progression from beginning to

Example 2 Steve Reich, *Music for Eighteen Musicians* (1976), rhythmic and registral expansion in Section I.

end. But Reich is able to channel and then release musical energy across several variations by using two musical devices not usually thought to exist in minimal music: a bass line that outlines semifunctional root progressions over large expanses of musical time; and a series of coherent, carefully controlled linear progressions in the soprano register.

Reich has made no secret of the fact that his later music reintroduced the concept of a bass line that, if not truly functional in a tonal sense, did at least have the function (which Reich traces back to Claude Debussy) of modifying the perceived "roots" of the complex pandiatonic sonorities above it:

Example 3 Steve Reich, *Music for Eighteen Musicians* (1976), basic chord cycle.

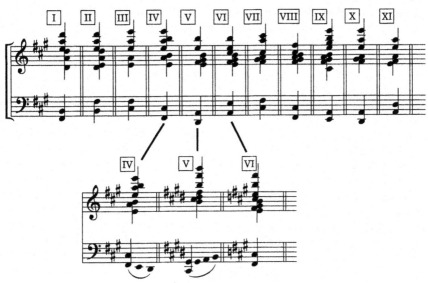

actual realization of cycle in Vars. IV-VI

> *Reich:* Harmonically speaking, what I've been doing right along has been taking something in the middle register and, when basses finally began appearing in my music, reharmonizing something that continues in the middle register with a changing bass . . . what this goes back to, unambiguously, is Claude Debussy.
>
> *[William] Duckworth:* Well, *Music for Eighteen Musicians* certainly has more of a bass line than any of your earlier works.
>
> *Reich:* To me it was, "How do you use the bass in this kind of music without using a drone? I don't want to use a drone." I mean, that part of Terry Riley I just completely rejected. That's foolishness to me.[65]

This is the signature sound of *Music for Eighteen Musicians:* a static middle-register pulsation of marimbas and pianos is repeatedly reinterpreted by waves of open fifths and fourths swelling in and out of silence underneath. That much Reich admits; but he makes no mention of tonal directionality. Naming Debussy as a model seems more to indicate a conscious avoidance of directional tonal progression, and (as various analysts have remarked)[66] there are in fact no strong tonic-dominant relations among the 11 chords that make up the work's basic cycle (Example 3).

Thus, since the 11 sections of the work are supposedly each built upon a single chord of the basic cycle, there would seem to be no possibility of long-range tonic-dominant progressions that could weld a succession of them into some recombinant version of harmonic teleology, however attenuated. The explanation of how this *does* in fact happen, quite clearly, also explains one of the more puzzling features of *Music for Eighteen Musicians,* obvious as soon as one actually looks at the score of the work: Reich's "basic" chord cycle is honored mostly in the breach. To take the most obvious example, there are *two* long sections theoretically based on Chord III, while Section X is vestigial, one-quarter the length of all others.

Reich also deviates consistently from the "correct" bass notes for each section. In expanding single chords into small process pieces he freely interpolates new "nonharmonic" tones — and sometimes entire step progressions — into the bass line. This new material is quite easily understood as prolonging (in some complex posttonal sense) the original bass note, as the pulsing chord above is prolonged and embellished through repetitive melodic process. But there are more radical departures from the rules of the game, departures that seem motivated by attempts to create teleological possibilities not implicit in the unfolding of the work's musical processes.

Consider Example 4, an overview that includes, at bottom, a loose reduction of the bass progressions underpinning Sections IV, V, and VI. Section IV does spend most of its time prolonging the correct F♯–C♯ fifth in the bass, alternating with an obviously "neighboring" fourth E–A. As expected, this neighbor then turns into a passing chord, leading to an arrival at bar 506 on the open D–A fifth that is the correct bass of the upcoming Section V. But Reich continues the bass progression an "extra" step down, and Section V actually begins over the "wrong" fifth C♯–G♯. This wrong fifth is, at least locally, functional — the key signature changes from three sharps to four, and Reich, indulging in an extremely rare moment of self-quotation, brings in the rocking arpeggiated pattern he had used in his 1967 *Violin Phase,* which outlines a C♯-minor seventh. The descending minor tetrachord F–E–D–C♯ in the bass could not be clearer or more traditionally tonal; the strong implication is that the C♯–G♯ displacing the expected D–A is to be heard as a move to the dominant of F♯ minor. Reich has flouted the rules of his minimalist process in order to indulge in the most traditional kind of teleology — tonic-dominant polarity — that Western music has to offer.

The pattern borrowed from *Violin Phase* signals the first appearance in *Music for Eighteen Musicians* of a technique initially developed in that

Example 4 Analytical overview of Steve Reich, *Music for Eighteen Musicians* (1976), Sections I–VI.

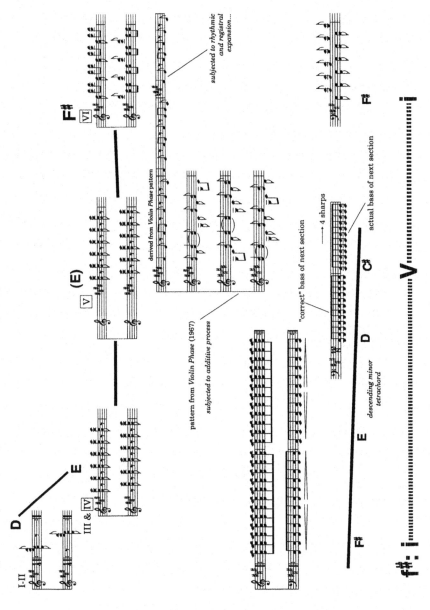

earlier work: new melodic material is derived by picking out sequential notes from within the contrapuntal complexes created by systematic phase shifting of the motive. Section V does this twice, throwing up first a sinuous compound arpeggio, and then a jazzy syncopated riff that spends most of its time oscillating between F♯ and E (see Example 4, *middle*). This riff is perfectly poised to execute the final gesture in a long, slow, linear ascent that spans almost the entirety of the piece thus far. As the melodic synopsis at the top of Example 4 attempts to demonstrate, the backbone of *Music for Eighteen Musicians,* the interlocking pulse material carried by the mallet instruments, has a "soprano line" that sits on D through the Pulse and Sections I–II, moves up to E at the beginning of Section IIIA, and remains on E through Sections IIIB, IV, and V. When Reich's derived riff begins to move between E and F♯, it raises the possibility that the soprano line, stuck on E for several hundred measures, will follow its example and climb another step.

The loose sense of dominant-tonic polarity and this equally loose linear progression coalesce for a single moment to create a dramatic move to F♯ at the beginning of Section VI. The mallet pulse does indeed move up from the open fifth E–B, which the bass of Section V led us to hear as upper partials of C♯m7, to F♯ and C♯, the tonic and dominant scale degrees of F♯, a motion prefigured by the sustained vibraphone figure E–(b–c♯–g♯)–F♯ that cues the ensemble to proceed into Section VI. This F♯–C♯ pulse recontextualizes the swingy derived melody below it: F♯'s that previously sounded like appoggiaturas to E now function as "tonic" embellished by a lowered-seventh neighbor. F♯-as-tonic is in turn contextually confirmed Debussy-style by a pounding ostinato in the fourth pianist's left hand that hammers out the tonic and dominant notes (F♯–C♯) of the key. (Section VI doesn't use A♮, the "correct" bass for the sixth chord of the Pulse, at all.)

The harmonic shift happens at the same time as a striking rhythmic modulation (the mallet pulse begins dividing 12-beat measures as 4×3 rather than 6×2) and the first use in the work of the maracas and their high rasping sound. A new funky rhythm and a dramatic new timbre signal a dramatic tonal shift; but the maracas might also be read as a coded reference to the famous maracas pulse in Reich's *Four Organs* — a piece that Reich himself has taken to calling "the longest V–I cadence in the history of Western music."[67] Is the hyper-extended tonic-dominant polarity of *Four Organs* the technique being "reprised" here?

In any case, the arrival at Section VI can be read as a moment of recombinant teleology. Within an overall experience that presents the listener with a series of gradual and partial tension-release arches (the assembly and disassembly of individual sections), harmony, rhythm, melody, and texture conspire to create a single disembodied moment that hails from within a much more traditional kind of teleological structure. The climax works to imply an all-encompassing teleology that the music does not actually provide. No one could "anticipate" the arrival at Section VI; and we are, remember, only halfway through a piece whose remaining sections neither pick up on the rising soprano line of the mallet pulse nor outline a directional root progression. In the moment this singular move to F♯ is exciting — but rather more in the manner of Frankie Knuckles than Ludwig van Beethoven, more like deciding to douse the lights and drop the needle on a moment of freight-train *telos* than like marshalling the *Tonwillen* of an entire *Satz* into a unified, "organic" formal structure.

LOVE TO LOVE YOU—THROUGH GRADUAL PROCESS—BABY
(READING DISCO THROUGH MINIMALISM)

We might thus refer, only somewhat facetiously, to *Music for Eighteen Musicians* as Steve Reich's "Dance Party for Eighteen Musicians": each section (i.e., each dance track) builds up, breaks down, and is mixed into the next, and at least once the *succession* of sections/tracks builds in a powerful wave of cumulative energy, as any good mixologist would try to arrange.

As I pointed out above, the overall structure of "Love to Love You Baby" in its 17-minute version is precisely analogous to that of *Music for Eighteen Musicians*: the original three-minute version of the song takes the place of the opening and closing Pulse section, while the intermediate 10 minutes are filled with a sectional set of "variations" on the song's basic groove, melodic material, and harmonic progressions. The use of process is most obvious in these middle sections; unlike later disco and most postdisco dance tracks, "Love to Love You Baby" was designed to work on its own as a kind of stand-alone dance floor set. Rather than a single build and breakdown of the basic groove, there are several, as if the track were a series of independent disco tunes strung together with textural cross fades. Later DJs would have the mixing technology and the vinyl raw material to do this in real time and at greater length — but Moroder's job was to create a *single track* that would allow people to immerse themselves in an unbroken groove for a full quarter hour, satisfying the requests for "more, more, more" filtering up in early 1975 from radio DJs and dancers through Neil Bogart and Casablanca records.

The next step would be for Moroder and Summer to make entire albums — and then double albums — that expanded the temporal scope of their premixed sets to the length of an actual night out at the disco. But by then DJs were doing it for themselves, and individual records were becoming simpler, not more complex. The complexity moved to the sets — totally transient constructions of desire, precursors of the dance floor and turntable edifices built and thrown away every night in the club world of today. A long underground proliferation of mix tapes and CDs has led to the recent mainstreaming of this phenomenon: with the release of dance floor sets DJ-ed by such luminaries as The Chemical Brothers, Fatboy Slim, and Boy George, this level of ephemeral musical architecture is finally available for general study and criticism.[68] Often the scale of desiring production and the breadth of semiotic reference rivals that of a Mahler symphony.

In effect, both *Music for Eighteen Musicians* and "Love to Love You Baby" are single compositions that exhibit the recombinant teleology of an entire DJ set — the complex of builds and breaks that can drive a room full of dancers (or an enthralled loft of listeners) into musical ecstasy. And, like Reich, Summer and Moroder manipulate musical parameters to create at least one overt moment of teleological drama in the mix. The middle section of "Love to Love You Baby" begins by setting out two consecutive builds that together structure almost five minutes of the piece; just as in the approach to Section VI of *Music for Eighteen Musicians*, their cumulative effect is to induce a sudden, dramatic harmonic shift and a strong release of musical energy.

The signal difference is — to put it delicately — that "Love to Love You Baby" does not sublimate its musical erotics. In the first, purely instrumental build section (3:54–7:18 of the track), Moroder produces musical teleology in a relatively familiar way. As Example 5 outlines, he uses systematic addition of rhythmic and melodic materials to move from a single bass line to a massive, fully orchestrated groove, layering on drums, guitar, funk organ, two different string sections (high and low), and finally a full horn complement. This *crescendo al disco molto* was much imitated and prefigures the structure of innumerable techno tracks; it is also reminiscent of nothing so much as that chestnut of rising sexual tension, Maurice Ravel's *Bolero*.

After this orchestral build has run its course and fallen back to nothing,

Example 5 Donna Summer, "Love to Love You Baby" (1975), layered orchestral "build" [3:55–7:15].

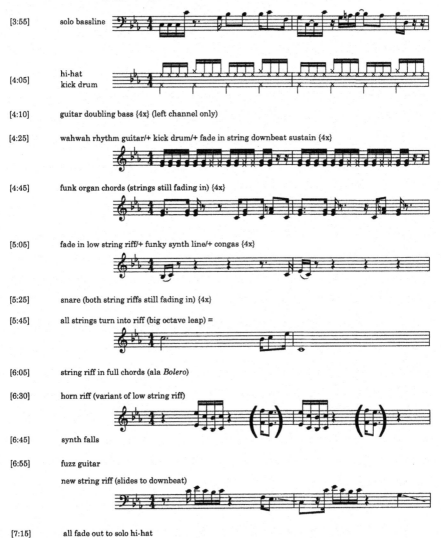

Moroder and Summer work in tandem to create a second, more intense, more overtly erotic build. Moroder, having stripped his groove down to a single ticking hi-hat, builds even more systematically than before, using an additive process uncannily similar to those in the exactly contemporaneous *Music for Eighteen Musicians* (see Example 6 for the overview).

Example 6 Donna Summer, "Love to Love You Baby" (1975), additive vocal "build" [7:15–8:30].

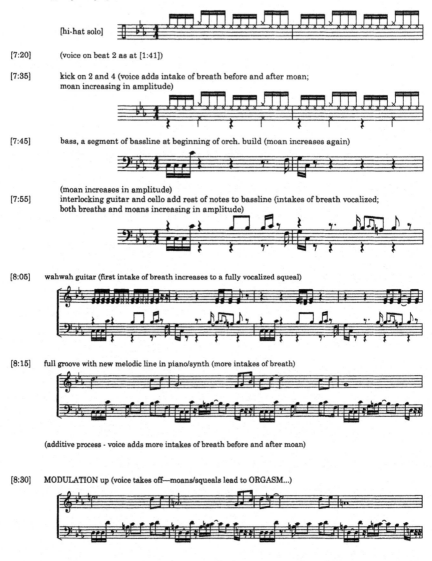

[hi-hat solo]

[7:20] (voice on beat 2 as at [1:41])

[7:35] kick on 2 and 4 (voice adds intake of breath before and after moan; moan increasing in amplitude)

[7:45] bass, a segment of bassline at beginning of orch. build (moan increases again)

(moan increases in amplitude)
[7:55] interlocking guitar and cello add rest of notes to bassline (intakes of breath vocalized; both breaths and moans increasing in amplitude)

[8:05] wahwah guitar (first intake of breath increases to a fully vocalized squeal)

[8:15] full groove with new melodic line in piano/synth (more intakes of breath)

(additive process - voice adds more intakes of breath before and after moan)

[8:30] MODULATION up (voice takes off—moans/squeals lead to ORGASM...)

Donna Summer begins to moan; a kick drum on two and four is added to the regular sixteenths of the hi-hat; and Giorgio Moroder unfolds his process, which a student of minimalism will have no trouble identifying as the technique of "substituting notes for rests," so familiar from works like *Drumming* and *Six Pianos*. The sparse bass line that begins to punctuate the stripped-down texture at 7:45 is a hollowed-out version of the funky original. In a particularly arty gesture, Moroder begins adding back the missing notes not in the electric bass, but in the cellos, creating a compound melody (7:55). By 8:15 the full groove has been restored in its original instrumentation — all the rests have been replaced by notes — and, as one might expect, something has to happen. Reich might change the chord at such a moment; or double the length of a rhythmic pattern; or recontextualize the melody he has just assembled by bringing in a new bass underneath. It is the bass that Moroder has been assembling, so he brings in a new soprano line that prolongs a mildly dissonant second scale degree, repeatedly moving from C to D while the bass circles around the notes of Cm7. (The same loosely teleological minor seventh chord is outlined insistently by the assembling patterns in Section V of *Music for Eighteen Musicians*.)

While all this is going on, Summer unleashes a steamy build of her own in perfect counterpoint, using an equally systematic additive process that works not with notes, but with gasps and moans. Her simulation of the sounds of intercourse was a virtuoso piece of studio stagecraft ("'Love to Love You' was approached as an acting piece. . . . My acting was done well, and people believed the story I was acting");[69] it is also a remarkable instance of controlled musical improvisation, a stretch of careful, gradual process leading to a clear teleological release that sounds, in this case, like exactly what it is supposed to be — a sexual orgasm.

At 7:20, over the neutral ticking of the hi-hat, a full octave below the breathy mezzo-soprano she uses for the rest of the song, Summer begins a masturbatory crooning: "oh . . . love to love you baby." The first syllable of this guttural two-measure phrase is more a moan than a pitch; entering on beat two of the first bar, it fills that bar with a slight, but distinct, upward pitch arc. This sets the symmetrical pattern: *rest;* moan on beats two and three; *rest;* sing "love to love you baby" on beats one, two, and three; *rest.* Summer proceeds — gradually — to expand the arc of her moan, and (like Steve Reich, like Giorgio Moroder) fill in the rests of her pattern, first with increasingly audible intakes of breath, and then with vocalized gasps of pleasure.

It is done with perfect rhythmic aplomb, in a carefully measured progression of intensity, and in precise synchronization with the ongoing instrumental build around her. Summer first expands the pitch range of her second-beat moan at the precise moment the kick drum enters (7:35); expands further and changes the vowel to an open "ah" as the electric bass enters (7:45); only allows herself to subvocalize the intake of breath filling the empty first beat as the cellos begin to fill in the fragmented bass pattern (7:55); fully vocalizes the first intake, and adds another sub-vocalized intake of breath *after* the moan, when rhythm guitar enters (8:05); and finally, dropping the "love to love you baby" of the second half altogether, creates a complex, syncopated, additive pattern of intakes and moans to fill the entire two-measure phrase — a really convincing simulation of orgasm — at the exact moment Moroder fills in the original funk bass and layers on his new soprano line (8:15–8:25).

The combination of these two teleological drives to climax — one sublimated into musical structure, the other boldly and transgressively explicit — are enough to dislodge "Love to Love You Baby" from its tonic key. After eight minutes at one pitch level, the music lurches up a whole step from C to D (a move foreshadowed by the D-over-C in Moroder's new soprano line). This is not a modulation in the traditional tonal sense — the bass moves right back down again. But it does represent the first time in the entire song that the harmonies have not been either the simple presentation of a chord based on C, or an obvious circle of fifths turnaround leading right back to C. Over the course of the next "variation" (8:30–10:45), this C–D bass oscillation recurs as the music for the first time explores other sonorities than Cm7 and its functional preparations. Here again the isomorphism with *Music for Eighteen Musicians* is clear and obvious. Both pieces use the systematic buildup and breakdown of a basic groove to gather musical energy that is released in a single, relatively isolated moment of teleological breakthrough: a single strongly articulated (but loosely functional) bass progression that stands out from a more static and nondirectional harmonic language.

Summer and Moroder got into a certain amount of trouble for "Love to Love You Baby," because its musical erotics are as virtuosic, exigent, and blunt as any ever committed to record; but have Steve Reich's compositional goals ("Obviously music should put all within listening range into a state of ecstasy") been so very different?[70]

Reich's 1970s colleague Philip Glass was right.

That's exactly what *they* were doing. How could you miss it?

———

Coda: "Love to Love You Baby" never went to number 1 on the Billboard charts. Summer and Moroder's first number-one hit was the icy Eurodisco funk of "I Feel Love" the next year. In the context of the entire album from which it was drawn, "I Feel Love" stands as a self-conscious prediction of the future of repetitive music. *I Remember Yesterday* was Moroder and Summer's first disco concept album, and, as the title might suggest, it was constructed as a chronological yet "disco-fied" survey of popular music styles from the 1940s on. Successive tracks fuse disco with swing ('40s), doo-wop ('50s), and Motown ('60s); then there are several straight disco numbers for the 1970s. "I Feel Love" is the final track, its cold computerized repetition assigned to the *next* decade, the uncharted 1980s. It is a self-conscious attempt to forecast *Zukunftsdisko* — the Dance Music of the Future.

Which it was. Disco + Minimalism = Techno. (Two separate collections tracing the prehistory of electronica nominate "I Feel Love" as the *Urpflanze* from which techno, rave, jungle, and ambient all sprang.)[71] The development of electronic dance music into the dominant art music of the twenty-first century is hardly a foregone conclusion — but the eventual dominance of 1970s-style "repetitive music" seems all but certain. We are all destined — privileged — to boogie on, and on, and on . . .

. . .

ONE TWO THREE FOUR . . .
Oooo, love to love you, baby . . .
ONE TWO THREE FOUR FIVE SIX . . .
Oooo, love to love you, baby . . .
ONE TWO THREE FOUR FIVE SIX SEVEN EIGHT . . .

TWO

"A COLORFUL INSTALLMENT IN THE TWENTIETH-CENTURY DRAMA OF CONSUMER SUBJECTIVITY"

Minimalism and the Phenomenology of Consumer Desire

Our frenetic earnestness to attack advertising, our fear of advertising, and our inability to fit advertising into old-time familiar cubbyholes of our significance — all these prevent us from seeing its all-encompassing significance as a touchstone of our changing concept of knowledge and of reality.

Daniel Boorstin, 1961

What is your thought about minimalist music?
I have a feeling about it that is very strong and it's probably not [politically] correct. And that is that we are surrounded by a world of minimalism. All that junk mail I get every single day repeats; when I look at television I see the same advertisement, and I try to follow the movie that's being shown, but I'm being told about cat food every five minutes. That is minimalism. I don't want it and I don't like it. And it's a way of making an impression that doesn't impress me. In fact, I do everything to avoid it. I turn off the television until it's over. I refuse to be advertised to.

Elliott Carter, 2001

THE BIRTH OF MINIMALISM FROM THE SPIRIT OF ADVERTISING

"I Refuse to Be Advertised To":
Interpreting Repetitive Music in a Consumer Society

Why compare minimal music to, of all things, *advertising?* As I observed in the Preface, it is hard to imagine *any* cultural interpretation breaching the radical formalism of minimalism's true believers; but to bypass all the attractive, exotic hermeneutic excursions that seem so close at hand — ecology, meditative spirituality, the influence of non-Western cultures, utopian race and gender politics — only to hone in on one of the least attractive features of our corporate consumer society might seem downright hostile. Delivered as a talk, an early version of this chapter had a noted oral historian of twentieth-century American music out of her seat before the applause died down, vibrating with anger. "You must really *hate* this music," was her accusation. As will become abundantly clear in the following pages, I am irresistibly attracted to minimal music and see this book as an affirmation of its cultural indispensability, but her instantly defensive reaction to the reading that is about to unfold does deserve an answer. Won't I play right into the hands of Elliott Carter, who only brings up advertising as a stick to beat with?

Carter's dark pronouncements on minimalism have been remarkably consistent over the years, returning again and again to what is clearly a preferred metaphorical register. In 1982, when, for a moment, repetitive music looked fair to sweep all before it, his bitterness knew no bounds, not even those of political correctness: "About one minute of minimalism is a lot, because it is all the same. Minimalists are not aware of the larger dimensions of life. One also hears constant repetition in the speeches of Hitler and in advertising. It has its dangerous aspects." Behind these blind attacks is an implacable hatred of repetition per se, an extreme musical snobbery that led Carter in 1973 to dismiss not only nascent minimalism, but the home-grown American modernism of Edgard Varèse and Charles Ives: "I cannot understand the popularity of that kind of music, which is based on repetition. In a civilized society things don't need to be said more than three times."[1]

Carter attacks repetitive music, which he loathes, by analogizing it to consumer advertising, another pervasive and repetitive phenomenon he assumes *everyone* loathes. The strategy is not new: advertising has been a useful scapegoat within Western culture ever since its rise to international prominence in the 1920s, constantly subject to withering dissection by humanists secretly (or not-so secretly) afraid that its repetitive rhythms will drown out the cultivated discourse of Carter's "civilized society." In an oft-anthologized article on the "unintended consequences of advertising," the *Journal of Marketing* boiled down decades of academic critique into a ringing indictment of such manifold complexity that only a multipage chart could do it justice. (The following is a loose narrative paraphrase of what author Richard Pollay thought were the most relevant counts.)

Because advertising is *pervasive* and *persuasive*, its presumed unintended effects are *profound, environmental, intrusive,* and *dominating; because it promotes goods*, it produces *materialism;* because it advocates through *incomplete truths and deceptions*, it creates *cynicism.* When advertising appeals to *mass markets,* it promotes *conformity;* when it appeals to *status,* it promotes *social stratification* and class conflict; when it appeals to *fear,* it promotes *anxiety;* when it appeals to *newness,* it creates *disrespect for authority;* when it appeals to *youth,* it *undermines the family;* and when it appeals to *sexuality,* it creates *erotic obsession* and dysfunction. Because it appeals to the *individual,* it makes people *selfish;* because it must be *simple* and easily understandable, it deals in *social stereotypes* and *debases language.* Because advertising is *emphatic* and repetitively *insistent,* it promotes *regression* and *irrationality,* putting consumers into a *hypnoid trance* that leads to *compulsive consumption,* inability to defer gratification and disregard of future consequences; at the same time, because it *idealizes "the good life,"* it creates *perpetual dissatisfaction* and feelings of lack.[2]

What artist would want to be associated with such a poisonous cultural phenomenon? This is the "dangerous aspect" of minimal music: because its repetitive structures can be analogized to repetitive selling, the style is implicated in the whole laundry list of social dysfunctions for which advertising has been blamed. Not surprisingly, minimalist composers and their advocates have shied away from advertising as a possible model for the style; Louis Andriessen, for example, devoted an entire seminar to erasing the invidious comparison from his students' minds: "A number of my students — say from the generation of Huib Emmer — were highly critical of the developments in American minimalism. Steve Reich, they thought, was like a television soap commercial. So I told them that they were free to think as they wished but that they should understand that the roots of this music sprouted from the true avant-garde attitude. Then we set up a minimal music project at The Hague."[3]

Andriessen's own first foray into minimalism (along with the avant-garde ensemble to perform it) was the product of that seminar. *Hoketus*

(1977–79) can be heard as a dialectical attempt to reclaim repetitive musical processes for European modernism, reworking them to generate dissonant, abrasive, and rhythmically complex sounds that no one would *ever* mistake for a soap commercial. (As we will see below, for all its surface anarchism, the large-scale structure of *Hoketus* is as "commercial" as the most ingratiating moments of American minimalism.) Even Philip Glass, the composer most directly in Carter's crosshairs, describes his theater music, designed as a deliberately unobtrusive ambience that creates "space" around charged images, as the nonmanipulative antithesis of advertising:

> If you didn't have that space there, if the music were too close and therefore immediately on top of the image, there wouldn't be anywhere for the viewer to place himself. In that case, it's like what you end up with on commercials. That's why television commercials end up looking more like propaganda than art. Really, I can't believe the music on most commercials. The music tells you exactly what to look at, at each and every second. It is as if the filmmaker and the composer were taking their hands and actually guiding your eyes around the screen. And this is exactly what you get in propaganda. They're not allowing you to look. They're *making* you look. They don't allow you to see and react or think for yourself.[4]

No high modernist could have put it better. It may have been self-righteous comments like these that caused musicologist Edward Strickland to disparage the later Glass so relentlessly in his 1993 study of the origins of minimalism. Strickland begins his book with a bitter elegy for a dead avant-garde style, observing that the decline in minimalism's potential subversive power is neatly indexed by the 1982 appearance of Glass's face in an ad for Cutty Sark whisky and the recycling, 10 years later, of his music for *The Photographer* in a swank commercial for Incognito perfume. Strickland's historical survey attempts to rescue minimalism by excluding everything that happened after 1976; like Andriessen, he'd rather ignore how repetitive music turned out, and concentrate exclusively on the avant-garde roots of the style.[5]

To undo this modernizing turn, and see minimalism as in any way comparable to advertising, may seem like a cynical attack on the style's countercultural aspirations. (The only question, to paraphrase my angry interlocutor above, is whether you hate this music — or just hate what it's become.) On the other hand, accept that minimalism's relation to "manipulative" late-capitalist cultural forms like advertising and television may be complicated, even equivocal, and you no longer find yourself apologizing quite so assiduously for the music's mainstream success in the 1980s. Let me be clear: I am emphatically not interested in arguing along with Elliott Carter the grim revisionist position that minimalism was a consumerist scam; that would mean that I not only hated this music, but also partook of the contempt that a revanchist like Strickland has for the Yuppie poseurs who (still) like it.[6] Even Susan McClary, who understands full well the potential power and complexity of musical hermeneutics, has recoiled from my earlier, provisional readings of minimalism through advertising culture, because they seemed to lead inexorably to such a nihilistic conclusion: "This pessimistic vision of a world peopled exclusively with hollowed-out subjects doesn't satisfy my old-fashioned humanist leanings. It also grates against my pride in my own time: do we truly like this music only because we're the mindless dupes of mass media?"[7]

If I argue in the following pages that the rise of repetitive music to cultural prominence is in fact one of the "unintended consequences" of advertising, it is without the intention of asserting that the two cultural phenomena, or the act of attending to them, are somehow morally equivalent. But I do not believe they are morally unrelated. It would be comforting to assume (along with its most vocal partisans) that minimalism is GOOD, because it is both the ascetic negation-from-within of late capitalism and a principled embrace of marginalized sensibilities at the non-Western peripheries of the system. Composers and listeners would then be absolved, musically at least, of responsibility for living in an extremely affluent society dominated by material consumption. But, by the same token, minimalism might be BAD, since its empty formalism and Romantic embrace of utopian otherness could as easily represent refusal to engage with the moral complexities of that same affluent consumer society.

In fact, I don't believe the structural isomorphisms between minimalism, advertising, and television, in search of which we will have to plunge deeply into the corporate minds of marketers and media moguls, have any single and necessary ethical implication. Repetitive music, like much avant-garde art since the 1960s, is best understood as a technology of sensation; it thus obeys the pragmatic morality of the tool. Identifying minimalist repetition as a simulation of advertising media does make that technology *signify:* it tells us how, and on what, the tool works. But it does not thereby tell us what the tool itself means, or whether we are fools to pick it up. Whether we use it for good or ill, for engagement or escape, is up to us. Process music that mirrors advertising's repetition — or, for that matter, any aspect of the culture of repetition — needn't only represent capitulation to its effects; the work might take on the burden of repetition as commentary, as critique, even as a kind of callisthenic mental toughening. (All these possibilities will be explored in the pages that follow.)

Suppose we accept that minimalism need not suffer directly for advertising's sins. Still, this new hermeneutic window seems to open onto an arid, uninspiring landscape of strip malls and billboards. What can tuning in to the low background hum of selling really add to our understanding of what are, after all, quite controversial, extreme, and sensuous musical experiences? As we shall see, the theory and phenomenology of advertising and advertising-dominated media reveal truly radical communication strategies, remappings of temporality, subjectivity, and information flow as "avant-garde" as any ever proposed by the denizens of Fluxus or Black Mountain College. Humanist scholars have consistently missed this countercultural aspect of advertising because their jeremiads tend to be based on little more than their own distaste for commercials and consumerism. As Pollay, a professor of marketing, gently points out, sweeping arguments about how ads work are often completely divorced from any real research into either advertising practice or consumer attitudes, and thus reify "the conventional wisdom of nonbusiness academics."[8]

Which Side Are You on?
(Counterculture vs. Corporate Culture)

In an interpretive gambit that will recur several times over the course of this book, I want to take a flippant disparagement of repetitive music, the sneer that it is "just like advertising," as the starting point for a serious historicist investigation. Exploring a business culture that has long been terra incognita for humanistic scholarship, we'll trek through dense thickets of advertising theory, discovering at their center a carefully researched and quite sophisticated discourse of desire, repetition, and subjectivity. The trail may seem to wind away from the authentic values of a musical counterculture toward a sterile corporate world of hollow subjects and media dupes; but, as Thomas Frank argues in his brilliant revisionist history of 1960s business culture, *The Conquest of Cool*, "the actual story is quite a bit messier":

> The cultural changes that would become identified as "counterculture"
> began well before 1960, with roots deep in bohemian and romantic thought,
> and the era of upheaval persisted long after 1970 rolled around. And while
> nearly every account of the decade's youth culture describes it as a reaction

to the stultifying economic and cultural environment of the postwar years, almost none have noted how that context — the world of business and of middle-class mores — was itself changing during the 1960s. The 1960s was the era of Vietnam, but it was also the high watermark of American prosperity and a time of fantastic ferment in managerial thought and corporate practice. Postwar American capitalism was hardly the unchanging and soulless machine imagined by countercultural leaders; it was as dynamic a force in its own way as the revolutionary youth movements of the period, undertaking dramatic transformations of both the way it operated and the way it imagined itself.[9]

It is all too easy for a historian of minimal music to become trapped in a retelling of the factional battles between Uptown (academic) and Downtown (avant-garde) composers in New York City; one way to place minimalism in a wider cultural perspective might be to weave into the story the ad executives and market researchers of Midtown (through which Madison Avenue runs). This will involve discarding conventional wisdom, not only on advertising and its effects, but also on the more narrow historiographic question of when, and in what cultural context, pulse-patterned repetition in music was actually invented. Minimal music is a product of the 1960s; but how well does a deliberately anti-expressive music based on repetition and process really relate to the countercultural ferment and utopian aspirations of "the Sixties"?

There is no doubt that the pioneers of process music saw themselves as part of the counterculture: "My generation grew up in the late sixties. We all went through the cultural crises of the sixties. It was civil rights, pop music, and drugs. . . . We saw our friends working in the field of popular music, living in a very connected way with their culture, and many of us wanted to have that same connection in our work."[10] Philip Glass, speaking here in a 1995 interview, is doubtless sincere in his identification; yet he was born in 1937, far too early for events of the late 1960s to have been formative for either his music or his generational identity. Like La Monte Young, Terry Riley, and Steve Reich (all born in 1935–36), Glass grew up in the sober '50s, not the psychedelic '60s. (Glass's early matriculation at the University of Chicago allowed him to graduate in 1956, take time out to work in a steel mill, and still complete postgraduate work at Juilliard in 1962. Reich had his Master's degree from Mills College in hand by 1963.)

The composers who eventually brought pulse-pattern minimalism into the mainstream might have dipped into the counterculture, especially if it meant getting acquainted with musicians like Ravi Shankar and the master drummers of Ghana, but they remained fundamentally true to their East Coast, 1950s-style training as upper-middle-class professionals. After prestigious university educations, both Reich and Glass ended up at Juilliard, which Glass laughingly remembers as the premier "trade school" for preprofessional composers. He and Reich independently recollect hearing Young's groundbreaking *String Trio* there at the turn of the 1960s — and dismissing it as nonsense. Glass in particular began as the ultimate musical insider, a gray-flannel composer whose well-mannered style and Juilliard connections got him fellowships, publications, and the BMI Young Composer of the Year award for 1960.[11]

For a few young establishment composers of the early 1960s — and that is what both Glass and Reich started as — the counterculture functioned much as it did for the equally buttoned-down young men of the business establishment, especially in the most "creative" corner of it, the advertising industry. Frank points out that advertising's Creative Revolution in the early 1960s (which, as we'll see in the next chapter, involved its own discovery of "minimalism") was not a cynical appropriation of authentic attacks on the consumerist status quo; admen "were drawn to the counterculture because it made sense to them, because they saw a reflection of the new values of consuming and managing to which they had been ministering for several years." The parallel is remarkably exact: both composers and marketers used countercultural energy to break free from — and this is Frank describing the business world, but it applies just as well to Columbia University and Pierre Boulez's *Domaine Musicale* — the stifling technocratic conformity of "over-organization and creative dullness."[12]

I don't want to push this analogy too far: as we'll see, "minimalism" in the design of advertisements actually meant a creative turn *away* from the repetitive "hard sell." It is at the level of the advertising campaign, not the individual ad, that we will make structural comparisons between the ways 1960s process music and advertising worked to create desire. The newly professionalized and computerized departments of "media planning" that oversaw those campaigns were serenely untroubled by either creativity or revolution and remained committed to massive doses of repetition in advertising media planning until well into the 1980s. Most consequentially, perhaps, minimalist composers were, whatever the structural implications of their music, self-consciously autonomous artists, while the "countercultural" energies of 1960s advertising were channeled into . . . more effective advertising. As Frank argues, the penetrating critique of consumer values foregrounded in "creative" advertising has operated since the 1960s as a veneer over the same old repetitive attempts to whip up consumer demand. (This is what he means by the "conquest of cool.") Minimal music, which foregrounds its grimly repetitive structure, might actually provide the immanent critique of consumerism — a look under the hood at the whirring, repetitive machinery of corporate desiring-production — from which ironic "minimalist" advertising is simply a flashy distraction.

Or — it might not. It is part of the postmodern critical position to be suspicious of countercultural utopias; indeed, one of its central questions is how to theorize oppositional politics now that modern industrial society has achieved the total colonization of every possible other utopian space: art, the unconscious, precapitalist (non-Western) societies, even nature itself. It may help to assuage a very real regret for the lost minimalist utopia if we see that it has been constituted in discourse from many if not all of the liberation fantasies of the utopian 1960s: deep ecology and the return to nature (Pauline Oliveros; La Monte Young in his log cabin); the revolutionary, bohemian, anti-Establishment strain (Uptown versus Downtown; Phil Glass driving a cab); the liberating subversion of cultural hierarchies (repetitive music's links to the cyclic structures of jazz, funk, disco, and hip-hop); and, most consistently, the emphasis on altered and non-Western states of consciousness and being-in-time (nonteleological "trance" or "hypnotic" music seen as the direct influence of drugs, Ravi Shankar, African drumming, or Balinese Gamelan).[13]

In fact — and this is the destabilizing conclusion of Frank's carefully researched work — the opposition between buttoned-down corporate-consumer culture and flamboyant 1960s counterculture may *itself* simply be a comforting piece of conventional wisdom, useful more for its ability to generate romantic nostalgia and easy-to-draw battle lines (right vs. left; square vs. hip; Uptown vs. Downtown) than for culture-historical accuracy. Perhaps it is time to stop asking, in the words of the old union ballad so popular in that countercultural decade, *which side are you on?* "Placing the culture of the 1960s in this corporate context does little to support any of the standard countercultural myths," writes Frank, "nor does it affirm the consensual notion of the 1960s as a time of fundamental cultural confrontation. It suggests instead that the counterculture may be more accurately understood as a stage in the development of the values of the American middle class, a colorful installment in the twentieth-century drama of consumer subjectivity."[14]

A pivotal episode in this ongoing drama of consumer subjectivity is precisely what a cultural reading of minimalist process music can illuminate. If the great drama of the 1950s and 1960s was not a titanic clash of political ideologies, but instead a profound yet subtle shift in capitalism as subjective experience, specifically as the experience of consumer desire, then what better hermeneutic index of that shift than the desiring-production encoded by contemporaneous music? Since the Renaissance and the "invention" of tonality, Western music has been uniquely concerned with constructing desire and subjectivity through its control of temporality and expectation; as we saw during our turn on the dance floor in the last chapter, pulse-pattern minimalism is no exception. Much recent work in critical musicology assumes two complementary historiographic propositions: that insight into how previous cultures construed desire and subjectivity can be induced analytically from the way their music moves through time; and that a knowledge of pertinent historical attitudes toward desire can and should have a critical effect on the way we appreciate and evaluate important musical texts.

The burden of this chapter and the next is thus to provide a historical context, perhaps even a pretext, for the emergence of the recombinant teleologies whose theoretical possibility we recently discovered in 1970s minimalism and disco. We will seek that context in the new models of consumer subjectivity and desiring-production developed by practitioners of advertising (and their critics) in the late 1950s and early 1960s; we will then attempt to confirm its relevance by comparing the way a specific structural device, pulsed repetition, is deployed by the corporate culture (advertising campaigns) and the counterculture (minimalist process music).

Midcentury reports on desire, repetition, and subjectivity in consumer society suggest that repetitive music, as important as it may have been to some segments of the late-1960s counterculture, actually bears the formative stamp of a different milieu and an earlier era. (This is a historiographic argument made quite convincingly, though to entirely different ideological ends, by Strickland.)[15] Reich and Glass came to musical maturity at a crucial inflection point within the post–World War II economic boom, a moment of public unease over the pervasive conformity and limitless production capacity of what John Kenneth Galbraith in 1957 christened *The Affluent Society*. Psychologists, social critics, and industrialists discerned a "crisis of desire," a failure of postwar subjects to produce enough authentic, inner-directed striving to keep the dynamos of economic prosperity turning. Advertising professionals, bolstered by new "sciences" of consumer cognition, motivation, and behavior, undertook to discipline the production of desire, mass-producing it with the same rationalized efficiency as their compatriots in manufacturing had achieved in the production of goods. Minimal music can be analyzed and interpreted culturally as the transposition of this rescue effort into sound. Repetitive processes, combined with more traditional constructions of musical *telos,* produce a perfect simulacrum of advertising: the mass production of musical desire.

Before we plunge into the discourse of consumer desire, I need to address two commonsense objections to what may still seem for some readers a twisted hermeneutic choice. At some point we are going to have to deal directly with the pervasive cultural reading of minimalist abstraction as *askesis,* as a turning away from the excess of consumer culture, as the dialectical opposite of Pop Art and its transgressive embrace of advertising imagery. On the other hand, what about the idea that pulse-pattern repetition in music is "trippy" and hallucinogenic? Young, Riley, Glass, and Reich were originally defined as the "New York Hypnotic School," purveyors not of minimalism, but of "trance music."[16] Young and Riley were disciples of Pandit Pran Nath; Reich studied yoga (until his back went out); Glass is still a practicing Tibetan Buddhist. Minimalism as meditative mantra: is that not countercultural enough?

Pop Art Redefined: Advertising, Technology, and Abstraction

> The authentic Pop image exists independent of any
> interpretations. It is simple, direct, and immediately
> comprehensible. We afforded priority to this kind of
> image deliberately, as part of our intention to re-define
> Pop Art as having a more direct relation to Minimal
> and Hard-edged abstract art than is frequently
> admitted.
>
> **Suzi Gablik, *Pop Art Redefined* (1969)**

One reason an attempt to read minimalism through advertising might seem perverse is that it bypasses Pop, the 1960s art movement that trumpeted its consuming interest in advertising culture and imagery.[17] In historical narratives of 1960s visual art, the Minimalist asceticism of mid-decade is often cast as a reaction against the campy Pop Art that immediately preceded it. In this reading, after Pop embraced the Beatles, the Ben Day dot, the Brillo box, and the Campbell's soup can, Minimalism turned away, emptying itself out in protest. Sculptor Carl Andre explained his infamous *Equivalent* series (piles of bricks on a gallery floor) not as a Dada-style attack on the museum, but as a revolt against the media-drenched culture outside, a world overrun by repetitive over-production of signs. For Andre, the creation of any art required "significant blankness . . . some *tabula rasa* . . . some space that suggests there is a significant exhaustion. When signs occupy every surface, then there is no place for the new signs."[18] In 1965 Barbara Rose portrayed Minimalism as offered to the unwilling critic like castor oil, a purgative cure for overconsumption: "If Pop Art is the reflection of our environment, perhaps the [highly reductive] art I have been describing is its antidote, even if it is a hard one to swallow."[19]

By the end of the decade, however, some art critics were becoming impatient with easy dichotomies between "figurative" Pop and "abstract" Minimalism. In an influential 1968 exhibition and subsequent book, curators John Russell and Suzi Gablik sought to "redefine" Pop Art by pointing out the strong formal affinities between its most representative American practitioners (Lichtenstein, Ruscha, Rosenquist, Warhol) and the hard-edged geometric works that both preceded and followed the early-1960s Pop explosion. Russell read Pop as the visual response to a specific historical moment that combined both abstraction *and* consumption: "Pop seems to me to have sprung from two distinct situations, neither of which was in existence before 1950. One is an economy of abundance, in which the password is 'I consume, therefore I am.' The other determinant historical factor was the predominance in both England and the USA of non-referential abstract painting."[20]

Unimpressed by puritanical attacks on Pop decadence, Gablik and Russell argued that American art incorporated commercial imagery not as an endorsement of advertising's hedonistic message, but as an ironic acknowledgment of its formal control. Advertisers, for their own selfish reasons, had developed a "simple, direct, and immediately comprehensible" visual language with all the iconic panache of modernist abstraction — and a vastly greater sphere of influence to boot. Gablik championed this risky formal engagement with commercial vernaculars, rather than "the purist attitudes of certain Abstract artists," as the courageous essence of immanent critique: "What I am attempting to suggest here is that the use of 'found' rather than invented images represents in America what really amounts to a moral strategy. . . . By a moral strategy I mean any means used to achieve a tougher art, to avoid tasteful choices, and to set the stakes higher."[21]

It is only a small step from a Pop Art so redefined to Minimalism, which now appears as the logical next step, honing the hard-edged illustrator's technique favored by Pop artists even as it eliminated their iconic use of branded images. For Gablik, Minimalism is just American Pop with the trademarks whited out: "Already [Pop Art's] main methodological assumptions are being expanded into a new dimension by the Minimalists, who have reduced its iconographic content to the essential structures which constitute the language of technology."[22] In effect, Pop induces the powerful abstracting force of technology, repetition, and mass-media exposure from their effect on what had once been "realistic" figuration; Minimalism then attempts the (perhaps impossible) task of representing those abstracting forces *themselves,* using nothing but the "technology" of advertising: the repetition of simple, flat, and abstract forms.

In a seminal essay quite misleadingly called "Advertising as Capitalist Realism," sociologist and communications scholar Michael Schudson argues toward the same point from the other side. He derives the minimalist aesthetic of mass-media advertising from its function as a repetitious mass reinforcer of consumer attitudes:

> The commercial for Coca-Cola or Alka-Seltzer does not presume a quick response of customers to its efforts. It does not presume that the consumers it wants to reach will see any given showing of the ad, or, seeing it, quickly respond by buying. It is a general reminder or reinforcer, not an urgent appeal to go out and buy. What the ad says or pictures, then, is obliged to be *relatively placeless and relatively timeless.* National consumer-goods advertising is *highly abstracted and self-contained.* This *flat, abstract world* of the advertisement is part of a deliberate effort to connect specific products in people's imaginations with certain demographic groupings or needs or occasions. Sometimes, in an effort not to exclude any potential customers from identifying with the product, advertisers choose not to show *any* people in their ads. *Thus abstraction is essential to the aesthetic and intention of contemporary national consumer-goods advertising.* It does not represent reality nor does it build a fully fictive world. It exists, instead, on its own plane of reality, a plane I will call capitalist realism. [23]

Schudson's 1984 coinage of the term "capitalist realism" neatly skewered both the tone (banal, optimistic) and the intended effect (propaganda) of advertising in terms that were sure to rankle Reagan-era conservatives. But the mass-media forms he describes are anything but "realistic" in the kitschy, Norman Rockwell sense. The flat, generalized, timeless, placeless, depersonalized world of the repetitive ad campaign more closely resembles (and perhaps illuminates) the geometric, empty spaces of Pop-Minimalist abstraction. The move from Pop to Minimalism can thus be read not as a move away from the consumer society, but as a move deeper into it. Pop abstracts the signifier-drenched surface of commodity culture; Minimalism models what Gablik calls its "technology," its underlying formal structure. One reflects the sharp-edged juxtaposition of images in a 30-second TV spot; the other, the endless, repetitious pulsation of the ad campaign that deploys 10,000 such spots every week.

The task of modeling abstract, repetitive structures in time is, of course, one for which music is particularly well suited. On the other hand, the direct equivalent of Pop Art in twentieth-century music, that is, the actual imitation of advertising slogans and jingles, has been extremely rare. The exceptions, almost all operatic, have tended to the puerile and self-congratulatory. (The tuneful singing commercials that comment on the action of Leonard Bernstein's 1955 *Trouble in Tahiti* are a rare early exception, as is the vintage 1967 Pop Art of the AM radio jingles on *The Who Sell Out*.) In a sense, the only true musical Pop Art is pulse-pattern minimalism, and its relation to advertising has little to do with programmatic imitation.[24] We need not violate minimal music's claims to pure abstraction to make our hermeneutic leap; counterintuitive as it may seem, the more relentlessly abstract and repetitious the music, the better its structures and effects model those underlying advertising. Minimalist composers like Glass and Reich were as perfectly positioned to capture advertising's "forms of extreme literalness and comprehensibility" as Warhol and Lichtenstein. Like their Pop Art counterparts, they forced the tradition of abstract experimentation within their chosen medium to confront the contemporary "capitalist realism" of the abundant society outside.

In the Prematurely Air-Conditioned Super Market: Advertising, Trance, and the Counterculture

I was in this prematurely air-conditioned super market
and there were all these aisles
and there were all these bathing caps you could buy
which had these kind of Fourth of July plumes on them
they were red and yellow and blue
I wasn't tempted to buy one
But I was reminded of the fact that I had been avoiding
    the beach.

Einstein on the Beach, act 3, scene 1, "Trial" (1976)

Distracting us from this rather hard-edged truth is the drug-induced funk of 1960s California. *Village Voice* critic Tom Johnson, a composer of process works himself, hazarded a still-popular cultural explanation for early minimalism in 1973: "A friend of mine suggested another theory.

According to him, this extreme form of California minimalism all has to do with acid. Tripping has always been big on the Coast, and people who trip a lot don't need much stimulation. They can be quite content just staring at the wallpaper or listening to one note." (Downtown legend recounts that La Monte Young dispensed some of the best hallucinogens in New York City.)[25] But what Johnson himself admits is an "extreme form" of semi-improvisatory drone minimalism has little in common with the popular pulsed pattern music that this book follows. Young and Riley, the "California" minimalists, tuned in to Indian music, turned on to psychedelics, and dropped out of the musical establishment; but they also dropped right out of "minimal music" as a mainstream cultural practice.

It was critics like Johnson who first popularized the idea that there was in fact a New York Hypnotic School whose process music was akin to the experience of drugs or meditative trance; the New York minimalists themselves have tended to resist the suggestion, often arguing for the most old-fashioned type of structural hearing: "You know, some critics of my earlier pieces thought I was intending to create some kind of 'hypnotic' or 'trance' music. And I always thought, 'No, no, no, no, I want you to be wide awake and hear details you've never heard before.'"[26] Steve Reich's 1984 disavowal was surpassed in vehemence by Philip Glass, who in a 1992 interview for the Buddhist journal *Tricycle* twisted and turned and ultimately refused to link his music with any kind of meditative state — even though the pretext for the friendly interview was his own long-term commitment to Tibetan Vajryana practice. Glass had always found the term "trance music" pejorative.[27] And there is no doubt that sympathetic voices like Johnson's have historically been drowned out by those of neo-conservative critics still fighting the battles of the 1960s: "Whether the experience of this music is meant to substitute for or enhance drug usage, the first impression a listener gains is boredom."[28]

For obvious political and generational reasons, neither Glass nor Reich is comfortable in the role of musical flower child. Still — better hippie than Yuppie, one might argue. If the "trance music" trope does nothing else, it at least wraps minimalism in a reassuring countercultural haze. The timeless, suspended state of altered consciousness that many listeners associate with pulse-pattern minimalism is also associated with rejection of consumer culture. Doesn't turning on, whether to marijuana or minimalism, lead inevitably to dropping out of capitalism's advertising-driven program of goal-directed striving?

Perhaps not. Consider the following anecdote from muckraking journalist Vance Packard's 1957 expose of advertising, *The Hidden Per-*

suaders. By the late 1950s, market researchers had uncovered the interesting fact that housewives no longer made lists when they went to the new "supermarkets," often buying much more than they intended; the new science of "motivational research" attempted to find out why. The (male) hypothesis was that the superabundance of consumer goods made people tense, and they were thus in a hurry to buy, just throwing purchases in the cart in order to get out fast. But sophisticated techniques of psychological monitoring showed that the reality was quite different:

> Mr. Vicary set up his cameras and started following the ladies as they entered the store. The results were startling, even to him. Their eye-blink rate, instead of going up to indicate mounting tension, went down and down, to a very subnormal fourteen blinks a minute. The ladies fell into what Mr. Vicary calls a hypnoidal trance, a kind of light trance that, he explains, is the first stage of hypnosis. Mr. Vicary has decided that the main cause of the trance is that the supermarket is packed with products. [A test by *The Progressive Grocer* showed that customers buy 22 percent more if the shelves are kept full.] Interestingly, many of these women were in such a trance that they passed by neighbors and old friends without noticing or greeting them. Some had a sort of glassy stare.[29]

We seem to have stumbled upon a previously unstudied corner of the 1960s Consciousness Revolution: while Junior was out behind the Piggly-Wiggly getting high on weed, and his sister was studying Transcendental Meditation at the local YMCA, Mom was getting stoned *inside* the supermarket by the endlessly repeating labels on the Campbell's soup cans. Meanwhile La Monte Young was becoming fascinated by the rhythmic pulsations of the electric motor that powered his tortoise's terrarium, and Steve Reich was listening to tape loops cycle in and out of phase for hours. Were all these trances the same trance? Clearly they are all in some way caught up with repetition. But Mom's trance encounter in the supermarket is also intimately bound up with consumption — and thus with the seemingly quite different experience of *desire*.

In the world of advertising there is no real conflict between these two states: timeless suspension in the present moment and diminution of the bounded, analytical ego are precisely the mental conditions under which consumer desire can be most effectively created and channeled. Consequently, perhaps, these are the mental conditions advertising-supported media like American television have evolved to foster. Richard Pollay reports that critics zero in on this phenomenological aspect of advertising, its seductive combination of trancelike suspension and goal-driven desire, as the most dangerous of all: "The repetitive, fantastic, one-sided, and often exhortative rhetorical styles of advertising combine, it is felt, to blur the distinction between reality and fantasy, producing hypnoid states of uncritical consciousness."[30]

James Vicary was by no means the last market researcher to employ elaborate psychological monitoring techniques to quantify the "altered states" of consciousness produced by repetitive advertising stimuli. In 1969 Herbert Krugman, a much-cited theorist of advertising response (and manager of corporate Public Opinion Research for the General Electric Company), went so far as to entice a consumer test subject into a neuropsychological laboratory to watch television advertising while hooked up to a medical electroencephalograph. Krugman, whose pioneering work on "low-involvement learning" from television we will meet again, had become curious about the trance-inducing effect of a dreamy Clairol Nice 'N Easy ad: "The commercial used a slow-motion technique borrowed from the movie film 'The Pawnbroker,' starring Rod Steiger. . . . It had exceptionally high recall scores, but aroused absolutely no pupil dilation response. This seemed quite unusual. Was the commercial learned without any excitement whatsoever, or was there another element present, an unmeasured response? Is the opposite of excitement just nothing? Is calm a flat emptiness?"[31]

Krugman's research protocol was simple: he took a baseline reading of brain activity while his test subject was reading a magazine advertisement, and then showed her the Clairol ad along with two GE spots, one quiet and gentle, the other fast and assaultive. The results were surprising, even to him: there was a "characteristic mode of response" to television ads, independent of content, that was quite distinct from the response to print advertising. The EEG showed that within 30 seconds the viewer of TV ads stops producing the beta waves that signal active mental work in favor of the alpha and delta waves that normally accompany sleep, drowsiness — or hypnotic trance. The effect was steady over all three ads, and neither increased nor decreased with repeated viewings.

Krugman saw his impromptu study as experimental confirmation of Marshall McLuhan's still-controversial dictum that "the medium is the message." As received, television advertising was hardly communication at all; what it really provided was ambience: "The subject was no more trying to learn something from television than she would be trying to learn something from a park landscape while resting on a park bench." But the ambience was loaded with information, huge quantities of information "*not thought about at the time of exposure,* but much of it capable of being stored for later activities."[32] These activities would undoubtedly include buying the products advertised — and at the point of sale, purchasers would testify, truthfully, that they *wanted* those products. But, if Krugman's data are any indication, purchasers would remain blissfully unaware of the gradual, repetitive process by which the cognitive parameters of that desire had been created. Krugman hypothesized that the information received during television's alpha-wave trance (brand identities, product claims, lifestyle images) is stored *unprocessed,* only to be experienced later, when we actually buy something, as part of the complex cognitive-emotional structure we call desire. *("I wasn't tempted to buy one/But I was reminded of the fact that I had been avoiding the beach.")*

I will have quite a bit more to say about the details of Krugman's "low-involvement" hypothesis below, particularly as they provide a cultural model for the long, static plateaus and sudden phase shifts of repetitive process music. For now, let the final "hip" metaphor of his article, so redolent of the heady countercultural year 1969 (and thus a perfect confirmation of Thomas Frank's thesis), remind us that the doors of perception could be cleansed not only by drugs, mantra, and music — but also by repetitious advertising: "The old theory [of mass communication] was concerned with the fact that a message was transported. The new theory must be concerned with the fact that the viewer is transported, taken on a trip, an instant trip — even to the moon and beyond."[33] Tripping may indeed have been big on the California coast, or in La Monte Young's Soho ashram; but the television trip was the biggest one of all. Why wouldn't music tag along?

THE SYSTEM OF OBJECTS: THEORIZING CONSUMER DESIRE FROM VEBLEN TO BAUDRILLARD

But already at a [very early] point in economic evolution, specialized consumption of goods as an evidence of pecuniary strength had begun to work out in a more or less elaborate system. It is traceable back to the initial phase of predatory culture.

Thorstein Veblen, *The Theory of the Leisure Class* (1899)

The basic lexicon that covers our walls and haunts our consciousness remains strictly asyntactic: different brands succeed one another, are juxtaposed, or replace

one another, without articulation or transition; this is
an erratic lexical system in which brands devour one
another and the lifeblood of each brand is interminable
repetition.

Jean Baudrillard, *The System of Objects* (1968)

Desires and Objects

The well-worn critical tropes around minimalist composition actually construct a chimera, the impossible new music that could be at the same time ascetic *and* narcotic.[34] Rather than choose one attribute over the other, I would prefer to set them both aside. But I am under no illusion that advertising, this chapter's ruling metaphor, does not also entail a full measure of complexities and contradictions. The claim that minimal music "is like" advertising could mean several things: that a certain recombinant teleology in music *feels like* the subjective desire for consumer goods stimulated by advertising; or that the process of minimalist music *works like* the process of stimulating that desire through repetitious advertising; or even that minimalism's repetitious overload *corresponds to* the force of mass-media advertising, as it piles up of huge masses of individual desires into what we have come to recognize as the driving force of the postindustrial economy, aggregate consumer demand.

In fact, I want to maintain the hermeneutic flexibility to argue that any or all of these mappings obtains at the appropriate moment of culture. But metaphoric flexibility, if it is not to degenerate into sheer scholarly sleight of hand, requires that the terms juxtaposed also be grounded in some direct human perception of sameness. This has been the transgressive power of a sexual hermeneutic for music: comparing musical teleology to sexual desire named a sensual similarity many already felt, but few were willing to discuss.[35] After all, we all (think we) know where sexual desire comes from — and what it feels like. Can we have the same immediate visceral understanding of consumer demand?

A persistent strain of leftist cultural critique would argue that we cannot, because the goal of consumer society is to alienate us from our "real" desires in order to replace them with an artificial and oppressive commodity fetishism. We will have occasion below to grapple with the economic essentialism of these "alienists of consumption," as post-Marxist sociologist Jean Baudrillard once dubbed them — but one must concede a structural point. Consumer desire is more complex than sexual desire, because it is mediated through a complex system of mass-marketed commodities. (This is not to imply that sexual desire is unmediated — just that the mediations *feel* simpler.) What is the place of "things" in the experience of consumer desire? Why compare the repetition in minimal music to advertising, rather than the endless series of interchangeable mass-produced objects, from soda cans to tract houses, that advertising was invented to promote?

Repetitive minimalism in the visual arts, the production of series like Andy Warhol's silk screens or Donald Judd's machined boxes, has often been seen as blank-ironic troping on industrial mass production, the kind of reading encouraged when Warhol bluntly renamed the studio where assistants cranked out copies of his work "The Factory"; or when Judd ordered hundreds of near-identical metal boxes from an actual factory, and then stored them in two abandoned artillery warehouses. But the very nature of music as an art form makes imitating industrial production at the same time too easy and too difficult for minimalist composers. Easy, because the orchestra has long been analogized to a factory: the multiplication of performances (and, even worse, recordings) is already inherently like industrial production. Difficult, because the musical "work" itself isn't really an object, and thus is hard to analogize to a consumer object. In fact, as Nyman pointed out in 1974, the experimental tradition within which minimalism grew was fundamentally averse to arresting musical creativity inside discrete, bounded "time-objects," preferring instead the fluidity of open-ended "situations, fields, and processes."[36] No minimalist composer ever turned out a series of identical musical "works" like Warhol; or directly engaged industrial mass production by ordering (ordering *what?*) from a factory like Judd.[37] It would be a serious epistemological misreading to see the repeated modules of minimalist process music as analogous to serial art, and thereby to the endless series of identical, material commodity-objects rolling off an assembly line.

But this is not to deny that one can construct a cultural hermeneutic that links minimal music to the structures and technologies of mass production. All that is required is a simple yet radical shift in perspective: from the production of things to the production of *desire-for-things*. Production of things happens in a factory; production of desire-for-things happens via magazines, billboards, television, the Internet — all those carriers of the manifold semiotic structures we can lump together and designate, after Michel Foucault, *discourse*. The central argument of this chapter will be that repetitive music arises with and mirrors a key historical transformation of the consumer society: the self-conscious postwar transfer of the repetitive structures of mass production from the material realm of the object into the symbolic realm of discourse. Instead of the mass production of *goods,* the affluent society became obsessed with the mass production of *discourse about goods,* specifically the mass production of both *discourse about the desire for goods,* and the mass production of *desire for goods through discourse.*

That last is, of course, just a fancy way of saying . . . advertising.

Systems of Desires, Systems of Objects

Put simply, repetitive music can be compared to advertising because, like advertising, it is an American discourse that uses structures in time to create and channel desire. But are the desires stirred up by music really "the same as" those engendered by advertising? Clearly the late-twentieth-century *desire-for-things* engages our subjectivity quite differently from the sexual urges commonly understood to be encoded in, for instance, Wagner's *Tristan und Isolde,* the nineteenth century's premier tonal discourse on bodily desire. And, just as clearly, Glass and Reich sound very different from Wagner — so radically different, as we have seen, that many critics have interpreted their music as encoding nothing less than liberation from late-Romantic tonality's dark desires for orgasm and violent annihilation. But if the linked analyses of the previous chapter have any persuasive force at all, they show how limiting a view of pulsed process music that excludes desiring-production can be.

Let's read minimal music through Donna Summer one last time. Along with the generalized sense that Eurodisco represented techno-fetishistic sexual perversity, there was in the late 1970s a strong critical subclaim that Summer and Moroder's collaboration was in fact a form of musical prostitution: "In one of the photos on the *[Bad Girls]* inner sleeve, Donna Summer's coproducer, Giorgio Moroder, poses as her pimp. That's as good a metaphor as any for their musical interaction."[38] The spectacle of prostitution — especially the streetwalking girls to whom Summer was compared (to some extent at her own instigation) — is the spectacle of (supposedly) natural desires not just commodified and industrialized through assembly-line repetition, but publicly *advertised* for sale. In popular parlance, advertising and prostitution are two sides of the same coin, stamped from an alloy of sexualized desire and manipulation: streetwalkers "advertise their wares," while ad executives "whore themselves" to sell products. To compare process music to advertising is thus to make two closely linked claims: first (interestingly) that the music deliberately uses its industrial-strength repetition to whip up desire; and second (invidiously) that the musical desire in question is "prostituted" — that is, debased and inauthentic.

This is why advertising is more useful as a metaphorical register for repetitive music than other repetitious public discourses, the most obvious being the twentieth-century fusion of mass media and propaganda that Elliott Carter evoked with his reference to "Hitler speeches." At issue here is not changing people's opinions — a task too concrete for musical structures alone — but changing the way they feel, the structure of their desires. Deny music that power, and you cut it off from almost any imaginable cultural agency. Accordingly, in the investigation that follows, I will accept the *minimalism-is-advertising* trope as cultural evidence that influential critics have perceived desiring-production in minimal music, while attempting to strip away their pejorative use of the trope to imply manipulation and prostitution. Commonsense ideas about "natural" desires for things will seem less and less relevant as we follow the sociology of consumption through its postmodern linguistic turn. Blithe assumptions about which desires are "real" and which "manipulated" evaporate when we see the consumption of mass-produced, branded consumer goods not just as satisfaction of somehow "innate" needs, but as our entry into what Baudrillard called "the system of objects": the endlessly stimulating game of consumption as signification.

It is by becoming enmeshed in this manufactured system of objects that consumer desire embarks on a quite different trajectory than that of the familiar sexual desires imputed to Poppea, Lucia, Tristan, Don José, Salome & Co., desires whose representation in sound and time has been the cornerstone of tonal evolution since the seventeenth century. Both urges begin together, with the instinctive pull toward homeostasis that has underpinned theories of desire since Freud postulated a biological drive in the human organism away from unpleasure (imbalance, tension) toward pleasure (balance, release). Almost all theorists agree that this type of instinctive physical drive is rarely, in advanced societies, experienced directly as such. In an influential move, French psychoanalysis made the linguistic implication of Freudian theories explicit, arguing that an essential part of our development as human subjects was the capture of irrational drives by the symbolic order, the world of language. Through the signifying power of language, to quote Jacques Lacan's familiar reformulation of Freud, the Oedipal "Law of the Father" transforms the implacability of biological *drive* into the complex cultural negotiations we experience as *desire*.[39]

Post-Lacanian psychoanalysis has tended to lose itself in constructing complex structural linkages among drives, desires, their various objects, the subject, and language itself, but the one distinction that has proved crucial for the hermeneutics of repetitive music has been between the experiences of time ascribed to drive and desire. Desire, the more symbolically complex phenomenon, has in practice been easier to describe and imagine musically. If "desire emerges when drive gets caught in the cobweb of Law/prohibition,"[40] then the experience of desire must always be teleological: an experience of delay, of circling around a forbidden object, of striving toward an ever-receding goal. The analogy to *Tristan*-style tonal structures of ever-more-prolonged tension and ever-more-delayed release is obvious — as is the relevance of Wagner's archetypal plot, with its biologically driven lovers in adulterous conflict with the Law. On the other hand, capturing the satisfaction of a pure, presymbolic drive in symbolic language has been more problematic, calling forth garbled intimations of an experience both instantaneous and endless. This is a feeling, one intuits, like the nonteleological, nonnegotiable short-circuit that follows contact with a high-voltage electrical wire. Or perhaps it has more to do, as 1970s French feminists famously testified, with the *petit mort*, the ecstatic, timeless, presubjective experience of the female orgasm.

Theoretical terminology for these experiential states has developed with a distinct French accent: symbolically mediated satisfaction of desire is *plaisir*, normally translated as "pleasure"; while the more exotic direct experience of the drive has been labeled as *jouissance*, which can mean either ecstasy or orgasm. The reader will recall how we approached this talismanic critical term during the previous chapter's exploration of disco teleology, and how dramatically I swerved away from using the concept to explain the effects of repetitive music. I am about to swerve again, but not simply back toward Lacanian desire and the entrapment of pleasure in language. Rather than oscillate helplessly between *plaisir* and *jouissance*, I want to introduce a third way. In late capitalism, it seems, there is another trajectory for the biological drive.

In French the word *jouissance* denotes not only — nor even usually — a timeless state of sexual ecstasy. Its mundane meaning is closer to "enjoyment," in its dual sense of *gaining pleasure from* and *possessing* something — more precisely, *gaining pleasure from possessing* something. *Jouissance* has, therefore, an irreducibly mercantile aspect. (*Jouis Coca-Cola!*) In a consumer society the satisfaction of biological drives is accomplished through consumption of commodities; economists call this drive to enjoy/possess commodities a *need*, and the perception of a need for a given commodity a *want*. These "wants and needs" are analogous to, but by no means the same as, Lacanian desire. If psychoanalytic desire is drive trapped within the system of language, then consumer desire may be conceptualized as that same drive captured by a very different system, the system of commodities. In the consumer society drives are not pent up within what Frederic Jameson once called (for quite different reasons) "the prison house of language"; they are set free within a huge department store, where they can crystallize onto the system's vast array of mass-produced branded objects. Forget the stern *Law* of the Father; consumer desire is drive enticed into the endlessly inviting *Store* of the Father.

Systemic Crises of Desire:
The "Other-Directed Personality" and the "Minimal Self"

The capturing of the drive by a sublinguistic system of objects is fundamental to Jean Baudrillard's iconoclastic analyses of consumption. Baudrillard's first major theoretical statement on the consumer society, *The System of Objects,* redefined consumption as a signifying act, and thus resonates strangely with the left-wing struggles that marked 1968, the turbulent year of its publication. Baudrillard's semiotic analysis of capitalist consumption deliberately removed it from the realm of political economy, neatly obsolescing not only Marxism, but an entire 1950s mandarin-liberal critique of industrial consumer culture as well. Intellectuals had worried for decades that "real" desire for commodities was largely absent in advanced capitalist societies, replaced by artificially created needs whose fulfillment made no economic sense, came largely without authentic pleasure, and undermined the very character structure that supported both the Enlightenment ego and the Protestant work ethic. Baudrillard swept these intimations of decline aside, announcing that consumption was *inherently* artificial, ritualistic, and repetitive; that the system of objects, a crude parody of the system of language, gave rise to what we had always thought of as "our" innermost desires; and — most relevant for the hermeneutics of minimal music — that consumption of objects, the "satisfaction" of those desires, didn't necessarily lead to anything immediately recognizable as personal agency or release of tension.

This is the same realization that conservative historian Christopher Lasch, from the opposite side of the political spectrum, would later articulate in a pair of powerful book-length jeremiads. In *The Culture of Narcissism* (1978) and *The Minimal Self* (1984), Lasch harnessed psychoanalytic object-relations theory to argue that a consumer society dominated by advertising would inevitably lead to a bad-postmodern collapse of subjectivity. Advertising and commodity culture had created a "dream world, a prefabricated environment that appeals directly to our inner fantasies," impoverishing our developmental environment and fatally enticing consumers into a narcissistic abandonment of self: "The commodity world stands as something completely separate from the self; yet it simultaneously takes on the appearance of a mirror of the self, a dazzling array of images in which we can see anything we wish to see. Instead of bridging the gap between the self and its surroundings, it obliterates the difference between them." As Lasch heard it, the minimalist tendency in art and music reflected this regressive narcissism directly: "It sees the surrounding world as an extension of the self or the self as something programmed by outside forces. It imagines a world in which everything is interchangeable, in which musical sounds, for example, are experienced as equivalent to any other kind of sound. It abolishes selfhood in favor of anonymity."[41]

By 1984 the critique leveled by *The Minimal Self* was at least 35 years old. Lasch echoes the standard set of generalizations about the "unintended consequences" of advertising, but he went further toward a cultural hermeneutics of music than most. It took the inexorable rise of minimalism to cultural ubiquity (1984 was already slightly past the apogee of repetitive pulse patterning in classical music) to make the connection with contemporaneous experimental art practices explicit. Earlier commentators, many of them like Baudrillard professional sociologists, were not yet aware of the minimalist tendencies in art and music that were gathering force deep underground: they simply registered a radical crisis of subjectivity and desire in the unprecedented economic and social conditions of postwar America.

The bland outlines of a new, disturbing character structure began to emerge in the middle 1950s. Both William Whyte, on the right, and Herbert Marcuse, on the left, wrote influential books bemoaning the deleterious effects of technocratic capitalism, specifically its habit of meddling with man's relationship to his "own" subjective desires. Whyte's *The Organization Man* (1956) inveighed against uncritical acceptance of what he called the "Social Ethic" — a set of collectivist ideas that encouraged men to sublimate themselves to large organizations, root out individualism, and conform at any cost to scientifically determined norms. His painstaking research into patterns of behavior in large companies — and in the new suburban housing tracts where their transient junior executives roosted — convinced him that too much of society's energy was being channeled into creating shallow, adaptable personalities, and that minor deviations from the organizational average, especially self-conscious attempts to exceed or challenge it, were ruthlessly and automatically punished. Whyte's prescription was a bit more rugged individualism and some covert individual resistance — his book ends with an appendix that tells the reader "How to Cheat on Personality Tests."

Marcuse's contemporaneous *Eros and Civilization* (1955) and his famous follow-up, *One-Dimensional Man* (1964), offered little hope that withholding a few answers on the next "personality inventory" from the Personnel Department would fix a fundamental flaw in the capitalist system. For Marcuse the sheer productivity of the new technological reality inevitably stunted developmental growth. Since, as he ruefully admitted, "the system delivers the goods" in abundance, there was now no need to repress desires, give up the Pleasure Principle, and internalize a painful Reality Principle. But this consumer nirvana (you can have whatever you want whenever you want it) has the nasty side effect of foreclosing subjectivity. Marcuse articulates the contradiction in classically Freudian terms: without the Reality Principle, there can be no Ego, and without the Ego there can be no true inner self. (Thus the "one-dimensional man" is parent to the "minimal self.") The system keeps us infantilized by encouraging us to act out every wish in seemingly liberated consumption.

> Thus diminishing erotic and intensifying sexual energy, the technological reality *limits the scope of sublimation*. It also reduces the *need* for sublimation. In the mental apparatus, the tension between that which is desired and that which is permitted seems considerably lowered, and the Reality Principle no longer seems to require a sweeping and painful transformation of instinctual needs. . . . The organism is thus being preconditioned for the unconditional acceptance of what is offered. Inasmuch as the greater liberty involves a contraction rather than an extension and development of instinctual needs, it works *for* rather than *against* the status quo of general repression.[42]

Marcuse coined the oxymoron "repressive desublimation" to describe the way a permissive and affluent society could close off any chance for dissent, by instantly gratifying all instinctual needs before they had a chance to be transformed into authentic (i.e., painful) inner subjectivity. A paradoxical side effect of this liberation of desire was the "weakening of Eros": a withdrawal of affect from all realms but the explicitly sexual, since no unsublimated libido remained to be channeled into work and creative activity. Marcuse was aware of, though not focused on, the implications for supposedly "autonomous" art and music: "If mass communications blend together harmoniously, and often unnoticeably, art, politics, religion, and philosophy with commercials, they bring these realms of culture to their common denominator — the commodity form. The music of the soul is also the music of salesmanship."[43]

Both Whyte and Marcuse agreed that the new character structures were determined by a new socioeconomic reality. For Whyte it was simply the self-protective impulse of large, scientifically managed bureaucracies; Marcuse's critique seems more penetrating, because it recognized, decades before *The Culture of Narcissism*, the painful fact that affluence — economic success itself — seemed to eat away at individual subjectivity. David Riesman's *The Lonely Crowd* (1950), with its pioneering definition of the "other-directed personality," was the first, and probably the most influential, formulation of this truth. Riesman postulated a single massive growth spurt in world economic history, and thus three economic stages of society: before growth, during growth, and after growth. Each stage gave rise to a distinctive character structure. During the extended and placid time before growth, personalities were *tradition-directed*: direction came from the stable consensus of a static culture. During the growth itself, a time of rapid change and scarcity of resources, personalities were *inner-directed*: direction internalized early from the parents allowed the conquest of a changing, often hostile environment with flexible strategies but fixed goals. Now, claimed Riesman, America was entering the postgrowth phase, with the concomitant rise of the *other-directed* personality. This type of person lacked strongly internalized goals and feelings, taking direction not from inner character structures (Marcuse's Ego) or strong "father" figures. Rather, each member of the group constantly took direction from others in the group: approval and belonging replaced success as the ultimate goal — as they must in a society of abundant resources where, for the first time, managing people was more important than transforming nature. In Riesman's elegant metaphor, the *gyroscope* by which the inner-directed personality navigates is replaced by the other-directed person's extremely sensitive *radar*.[44]

Riesman purposely refused to romanticize the inner-directed personality, or condemn the other-directed. Still, combining his portrait with the less flattering ones by Marcuse and Whyte lets us identify an accelerating crisis of desire and subjectivity in the late 1950s and early 1960s. Some artists lived the crisis directly and personally: is there any real doubt that

Andy Warhol, for instance, was an other-directed personality? Minimalists (as we might expect, given Gablik and Russell's arguments above) picked up on the crisis structurally, turning all its characterological traits into abstract formal devices: the waning of affect, the emphasis on order and "consonance," the deliberate emphasis on surface, externalized relationships, the lack of any attempt to represent subjectivity or inwardness. And above all, in music, the repetitious collapse of traditional teleology, a mimetic response to the collapse of the internalized goals and "real" inner desires — the "gyroscope" — that supposedly guaranteed an independent, directed subjectivity.

In the next chapter I will follow up in some detail the analytical consequences of a music that attempts to mirror this collapse — as we'll see, perhaps better seen as a recombinant mutation — of desiring-production. But even a cursory look at the performing instructions for an early minimalist work like Terry Riley's *In C* turns up phrase after phrase emphasizing an unprecedented degree of other-direction in musical performance. Executants are urged to keep their antennae always up ("Listen very carefully to one another"), since the challenge of the piece is managing the complex polyrhythmic interaction of their individual patterns. No authority figure tells them when to move from pattern to pattern — but the piece works only if they use that freedom responsibly, to stay close to the statistical norm, within earshot of the group ("It is important not to race too far ahead or to lag too far behind"). Playing is a constant process of adjusting individual patterns to the group dynamic, whether through accentuation ("when you reenter you [should be] aware of what effect your entrance will have on the music's flow") or metric placement ("if the players seem to be consistently too much in the same alignment of a pattern, they should try shifting their alignment by an eighth note or quarter note with what's going on in the ensemble").

In C represents a type of musicking that had not previously been a feature of the European classical tradition, which has tended to favor — no surprise — the tradition-directed personality type, ready to submit completely to a score, a teacher, or a conductor's will. Riley's loose musical framework obviously has more to do with the improvisatory pragmatics of jazz, and it is true that the overall shape of a jazz performance, when not dictated by a leader, is arrived at democratically by group consensus.[45] Still, jazz musicians are judged not by their ability to stay in the collective groove, which is taken for granted, but by their solo improvisatory prowess. African American jazz, if it does not altogether transcend Riesman's typology, seems a music of deep inner-direction, appropriate for a culture undergoing a grievously delayed entrance into modernity.[46]

In performance, the modular repetition of *In C* is emphatically not, as Tom Johnson once hypothesized, "more like a raga than a piece"; the Hindustani melodic world in which *rāgā* operate emphasizes free-flowing yet tradition-directed improvisation. To read *In C* as an exotic "tribal" experience is to confuse the superficially similar group orientations of tradition and other-directedness. Sitting at the feet of a guru, one internalizes what Riesman analogizes as the "cultural monotone" of tradition. (When Riley became a formal disciple of Pandit Pran Nath, he stopped composing repetitive music.) But a performance of *In C* demands much more contrapuntal, cosmopolitan skill at working with people: "The other-directed person must be able to receive signals from far and near; the sources are many, the changes rapid."[47] Only the reflexive alignment of *In C* with the psychedelic and exotic could justify labeling as countercultural "freedom" the constant web of minor negotiations necessary to navigate even a moderate-sized group through its interactive structure.[48]

As anyone who has tried to perform in it can attest, *In C* is, at root, an exercise in human relations. Riley's performance instructions don't have much in common with the autocratic musical traditions of north India (or Young's Soho loft, for that matter); what they *do* resemble are the results of the reigning 1960s liberal assumptions about people management known, thanks to the popularity of Douglas McGregor's 1960 business bestseller, *The Human Side of Enterprise,* as "Theory Y."[49] McGregor rejected traditional Taylorist management strategies based on what he called "Theory X": that most people hate their work, avoid responsibility, and must be coerced or controlled into achieving organization goals. Theory Y, conversely, takes other-direction as its starting point: it assumes that employees respond to peer pressure more than authority; that work is as natural a human endeavor as play; that most groups are capable of taking responsibility for their own performance; and that well-managed, committed employees will motivate themselves to work together and achieve corporate goals.

As Riley pitches it to his players, *In C* might as well have been titled *In Y;* the "freedom" it offers is a perfect antidote to the rigid Theory X orientation of the traditional symphony orchestra.[50] And as such, it is the perfect index of the strange attraction that corporate and countercultures had in the 1960s. Thomas Frank has noted the fusion of corporate Theory Y rhetoric with countercultural attitudes in "revolutionary" business literature of the late 1960s; the remarkably successful other-directed performing ensembles of minimalism show a homegrown version of Theory Y at work in the musical counterculture as well. Robert Townsend's *Up the Organization* (1970) ironically hypothesized that Ho Chi Minh subscribed to Theory Y; had the author been a devotee of experimental music, he could have praised the equally "subversive" guerilla management skills of Terry Riley, Steve Reich, and Philip Glass.[51]

Homo economicus Meets the Society of Affluence

How, then, does desire work, what does it *feel* like, in an affluent world full of other-directed personalities? At a key moment in his 1970 study of *Consumer Society*, Jean Baudrillard spins a fable: "There once was a man who lived in Scarcity. After many adventures and a long voyage in the Science of Economics, he encountered the Society of Affluence. They were married and had many needs."[52] The man in this little fable is *homo economicus*, the rational subject beloved by economists because, as Baudrillard recalls, "you always knew what he wanted." By 1968, after his colleagues had announced the Death of the Subject in almost every other realm, Baudrillard was ready to hold "an autopsy of *homo economicus*." We'll observe that autopsy in detail below, but first we must establish the cause of death. *Homo economicus* was laid to rest by the very same economic profession that created him; and they killed him by taking away his "authentic" needs. By the early 1970s all the comforting economic fictions about "needs" — that our desires for certain goods are natural, that they come from inside us, that they somehow belong to us, and that the way we handle them can define our individual identity — were in tatters. As long as those needs appeared likely to exceed the productive capacity of society, they created a society of scarcity, with a fundamental "economic problem." Solving the economic problem — increasing production — gave purpose to both human endeavor and the science of economics. The inalienable, inexhaustible desires of *homo economicus* provided the teleology of social progress.

But as early as 1930, in the depths of a world depression, John Maynard Keynes had the temerity to predict the solution of the economic problem: "assuming no important wars and no important increase in population, the *economic problem* may be solved, or at least within sight of solution, within a hundred years." Keynes's donnish image of the future was a cultured, leisured society struggling to find outlets for human energy. Since all needs could effortlessly be met, *homo economicus* would die, to be replaced by *homo aestheticus*. But along the way, we would have to learn to make nice distinctions among our needs: "Now it is true that the needs of human beings may seem to be insatiable. But they fall into two classes — those needs which are *absolute* in the sense that we feel them whatever the situation of our fellow human beings may be, and those which are *relative* in the sense that we feel them only if their satisfaction lifts us above, makes us feel superior to, our fellows. Needs of the second class may indeed be insatiable, [but] a point may soon be reached . . . when [absolute] needs are satisfied."[53]

I'll ask you to remember this gambit. Keynes is raising the specter of what Thorstein Veblen, in his sociological classic *The Theory of the Leisure Class,* had called "invidious" or (the term that stuck) "conspicuous" consumption: the never-ending desire to keep up with the proverbial Joneses. (Or, rather, keep up with the Vanderbilts: in 1899 Veblen hardly thought his study of the idle rich had any relevance to society at large.) To proclaim the general solution of the economic problem, Keynes has to declare that invidious desire is in some way inauthentic desire. We can longer depend on *homo economicus* knowing what he needs; he might be consuming just for display, looking to the consumption of his neighbors to tell him what he needs to be satisfied. He might be a little too — other-directed.

Keynes was wrong about the wars and population, but he appeared, at least by the mid-1950s, to have been even more spectacularly right than he could have imagined about staggering increases in productivity. Only 28 years later, his one-time disciple John Kenneth Galbraith could take the solution of the economic problem as the starting place for a bestselling indictment of what he indelibly labeled *The Affluent Society.* Breaking with conventional economic wisdom, Galbraith argued that an ever-increasing volume of consumer production did not guarantee a utopian, just, or even tolerable society. To make his case, he systematically dismantled every justification he could see for more and more productive capacity: to increase economic (job) security, to lessen inequality — or as a last defense, to obey the dubious "imperatives of consumer demand." Galbraith was openly impatient with those who justified everincreasing production of consumer goods simply because people seemed to want the stuff. He went Keynes one better — not only were more and more of those desires invidious and thus inauthentic, but the entire relationship between demand and supply seemed to have been inverted: "As a society becomes increasingly affluent, wants are increasingly created by the process by which they are satisfied. This may operate passively.

Increases in consumption, the counterpart of increases in production, act by suggestion or emulation to create wants. . . . Or producers may proceed actively to create wants through advertising and salesmanship. Wants thus come to depend on output. It will be convenient to call [this] the Dependence Effect."[54]

Galbraith's Dependence Effect led to what he called the *revised sequence* of economic expansion: in the traditional sequence it was people's latent (authentic) desires that justified increases in production; now increases in production actually created wants in people that production then rushed to fulfill. Every shiny, newly created desire for a shiny, newly created Maytag refrigerator or Delco TV set was by definition inauthentic. *Homo economicus* was out of a job. Galbraith assumed that the pointlessness of what he exposed as the vicious circle of consumption ("the effort of the squirrel to keep abreast of the wheel that is propelled by his own efforts") would be obvious.[55] His prescription was a moratorium on increased consumer production, and massive governmental investment to meet real needs (education, poverty, housing, scientific research, etc.) in the public sector.

The providential appearance of *Sputnik* in late 1957 gave Galbraith's rather sober economic treatise instant notoriety, but it took a professional muckraker to dramatize the blistering critique of advertising-as-(inauthentic)-want-creation implied in Galbraith's revised sequence. In 1957, a few months before *The Affluent Society*, Vance Packard published *The Hidden Persuaders*, the first sustained attack on advertising in a decade. In an introductory chapter called "The Trouble with People," Packard mordantly noted that *homo economicus*, now on his last legs, had become "perverse and unpredictable." There was simply not enough consumer demand *of any kind* to go around. Packard outlined the panic in executive suites caused by the disappearance of what had seemed like endless reserves of consumer desire: "In the early fifties, with overproduction threatening on many fronts, a fundamental shift occurred in the preoccupation of people in executive suites. Production now became a relatively secondary concern. Executive planners changed from being maker-minded to market-minded. The president of the National Sales Executives in fact exclaimed: 'Capitalism is dead — consumerism is king!'" The solution? Admen needed to roll up their sleeves and get cracking at making the revised sequence work as well for business as the traditional one had: "One ad executive exclaimed with fervor: 'What makes this country great is the creation of wants and desires.'"[56]

The Ideological Genesis of Needs

Packard's *The Hidden Persuaders* was actually sold as an exposé of how advertising men were exploiting the new "sciences" of depth psychology and motivational research to mobilize steady new streams of consumer desire. Packard saw this as an escalation in the eternal war between hucksters and the unsuspecting public, with the new Freudian heavy artillery fired from hidden bunkers far behind the lines: "The trend in marketing to the depth approach was largely impelled by difficulties the marketers kept encountering in trying to persuade people to buy all the products their companies could fabricate. Thus it was that merchandisers of many different products began developing a startling new view of their prospective customers. People's subsurface desires, needs, and drives were probed in order to find their points of vulnerability. . . . Once these points of vulnerability were isolated, the psychological hooks were fashioned and baited and placed deep in the merchandising sea for unwary prospective customers."[57] Previous critiques of advertising had always attacked deceptive claims; Packard's book provides the first indignant discussion of the many familiar advertising strategies that do not lie, but manipulate: image or lifestyle ads, the sexual sell, the appeal to hidden needs, ads that encourage infantile regression, appeals to subconscious class and race anxieties, and so on.

The most sensational revelation in *The Hidden Persuaders* was that advertisers were experimenting with *subliminal* advertising: brief messages flashed for a fraction of a second on a movie or television screen could implant desires directly into our brains without ever impinging on our conscious minds. (Tests at the time showed that a subliminal message like "You are hungry" at the movies could increase traffic at the refreshment stand by up to 10 percent.) It is difficult to imagine a more powerful image around which pervasive anxiety about the affluent consumer society and its inauthentic, advertising-created needs could crystallize. Packard stirred up enough indignation to get the practice banned by law from moving pictures and television, but an irrational fear of subliminal media persists. The voice crying in the wilderness in this regard has always belonged to Wilson Bryan Key, whose 1972 camp classic *Subliminal Seduction* is still in print. Key, a deeply obsessive paranoid, has been warning readers for over 25 years against subliminal "media rape": the nine naked women airbrushed into the ice cubes in the Cutty Sark ad, the penis and vagina concealed in the swirls of the Betty Crocker cake frosting, the letters S-E-X . . . basically everywhere. According to Key, we consume in an erotic haze; any conscious decision we might come to about the products in the ads will be totally swamped by carefully planned — and carefully disguised — subliminal sexual arousal.[58]

And yet, for all the hysterical anxiety of these so-called exposés, they were then and remain now profoundly reassuring to anyone worried about the loss of authentic desire. (They are also a source of great amusement to advertising executives.) As one might predict, the hysteria is a defense against a repressed truth too painful to face: the fact that advertisers don't need subliminal advertising to create desire. The discourse of subliminal seduction magically recuperates all desire as fundamentally authentic. It implies that admen cannot simply implant desires in us through brute repetition of stimuli; they have to piggyback their artificial desires on top of absolute, if unconscious, desires we already have for primal satisfactions like sex, security, and status. But perhaps there is no need for skullduggery. If what we consume in consumer society is not goods, but the structures of meaning embodied in goods, that would imply that all desire is actually relative, and thus invidious. *Homo economicus* turns out to be a pleasant fiction; in Baudrillard's analysis of consumption, his place will be taken by *homo significans*.

Baudrillard had surveyed the same American landscape as Whyte and Marcuse. He had actually read both Galbraith and Packard, and he was not impressed. They had both missed the fundamental fact that consumption is not just an economic function: it is also a discourse, and thus must be organized like a language: "The truth is not that 'needs are the fruits of production,' [Galbraith] but that *the system of needs* is *the product of the system of production,* which is quite a different matter."[59] Galbraith's revised sequence was correct, but it was also inevitable, since the system of objects organized by mass production and mass marketing was more coherent and better able to signify than what Baudrillard disparaged as the "less integrated" system of needs. Baudrillard was one of the first to see that the system of mass production, the structural play of competition, and brand differentiation through advertising allowed everyone to play the game that Veblen had restricted to the leisure class: consumption as invidious display, or, taking the semiotic view, consumption as signifying act. There was no need for subliminal seduction: the seductive power to provide coherent meaning and structure to our "incoherent" desires was quite enough. As Baudrillard put it, this signifying system of objects "imposes its own coherence and thus acquires the capacity to fashion an entire society."[60]

Here is perhaps the most fundamental structural link between the cultural practices of music and advertising in advanced capitalism. Music may not have the power to fashion an entire society, but it does help fashion subjectivities, through precisely the same means that Baudrillard attributes to advertising: the power to impose discursive coherence and structure on needs that would otherwise remain disorganized and inchoate. Susan McClary's formulation remains unsurpassed in forthright clarity: "Music teaches us how to experience our own emotions, our own desires, and even our own bodies. For better or for worse, it socializes us."[61] And nowhere is this social construction of desires more obvious and arbitrary than in music — after all, why should we desire the tonic without a composer to advertise its necessity by harping on the dominant? When Galbraith complained that "wants are increasingly created by the process by which they are satisfied," he didn't have Beethoven in his sights; and yet musical artworks give us pleasure only insofar as they can fulfill the precise desires that they themselves have worked painstakingly to create. The Dependence Effect, new and confusing to postwar economists, turns out to have been a not-so-hidden cornerstone of musical aesthetics since the birth of tonal rhetoric and expression in seventeenth-century Italy.

But back in the "real world" of production and consumption, what about authentic, absolute needs? *They do not exist.* In a pitiless passage from his 1969 essay on "The Ideological Genesis of Needs," Baudrillard took the idea of consumption as degraded language to its logical conclusion:

> Consumption is exchange. A consumer is never isolated, any more than a speaker. It is here that total revolution in the analysis of consumption must intervene: *Language cannot be explained by postulating an individual need to speak* (which would pose the insoluble double problem of establishing this need on an individual basis and then of articulating it in a possible exchange). Before such questions can even be put, there is, simply, language — not as an absolute, autonomous system, but as a structure of exchange contemporaneous with meaning itself, and on which is articulated the individual intention of speech. Similarly, consumption does not arise from an objective need of the consumer, a final intention of the subject towards the object; rather, there is social production, in a system of exchange, of a material of differences, a code of significations and invidious values.[62]

"Consumption does not arise from an objective need of the consumer"; by 1969 *homo economicus* was truly dead and gone. Baudrillard drove the nails into his coffin with poststructuralist flair: "One can generalize this conclusion by saying that needs — such as they are — can no longer be defined adequately in terms of a naturalist-idealist thesis — as innate, instinctive power, spontaneous craving, anthropological personality. There are needs only because the system needs them." There is no authentic desire, and thus no need for paranoid attacks on inauthentic ways of creating desire: "[One must refute] all of the 'alienists' of consumption, who persist in their attempts to demonstrate that *people's relation to objects, and their relation to themselves is falsified,* mystified, and manipulated. . . . Once having stated the universal postulate of the free and conscious subject, they are forced to attribute all the 'dysfunctions' they have discovered to a diabolic power — in this case to the technostructure, armed with advertising, public relations, and motivation research. . . . They do not see that, taken one at a time, needs are *nothing;* that there is only the system of needs."[63]

No wonder consumer desires had become so "perverse and unpredictable": like subjectivity itself, they are a product/effect of discourse, a frantic search not for satisfaction, but for *significance* within an ever-receding network of difference. To believe with Keynes and Galbraith that the desire to consume could ever be satisfied would be as naive as assuming one can cure a hysteric by treating his symptoms. The need acted out is a need for social meaning, not a particular object — and thus can never be fulfilled. As Baudrillard proclaims in stentorian capitals on the final pages of *The System of Objects,* "THERE ARE NO LIMITS TO CONSUMPTION."[64]

Let us summarize Baudrillard's new image of desire within consumer society: it is inauthentic (there is no "anthropological need"); collective and relative; produced by the system; an instrument of control, not liberation; detached from objects; and, counterintuitively enough, detached logically from the feeling of pleasure: "paradoxical though it may appear, consumption is defined as *exclusive of pleasure.* Pleasure no longer appears as an objective, as a rational end, but as the individual rationalization of a process whose objectives lie elsewhere. Pleasure would define consumption *for itself,* as autonomous and final. But consumption is never thus: [it] is a system of meaning."[65]

This is a long, *long* way from Wagner and Schopenhauer. And it is no less distant from the utopianism of a countercultural minimal music that celebrates freedom from desire, pure "being in time." It would be as radical a critical notion (and probably more accurate) to claim that minimal music represents the *triumph* of desire over all other signifying systems in music. But it is not wrong to see a fundamental shift in the subjective "feel" of this desire. In the society of scarcity (basically all of human society except post–World War II America), human needs and wants are disruptive, leading inevitably to interpersonal or interclass conflict. In the society of affluence, on the other hand, consumer needs are essential and, in fact, are society's most powerful controlling force. The (normatively male) creative artist has always tended to identify with disruptive desire and to depict it as heroic, destructive, even annihilating (thus the penetrating analyses of musical desire and violence in recent musicological criticism). Minimal music presents us with a constructed desire that is just as real, as physical — but that has no melodramatic or rebellious heroics to back it up:

> Even drives are dangerous however, and the neo-sorcerers of consumption are careful not to liberate people in accordance with some explosive end state of happiness. They only offer the resolution of tensions, that is to say, a freedom *by default*. The goal is to allow the drives that were previously blocked by mental determinants (taboo, superego, guilt) to crystallize on objects, concrete determinants where the explosive force of desire is annulled and the ritual repressive function of social organization is materialized. The freedom of existence that pits the individual against society is dangerous. But the freedom to possess is harmless, since it enters the game without knowing it.[66]

I do not want to replace the minimalist utopia with my own Huxleyan consumer dystopia, a *Brave New (Minimal) World*. If Baudrillard's tone in the quotations above is censorious, that is only because in 1968 he is still trying to be a both a poststructuralist culture critic and a good Marxist — in other words, a "postmodern modernist." This did not prove possible, as a reading of his later works can confirm. We may not want to follow his hyperbolic intellectual trajectory, but it is clearly true that "[Baudrillard's] work shatters the existing foundations of critical social theory, showing how the privilege they give to labor and their rationalist epistemologies are inadequate for the analysis of the media and other new social activities."[67] I believe that minimalist music is very much one of those "new social activities." As we shall see below, one of the first articles of faith Baudrillard jettisoned was belief in an authentic "explosive force of desire"; to appreciate the music of Glass and Reich, we will have to follow suit. If we don't, we will see it and reject it as either pop trivia or incipient totalitarianism — or even both at once.[68]

I hope that this extended critical prolegomenon outlines a different, perhaps postmodern, way of relating musical desire to politics, morals, and ultimately musical style. The first step is to replace the *desire-autonomy-violence* narrative that structures our understanding of mod-

ern society. In this story, told both through and about art, explosive
desire is first good because it is an index of individual autonomy against
society, and then bad because that same drive leads inevitably to violence,
annihilation, and loss of self. If Baudrillard is at all relevant to this discussion, it is because he explodes, as only a Lacanian post-Marxist can,
the necessary connection between desire and freedom — and thus
between desire and destruction. It appears that in minimalist music we
have a new form of desire that models a new postmodern musical world:
not the utopian world without desire, but a world of totalized desire that
is neither violent nor free.

MINIMALISM AND THE PHENOMENOLOGY OF CONSUMER DESIRE

> Ils voulaient jouir de la vie, mais, partout autour d'eux,
> la jouissance se confondait avec la propriété.
>
> [They wanted to enjoy life, but all around them
> enjoyment was confused with owning things.]
>
> **Georges Perec, Les Choses: une histoire des années**
> **soixante (Things: A Story of the Sixties) (1965)**

The experience of living in that world is what novelist Georges Perec cap-
tures when he observes in the epigraph above that, for the protagonists of
Les Choses (Things), his extraordinary 1965 novel of ideas, "enjoyment
[jouissance] was confused with owning things."[69] It is no accident that
Perec's "Story of the Sixties" is the story of an acquisitive young Parisian
couple who make ends meet as market researchers in the employ of a
large advertising agency. Advertising is the school in which we learn to
"confuse" enjoyment with assembling correct fashion statements out of
a complex system of things, and, like Perec's novel, pulse-pattern music
shows it happening to us, the same way *Tristan* shows us biological drive
turning into symbolic desire, endless yearning, love-death.

Interestingly, Perec denied that *Les Choses* was a critique of the
"emptiness" of consumer culture; his stated goal was to examine, imaginatively, how "the language of advertising is reflected in us."[70] In a virtuoso opening chapter remarked on by Baudrillard, Perec describes a
house and its furnishings at great length, in the second person, with a
maniacal, hallucinatory exactitude:

Your eye, first of all, would glide over the gray fitted carpet in the narrow,
long, and high-ceilinged corridor. Its walls would be cupboards, in light colored wood, with fittings of gleaming brass. Three prints, depicting respec-

tively, the Derby winner Thunderbird, a paddle-steamer named *Ville-de-Montereau,* and a Stephenson locomotive would lead to a leather curtain hanging on thick, black, grainy wooden rings which would slide back at the merest touch. There, the carpet would give way to an almost yellow wood-block floor, partly covered by three faded rugs.

It would be a living room about twenty-three feet long by ten feet wide.[71]

Perec, an author who values fastidious formal control, uses nothing but the conditional tense for five pages, for he is describing not a house, but an entire desire-for-a-house, in microscopic, almost pornographic detail. We meet Jérôme and Sylvie's system of objects — the universe of consumer goods they desire — before we meet them. Or rather, that is *how* we meet them, because that system defines, quite literally, *who they are.*

These young, hip, marketing executives appear to have no identities other than those defined by their desires for consumer goods. And their desires are anything but "natural" or "innate" — they are carefully learned, carefully constructed. The author's early-1960s French view has his characters doing a lot of window shopping in the seductive boutiques and antique shops of Paris, testing their sense of self against displays of tasteful goods. (Perec's only weakness is his slighting of mass media. A 1960s American version of *Things* would have to show its protagonists not strolling the boulevards, but reading magazines and watching television.) Late in the book, when the sheer impossibility of achieving consumer *jouissance* on lower-middle class Parisian salaries begins to oppress them, the couple attempts to run away to a small Tunisian village where they can live more "naturally." The result is disaster, a complete collapse of personality: "A world without memories, without memory. More time passed, days and weeks of desert waste, which did not count. They had stopped wanting. An indifferent world. . . . They were walking in their sleep. They no longer knew what they wanted. They were dispossessed."[72]

"A Pleasure So Intense as to Verge on Numbness"

Sociological analyses of consumption, however elegantly theorized, cannot engage our visceral sympathies in the way even the most arcane discussions of sexuality do. There is a term missing: how does this consumer desire actually *feel?* Answering that question is the great achievement of Perec's novel, one of the most striking imaginative leaps in contemporary literature. *Les Choses* is studded with set-piece evocations of the precise phenomenology of 1960s consumer desire, extended passages of extravagant description in which the author attempts to capture and describe the most mundane mercantile pleasures. Perec fixes fleeting, inarticulate glimmers of sensibility in language so concrete and tactile one wants to cry out, *Yes, that's it, that's exactly how it feels!*

> They would push open a door into a small restaurant and joyfully, almost ritually, absorb the ambient warmth, the clutter of cutlery, the clinking of glasses, the muffled sound of conversation, the inviting whiteness of napkins. They would select their wine punctiliously, unfold their napkins, and then it would seem to them, as they sat in the warm, in a close huddle, smoking a cigarette to be stubbed out in a moment's time when the hors d'oeuvres would arrive, that their life was going to be only the infinite sum of such auspicious moments, and that they would always be happy, because they deserved to be happy, because they would manage to stay free, because happiness was within them. They would sit facing each other, they were going to eat after having been hungry, and all these things — the thick white tablecloth, the blue blot of a packet of *Gitanes*, the earthenware plates, the rather heavy cutlery, the stem glasses, the wicker basket full of newly baked bread — constituted the ever-fresh setting of *an almost visceral pleasure, a pleasure so intense as to verge on numbness: an impression, almost exactly opposite and almost exactly identical to the experience of speed, of a tremendous stability, of tremendous plenitude.* From this table set for dinner arose for them the feeling of perfect synchrony: they were in tune with the world, they were swimming in it, in their element, with nothing to fear from it . . .
>
> But when they surrendered to *those feelings of unruffled beatitude, of eternity undisturbed by the slightest ripple, when everything was in balance, deliciously slow, the very intensity of their bliss underlined the ephemerality and fragility of such instants.* It did not take much to make it all crumble: the slightest false note, a mere moment's hesitation, a sign that was perhaps too vulgar, and their happiness would be put out of joint; it went back to being what it had always been, a kind of deal, a thing they had bought, a pitiful and flimsy thing, just a second's respite which returned them all the more forcefully to the real dangers, the real uncertainties in their lives, in their history.[73]

The epic climax of *Les Choses* is an extended descriptive rhapsody (seven full pages in a book that is just over 125 pages long) on consumer desire. Sylvie and Jérôme, in the midst of a marketing survey in the French countryside, surrender themselves to what can only be described as the *jouissance* of consumption, an unstoppable, fantastic excess of desire-for-things that, rapidly expanding past the contents of homes, rural markets, entire urban complexes, literally takes over the world:

> They would drift from marvel to marvel, from surprise to surprise. All they had to do was live, to be there, for the world to offer itself to them whole. Their ships, their trains, their rockets crisscrossed the planet. The world was

in their arms, with its wheat-covered counties, its fish-filled seas, its peaks and its deserts, its flowery landscapes, beaches, islands, trees, and treasures, with its huge and long-abandoned factories buried underground making the finest woolen cloths and the brightest silks for them alone . . .

But *these glittering visions, all these visions which came surging and rushing towards them, which flowed in unstoppable bursts, these vertiginous images of speed, light and triumph,* seemed to them at first to be connected to each other in a surprisingly necessary sequence, in an unbounded harmony. It was as if before their bedazzled eyes a finished landscape had suddenly risen up, *a total picture of the world, a coherent structure which they could at last grasp and decipher.* At first it felt as if their sensations were multiplied by ten, as if their faculties of sight and sense had been amplified to infinite powers, as if a magical bliss accompanied their smallest gesture, kept in time with their steps, suffused their lives: *the world was coming towards them, they were going towards the world, they would go on and on discovering it.* Their passion knew no bounds; their freedom was without constraint.[74]

As their minds race along and over the entirety of the system of objects ("a total picture of the world, a coherent structure which they could at last grasp"), Perec's two protagonists experience a more intense, hallucinatory version of the consumer trance that held James Vicary's supermarket shoppers in its grip. They are stoned by the sheer excess of it all, deriving the kind of ecstatic pleasure from mentally encompassing a physically overwhelming phenomenon that Kant identified as the emotional core of the aesthetic sublime.[75] But . . . after the high comes the crash: this moment of what one might dub the *mercantile sublime* is as fragile as the spurious syntax of their desires. The system fails to maintain coherence ("They were choking under the mass of detail. The visions blurred, became jumbles; they could retain only a few vague and muddled bits, tenuous, persistent, brainless, impoverished wisps"), and they are left unprotected against the terrifying insatiability of their desires: "Later on, they were themselves on the gray track lined with plane trees. They were themselves the little passing glint on the long black road. They were a tiny blot of poverty on the great sea of plenty. They looked around at the great yellow fields with their little red splashes of poppies. And they felt crushed."[76] (It is after this passage that Jérôme and Sylvie flee the affluent society altogether.)

We are on the verge of posing a question that the early, sociologically oriented Baudrillard never thought to ask: What are the *aesthetic* implications of the system of (consumer) objects? Can the system and its effects on desiring-production be represented in a work of art? If, as Perec's novel implies, looking straight on at the vast immensities of consumer demand mobilized by the "system as a whole" has the potential to crush subjectivity, then a work of art that strove to reproduce that effect would be attempting to represent the frankly unrepresentable, to, as one apologist for the "postmodern sublime" memorably phrased it, "put forward the unpresentable in presentation itself."[77] The mercantile sublime is a structuralist postmodern sublime, and in late-twentieth-century music it is the unique province of pulse-pattern minimalism.

What might the mercantile sublime, the impossible attempt to represent the system of objects in its full immensity and effect, sound like? One could explore a rigid, drastically impoverished tonal syntax, since the system of objects signifies in a crude, reductive way but does not possess the flexible syntactic power of language. One would avoid traditional teleology, since, as Baudrillard observed in the epigraph above, consumer objects form "an erratic lexical system in which brands devour one another." Crucially, one should use a musical style that features immense amounts of repetition, since, thanks to the pervasiveness of advertising, "the lifeblood of each brand is interminable repetition."

This suggestive series of isomorphisms, easily deducible from even a superficial acquaintance with minimalism as ideology and musical style, seems to indicate that our hermeneutic expedition has found a promising track; but there is danger, too. I am particularly anxious not to give the impression that musical minimalism is to be dryly decoded as an abstract *symbolization* of the system of consumer objects — that is, that the modules in a minimalist work simply "stand for" various brand images, their repetition is like advertising, and so on. Certainly no minimalist composer has ever set out to create such an arid allegory. What minimalism points to, intentionally or not, is what Raymond Williams famously called a "structure of feeling": a complex embodied hypothesis about how consumer desire within the system of objects is *actually felt*. Minimal music can sometimes be read as abstractly symbolizing repetitive processes in the larger culture that are constitutive of the system of objects (see the following chapter); but more importantly, through its direct effects on the listener's body, it holds up to us in a sonic-temporal mirror our own experience of that system and its processes. McClary argues that music socializes us, training us in the structure of desires. But, in advanced industrial capitalism, advertising and consumer culture now also perform that function — and with vastly greater amplitude and intensity, an intensity so great that it is literally inconceivable. Repetitive music may well provide an echo of that deafening roar, an echo of our common predicament, at a volume we can actually hear.

What is the general structure of feeling that desire-for-objects and minimalism share? Perec's descriptive language for consumer desire usually involves elaborate, multilayered metaphors of time. In *Les Choses* the mercantile sublime creates a kind of relativistic temporal distortion, an extreme experience of being in time that feels either very fast or very slow. Often the experience is analogized as accelerating forward motion taking place high above a vast landscape (system?) of objects ("the world was coming towards them, they were going towards the world, they would go on and on discovering it"), with images of consumption approaching at the speed of desire: "these glittering visions, all these visions which came surging and rushing towards them, which flowed in unstoppable bursts, these vertiginous images of speed, light and triumph." On the other hand, there are equally vivid moments in *Les Choses* that seem to argue that consumer desire congeals time into an unnatural, hallucinatory slow motion, "those feelings of unruffled beatitude, of eternity undisturbed by the slightest ripple, when everything was in balance, deliciously slow." In fact, as Perec hastens to point out, such suspended moments of intense desire are delicate and fleeting ("the very intensity of their bliss underlined the ephemerality and fragility of such instants"), and his master trope for consumer desire encompasses this ephemerality while mediating between contradictory images of motion and stasis. As Sylvie and Jérôme sit down to consume dinner at a local bistro, they experience "an almost visceral pleasure, a pleasure so intense as to verge on numbness: an impression, almost exactly opposite and almost exactly identical to the experience of speed."

The recombinant teleology of consumer desire manifests itself in *Les Choses* as an intense, self-contradictory, fast-and-yet-slow experience of passing time, and there is no art form better at conveying that complexity of experience than music, the temporal art par excellence. Furthermore, no genre of art music is more concerned with interpenetrated extremes of temporality than pulse-pattern minimalism. Contradictory images of speeding across a wide, slowly changing landscape are clichés of minimalist reception, whether it is the members of an alternative rock band reacting to Reich ("Man, you should get that record and drive through New Mexico") or the composer himself explaining why he titled his 1984 oratorio *The Desert Music:* "When I first played a taped version of that [final] section to David Drew, I remember turning to him and saying, 'Out on the plain, running like hell.' And that's the image — it's as if you're in the desert and you're running as fast as you can." One critic analogized listening to early John Adams as "flying or gliding over a landscape of gently changing colors and textures"; Adams himself confessed that a particularly surreal road-trip fantasy was the inspiration behind his *Grand Pianola Music:* "[It] started with a dream image in which while driving down Interstate 5, I was approached from behind by two long, gleaming, black stretch limousines. As the vehicles drew up beside me they transformed into the world's longest Steinways, twenty, maybe even thirty feet long. Screaming down the highway at 90 mph, they gave off volleys of B-flat and E-flat major arpeggios."[78]

We can be even more precise. With minimalism, as in Perec's novel, the key feature of the experience is the *interpenetration* of fast and slow. Kaleidoscopic arpeggios over slow harmonic rhythms afford many experimental musicians the same experience undergone by Jérôme and Sylvie, that impression "almost exactly opposite and almost exactly identical to the experience of speed." Wim Mertens remarked that "the very rapid patterns that Riley uses produce slow movements that nevertheless feel like a vibrating motionless trance," echoing analytical descriptions of Steve Reich by Brian Eno ("Either you can hear it as slow music with rapid ornaments or as fast music with slow underpinnings") and Joan La Barbara ("*Variations for Winds, Strings and Keyboards* is rich in timbre, slightly oriental in flavor, melodically alive, in a constant state of motion while giving an overall feeling of peace and rest"). An avant-garde computer music collective concurs, reporting that Reich's phasing process generates a music that sounds to them "like a fast forward movement and a slow backward movement at the same time." Some hypothesize that this fast-yet-slow effect is built into the music at a very deep level: "the structure of the piece gives you no idea as to whether it is moving very fast, very slowly, or not at all."[79] I would agree; and one need not argue the fundamental importance of this fast-yet-slow structural trope for minimal music based only on scattered listener responses. We have testimony from Steve Reich that creating a complex musico-temporal experience that allows fast and slow tempi to interpenetrate was a central part of his compositional intent: "What I asked that person [who complained, 'Don't you write any *slow* music?'] in response was: 'In my *Octet,* are you going to concentrate on listening to the pianos — that's the rhythm section of fast eighth notes that never let up — or to the strings, which are playing much more spaciously?' What I'm trying to do is present a slow movement and a fast movement simultaneously in such a way that they make music together."[80]

Steve Reich's *Music for Mallet Instruments, Voices, and Organ* (1973)

In fact, Reich made this discovery—that by deploying temporally opposed processes, he could construct musical experiences that would be heard simultaneously as slow (getting slower), and fast (getting faster)—at a crucial turning point in his compositional career.[81] In the later 1960s he had been exhausting the structural possibilities of two musical processes with quite different temporal implications. The first is familiar from eponymous works like *Piano Phase* and *Violin Phase*, what Reich himself would later call "gradual phase shifting." On a purely phenomenological level, phase shifting creates an imprecise doubling of rhythmic activity toward the halfway point of a shift, when the patterns are maximally out of phase. This perceptual pseudo-accelerando is matched by a hidden, conceptual one mandated by Reich's actual performance directions. In the score for *Piano Phase* (1967), the composer instructs the second, phasing player to "increase his tempo very slightly" so as to "move ahead of the first until . . . he is one sixteenth ahead."[82]

Why ahead, and not behind? No one, not even Reich himself, seems ever to have considered the expressive implications of this choice. There is no practical or perceptual reason why the phasing player should not slow down very slightly as he initiates the shift; every acceleration could be replaced by a corresponding deceleration, and the entire phase process would proceed without a whit of difference. In fact, this is how the phase process had originally worked, in the electronic pieces of 1965–66. Reich's studio technique in *It's Gonna Rain* and *Come Out* was an extension of a soon-to-be standard recording trick called "flanging": running the same music through two tape recorders, he put thumb pressure on the flange of one take-up reel to slow it down. Recording engineers found that this trick, used sparingly, could produce "trippy" echo, pan, and filter-sweep effects; Reich simply flanged his tape loops much more heavily, repeatedly letting the loop with his thumb on it fall behind, until the phase period reached one beat-unit and the patterns remeshed in what suddenly began to sound like canonical imitation.

As he himself learned to play through a phase process, Reich *inverted* the temporal relation of the two voices: he instinctively transferred the "speeding up" feeling of phase interference into an actual acceleration of the phasing voice. (He appears to have been predisposed to hear the effect as an acceleration. Describing his accidental discovery of phasing during the remixing of *It's Gonna Rain*, he explained that his attention was caught when one of two tape recorders, playing the same material, "gradually began to get ahead [not *behind*] of the other.")[83] The effect was to turn his early phase music into an endless accelerando that never actually gets any faster, a new kind of recombinant musical teleology, a sonic impression — à la Georges Perec — almost exactly opposite and exactly identical to the experience of speed.

Reich had exhausted this phase process by about 1970; in *Drumming* (1971), he introduced a the new type of short-range rhythmic process we encountered in *Music for Eighteen Musicians*. The "process of substituting beats for rests," as Reich would later call it, was much simpler to perform, and much more obviously based on metric acceleration. *Drumming* begins by setting out this process with didactic clarity: from a single eighth-note attack surrounded by the rests of an otherwise empty 12-beat bar, tuned drums in unison fill the metric space, building up to an eight-note paradiddle pattern (Example 7). This accretion of attacks already feels like acceleration, a perception that the composer has enhanced by careful control of the order in which pitched drum beats enter. If at the opening we hear an A every 12 beats, by the sixth cycle we notice that four of the six pitches sounding are repeated B♮'s, evenly spaced once every three beats. The distinctively African cross-rhythm creates a fourfold acceleration of pulse — and as the full pattern swings back into a steady quarter-note beat, the implied pulse slides up another notch. When Reich then phase shifts the freshly constructed pattern against itself (Example 8), not only does he create the fast spatter of attacks characteristic of the earlier procedure (virtual sixteenth notes, in this case); the resulting canonic patterns, once they lock back in one beat apart, provide an attack on every beat, and thus sound as if moving 12 times faster than at the opening.

Reich saw *Drumming* as an extended valedictory to phasing; his next major piece, the 1973 *Music for Mallet Instruments, Voices, and Organ*, combines the constant acceleration of "substituting beats for rests" with a diametrically opposite rhythmic process, one that had haunted him as an unrealizable concept for almost a decade. In 1967, just as he was sinking his hands deep into the whirring sixteenth notes of *Piano Phase*, Reich first wrote down an idea for a completely different kind of experiment with musical time. *Slow Motion Sound* consists of a simple one-sentence instruction outlining a technical impossibility, at least for 1967: "Very gradually slow down a recorded sound to many times its original length without changing its frequency or spectrum at all."[84] A literal realization would have to wait until inexpensive digital sampling made

Example 7 Steve Reich, *Drumming* (1971), Modules 1–8.

such time-stretching routine;[85] but in 1970, quite separately from his live explorations of phase acceleration, Reich created a live "slow-motion" piece. *Four Organs,* as Reich understood it, was a metaphor for *Slow Motion Sound:* "if a group of tones were all pulsing together in a repeating chord, one tone at a time could gradually get longer and longer in

Example 8 Steve Reich, *Drumming* (1971), first phase shift.

*Complete resulting
pattern of drummers
1 and 2

**Individual resulting patterns
for drummers 3 and 4
and/or male voices

duration until the gradual augmentation of durations produced a sort of slow motion music."[86]

Music for Mallet Instruments, Voices, and Organ is the first piece in which Reich combined and balanced both accelerating and decelerating musical processes.[87] As it unfolds, the work forges beat substitution and rhythmic augmentation processes into a complex oscillating musical mechanism. The opening section is paradigmatic (Example 9). While voices and organ alternate two jazz-inflected chords, three marimbas and a glockenspiel cycle through an interlocking rhythmic pattern moving four times as fast. A fourth marimba then builds up, note by note, a copy of the

Example 9 Steve Reich, *Music for Mallet Instruments, Voices, and Organ* (1973), Modules 1–5 (continued on pp. 111–13).

pattern, three eighth notes out of phase. The two textural layers (marimbas, voices-organ) are not merely stratified; they are causally linked in a distinctive negative feedback loop. The "process of rhythmic construction," Reich explains, "has the effect of creating more fast-moving activity, which then triggers the voices and organ into doubling, quadrupling, and further elongating the duration of the notes they sing and play."[88] The length of a cycle, marked by the two-chord alternation in voices and organ, doubles—and then more than doubles again, so that by module three the mallet instruments are cycling through their material 11 times faster than the long sustained tones of the singers and keyboard.

Example 9 (cont.) Steve Reich, *Music for Mallet Instruments, Voices, and Organ* (1973), Modules 1–5.

Let us zero in on a fine detail, symbolic, perhaps, of the complex temporal balancing act the work enacts. At this precise moment of greatest expansion, the vibraphone player — whose part, supporting the singers, has had the longest and slowest notes of all — abruptly rejoins the other mallet instruments with a barrage of interlocking sixteenth notes. He is now playing *faster* than anyone else. Even more than the nervous hurry-up-and-wait of Reich's early phase works, such elaborate interpenetration of acceleration and deceleration seems custom-designed to create an impression that is both exactly like (mallet instruments) and exactly opposite (voices, organ) the experience of speed.

Example 9 (cont.) Steve Reich, *Music for Mallet Instruments, Voices, and Organ* (1973), Modules 1–5.

Example 9 (cont.) Steve Reich, *Music for Mallet Instruments, Voices, and Organ* (1973), Modules 1–5.

Counterbalanced acceleration/augmentation is arguably the single most important structural principle in Reich's music after 1973 — he has never grown tired of its ramifications, as he did so quickly with the gradual phase shifting that defined his style. (The same stratified texture and endlessly augmenting canons structure a recent work like *Proverb* [1995], whose Wittgensteinian text, "How small a thought it takes to fill a whole life," takes on in this context a rather interesting self-reflexivity.) Nor is Reich the only minimalist composer whose works can be parsed this way: a piece like Glass's *Music in Similar Motion* (1969) takes short, fast-moving melodic fragments and stretches their repetitive cycling through additive process, forcing on the listener the same split temporal perspective. As new pitches are added, what was once a straightforward melodic line seems to speed up as it twists and turns in ever-more-

Baroque complexity; but the same process increases the length of each successive cycle — and thus slows down the "tempo" of the work as a whole.

After the first cycle of *Music for Mallet Instruments* contracts to its original two-bar length, Reich changes pitch collection and begins anew. (We'll ask why he needed to change pitches in the following chapter.) But the next section is not just a rhythmic recapitulation with fresh tonal materials; in a virtuosic display of compositional craft, Reich uses the processes of acceleration and deceleration operating *within* sections to determine as well the overarching rhythmic relationships *among* the work's four large sections. Thus the second section presents both "faster" and "slower" motion than the first. The new section moves faster because the pattern in the mallet instruments has lost a beat, shrinking from six notes to four. It thus cycles more quickly — and lends itself to a quicker process of rhythmic construction: what took five submodular steps (1a–1e) in the first module of section one now takes only three.

The speed-up is characteristic: throughout his career Reich has consistently used the proportional acceleration of ever-shortening patterns to drive his extended process pieces. For instance, each of the four large sections of *Piano Phase* is shorter and moves faster than the previous one, because the length in sixteenth notes of the patterns subjected to gradual phase processing shrinks in the strict prolational ratio 16:12:8:4. Yet the second section of *Music for Mallet Instruments* is actually *longer* than the first — in effect, even slower — because there is now another step in the counterpoised augmentation process. Reich lets the voices and organ double their doubling: sustained tones sprawl over two, four, eight, and finally *18* cycles of the mallet patterns, totaling up, with symmetrical expansion and contraction, to exactly double the number of bars in section one (i.e. 2 + 4 + 11 + 4 + 2 = 23, while 2 + 4 + 8 + 18 + 8 + 4 + 2 = 46; see Example 10). The third section has the same rhythmic structure as the first; the final section, interestingly enough, presents the triple augmentation of section two without recoil and subsequent diminution, as if a potentially infinite process of doubling and redoubling had simply broken off at the limits of human endurance.

Which leads a historian of consumer subjectivity to ask: Why should *Music for Mallet Instruments* ever come to anything other than an arbitrary, unfulfilled stop? After all, as Baudrillard pointed out in 1969, the very year Reich began to assemble the musical techniques that set the work in complex motion, there is no theoretical limit to consumption, no cadential formula for the consumer society. Minimalism's abandonment

Example 10 Steve Reich, *Music for Mallet Instruments, Voices, and Organ* (1973), Module 9.

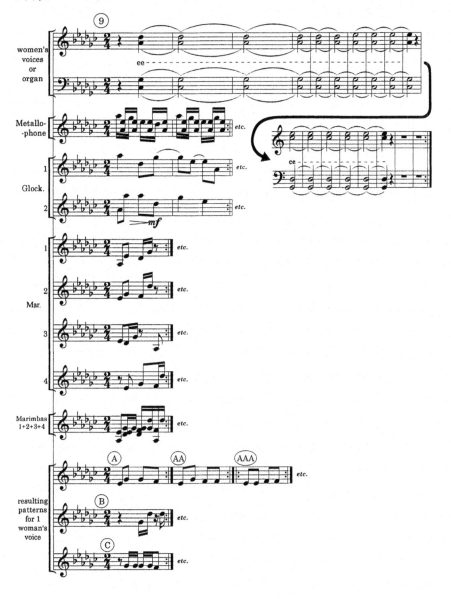

of traditional teleological form has usually been seen as an attempt to represent a subjectivity that has transcended desire; we would do better, perhaps, to imagine minimalism as the sound of a desire that has transcended individual subjectivity. The endless expansion, the "mindless" repetition — these are the markers of the mercantile sublime, of the attempt to represent desire *as it is truly experienced within the consumer society:* as a transsubjective effect of the system of objects, a system whose scale, scope, and discursive intensity dwarfs human consciousness. Even Wagner's *Tristan und Isolde,* the canonical portrayal of biological drive metastasized into the "endless yearning" of symbolic desire, does finally cadence — the desires in question, however mythic and excessive, are still contained within the bodies and wills of its protagonists. When they die, their desire dies too. But the system need never die, need never stop producing desire, in fact, *cannot* stop producing desire if our consumer society is to continue functioning. As we shall see in the next chapter, the system voices its desire, performatively, through mass-media advertising. Close reading of 1960s advertising theory will demonstrate how this unique systemic speech-act — an endless, impersonal, and incredibly repetitious "lover's discourse" whose immense force is calibrated not for any single consumer but for the market as a whole — was consciously designed to use the same pulsating rhythms and recombinant teleology that musicological analysis can discover in contemporaneous minimal music.

So, finally, how do we listen to a work like *Music for Mallet Instruments, Voices, and Organ?* Does its repetitious cycling betoken the complete collapse of subjectivity that Lasch and Marcuse so feared? Perhaps minimalism simply lets us tune in to the real discourse of consumer society, the sound of an immense array of commodified objects talking endlessly, repetitively, to each other, a continuous whirring noise that, according to Jacques Attali, "heralds the general silence of men before the spectacle of commodities . . . the radical jamming of codes by the economic machine."[89] That reading is not only, as Susan McClary complained above, pretty damn depressing; I would argue that it is a serious oversimplification. Minimalism is not simply an artistic translation of the language of advertising; it is an artistic exploration, much like Perec's novel, of how "the language of advertising is reflected in us."

If the language of advertising is reflected in us, then we are indeed "there" in the music, if only as hungry ghosts in the machine. One can pinpoint the moment in *Music for Mallet Instruments* when the ghost of the consumer subject makes itself audible; subjective desire is associated, as it has been so often in Western music, with a "solo" for the female voice: "When the marimbas and glockenspiels have built up to maximum activity, causing the voices and organ to elongate to maximum length and slowness, then a third woman's voice doubles some of the short melodic patterns resulting from the interlocking of the four marimba players, using her voice to precisely imitate the sound of these instruments."[90]

It's not really a solo, of course: Reich places great emphasis on the fact that this "new timbre" is "both instrumental and vocal at the same time." But the symbolic import of this third woman's musicking is much more than a simple submission to instrumentality. ("Now I am a marimba.") She assembles a melodic identity for herself — one *not* predetermined by the composer — by choosing freely among the pitches sounding in the complex, interlocking web of notes that surrounds her, at precisely the moments when the repetitive process that might well represent consumer desire has peaked (the fastest-and-yet-slowest moments of the work). It is as if, to make the analogy explicit, one were to assemble an identity for oneself out of the complex web of consumer objects, at the moment when the power of that web to create desire was at its peak.

This melodic identity is not oppositional or antisocial, nor does it act out any individual striving. In fact, the "resulting patterns" have no *Tonwille,* no melodic independence, at all: they are nothing more than an arbitrary effect arising within the complex canonic system that completely determines the narrow parameters within which they move. In a way these patterns, and the singer who sings them, are acting out the fate of the ghostly protagonists of *Les Choses,* seen through the eyes of Baudrillard: "Jérôme and Sylvie do not exist as a couple; their sole reality is as 'Jérôme-and-Sylvie' — as a pure complicity surfacing within the system of objects that signifies it."[91] How that complicity is produced, and mass-produced, will be the subject of our next chapter.

———

Vance Packard published *The Hidden Persuaders* in the summer of 1957; Galbraith's *The Affluent Society* appeared in the spring of 1958; La Monte Young wrote his *String Trio,* generally accepted as the first American minimalist musical composition, during the last months of 1958; Frank Stella began his famous series of black pinstripe paintings in early 1959. Is it any wonder an art of emptying-out, of radical impoverishment, an art that enacted the denial of subjectivity and the collapse of goal-directed desire, should arise in the United States at precisely the right moment — as if the lonely crowds of one-dimensional organization men and women, drifting through the system of objects, needed some kind of repetitious, low-key anthem? The birth of minimalism appears in historical perspective to be the aesthetic reflection of the death of *homo authenticus* and *homo economicus*, a sonic mirror of the profound crisis in subjectivity and desire that we have just attempted to trace and historicize.

But, as Packard's tongue-in-cheek reportage foreshadowed, powerful reactions to the crisis of desire were brewing, both from within and without the business world. An accelerating transformation of the practical discourse of desire culminated during the mid-1960s. The shape of musical minimalism — remember, pulsed process music was still at least six years away in 1958 — will have as much to do with corporate reactions to the crisis of desire as with the crisis itself. As we have seen, there are deliberate, systematic constructions of desire in minimal music, constructions that are often miles away from familiar romantic patterns of painful tension and pleasurable release. The new, inauthentic musical "needs" reflect increasingly sophisticated attempts to construct consumer needs through advanced scientific use of mass media. Music, like advertising, will get into the business of mass-producing desire.

But before we move on to the ad factory, let us pause to reconsider the hermeneutic objections that opened this long chapter. I hope that comparing minimalism to advertising now seems somewhat less bizarre; if, as Elliott Carter assumes, a critique of the music is implicit in the comparison, there is no reason to assume the critique is not *in* the music, too — a critique that encompasses the entire lived experience of late-capitalist consumer society. Listening to repetitive music is, in a very real sense, listening directly to the most powerful forces shaping American culture into a culture of repetition, and, from time to time, some minimalist composers seem to have sensed this. Thus Steve Reich, explaining to Edward Strickland in 1987 why he didn't write elite European-style serial music, argued that his repetitive, low-affect music was true to the popular experience of postwar consumer America: "Stockhausen, Berio, and Boulez were portraying in very honest terms what it was like to pick up the pieces after World War II. But for some American in 1948 or 1958 or 1968 — in the real context of tailfins, Chuck Berry and millions of burgers sold — to pretend that instead we're really going to have the dark-brown Angst of Vienna is a lie, a musical lie."[92] Tailfins are long gone, and Chuck Berry is a golden oldie, but the millions have turned to hundreds of billions — because the mercantile sublime, we have ever with us.

Say what you will about it, minimalism is at least not a musical lie; it carries a profound cultural truth in its very structure; it is the sound of millions of burgers being sold.

Would you like fries with that?

THREE

THE MEDIA SUBLIME

Minimalism, Advertising, and Television

The first time a man looks at an advertisement, he does not
    see it.
The second time he does not notice it.
The third time he is conscious of its existence.
The fourth time he faintly remembers having seen it before.
The fifth time he reads it.
The sixth time he turns up his nose at it.
The seventh time he reads it through and says, "Oh bother!"
The eighth time he says, "Here's that confounded thing again!"
The ninth time he wonders if it amounts to anything.
The tenth time he thinks he will ask his neighbor if he has
    tried it.
The eleventh time he wonders how the advertiser makes it pay.
The twelfth time he thinks perhaps it may be worth something.
The thirteenth time he thinks it must be a good thing.
The fourteenth time he remembers that he has wanted such a
    thing for a long time.
The fifteenth time he is tantalized because he cannot afford to
    buy it.
The sixteenth time he thinks he will buy it some day.
The seventeenth time he makes a memorandum of it.
The eighteenth time he swears at his poverty.
The nineteenth time he counts his money carefully.
The twentieth time he sees it, he buys the article, or instructs his
    wife to do so.

Thomas Smith, "Hints to Intending Advertisers" (1885)

CULTURAL CONTEXT:
MASS-PRODUCING DESIRE IN CONSUMER SOCIETY

"Advertising as a Gradual Process": A Brief History
of Repetition in Marketing Communications

The fundamental truth of advertising as a cultural form is that it has been designed, through most of its history, by what to its practitioners seemed stark, scientific necessity, to be highly repetitive. Conceptualized as incremental in its effect, advertising has always been understood as a gradual process requiring multiple iterations of the same stimulus to produce a rising curve of attention, interest, and desire — leading, ultimately, to a successful transaction at the point of sale. Thus advertisers have always incorporated large amounts of redundancy into their communication strategies. Consider the epigraph above, which reproduces one of the foundational texts of Anglophone advertising history, Thomas Smith's 1885 "Hints to Intending Advertisers." Although nobody seems to know who Smith was, or in what context he devised it, his rubric is still being quoted in advertising media planning texts to this day, a rueful admission of just how much advertising it really takes to change consumer attitudes. (Even more famous, perhaps, is 1920s department store magnate John Wanamaker's lament, "I know half my advertising is wasted; I just don't know which half!") We'll come back to Smith's little saga; let it stand now as evidence of how central repetition and process have always been to theories of desire creation in advertising.

Actually, nineteenth-century newspaper advertisers, driven to distraction by the *New York Herald Examiner*'s so-called agate rule (publisher James Gordon Bennett, to keep deep-pocketed advertisers from monopolizing space and gaining what he saw as "unfair advantage," had decreed that no type in classified advertising could be larger than that very small size of font, about 5½ points), were already creating some truly impressive typographic process pieces in the mid-1850s. In 1856 a Manhattan furrier sought a way to get around the rule and dramatize a pre-Christmas sale on winter clothing. He dismembered the single word "overcoats" and subjected it to a Glass-style additive process, repeating lines of agate-sized type and torturing them into the seasonal silhouette of a church steeple (Figure 1). Rival publisher Robert Bonner, a true tabloid minimalist, made a sensation (and advertised himself into the history books) when he filled an entire broadsheet of the *Herald* with over 600 iterations of a single come-on phrase for his literary weekly, the *New York Ledger* (Figure 2).[1] Such absurdities led directly to the introduction

Figure 1 An early advertising process piece.
1856 overcoat ad from the *New York Herald
Examiner*. Reproduced in Frank Presbey, *The
History and Development of Advertising* (New
York: Greenwood Press, 1968), p. 243.

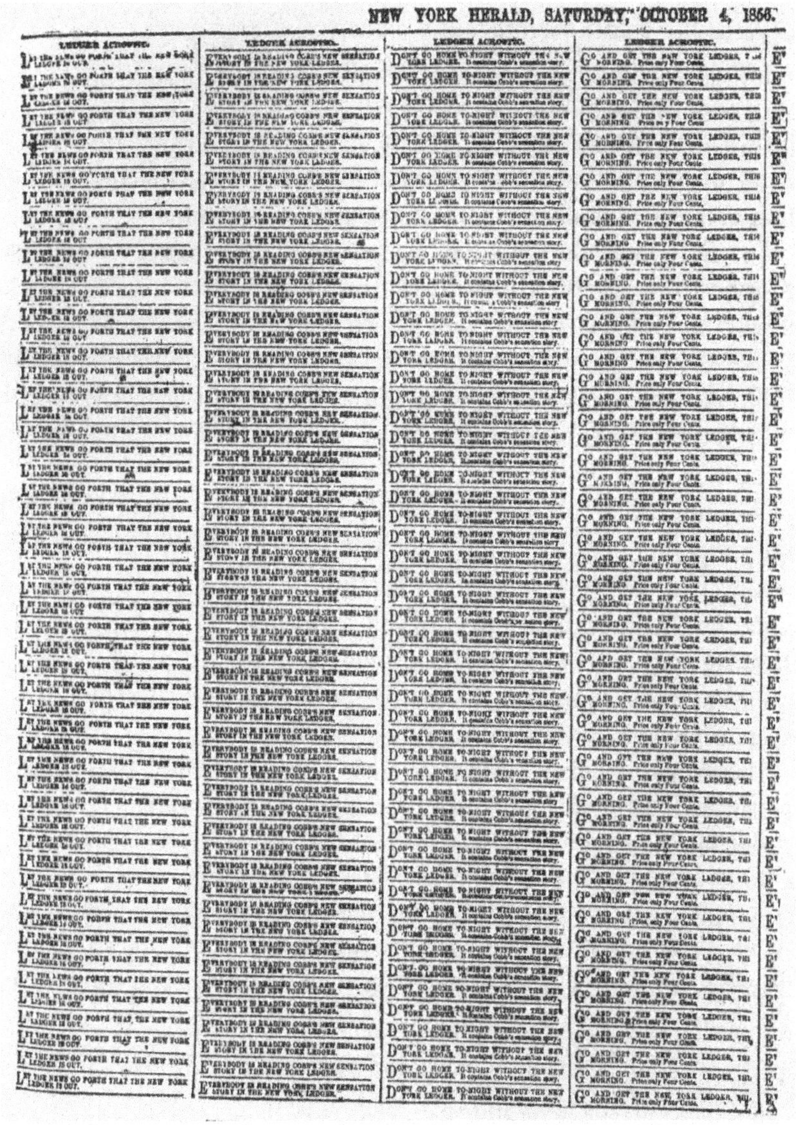
NEW YORK HERALD, SATURDAY, OCTOBER 4, 1856.

LEDGER ACROSTIC.

LET THE NEWS GO FORTH THAT THE NEW YORK LEDGER IS OUT.

LEDGER ACROSTIC.

EVERYBODY IS READING COBB'S NEW SENSATION STORY IN THE NEW YORK LEDGER.

LEDGER ACROSTIC.

DON'T GO HOME TO-NIGHT WITHOUT THE NEW YORK LEDGER. It contains Cobb's sensation story.

LEDGER ACROSTIC.

GO AND GET THE NEW YORK LEDGER, THIS MORNING. Price only Four Cents.

Figure 2 Repetition in advertising, ca. 1856. Reproduced in Frank Presbey, *The History and Development of Advertising* (New York: Greenwood Press, 1968), p. 236.

of display advertising, what we now think of as "ads," as opposed to "the classifieds," which still use nothing but agate-sized type.

In moving from Smith's "Hints" to these proto–display ads, I am already in danger of blurring a distinction that will become crucial as the argument proceeds: the difference between the repetitious use of an advertisement, and an ad that is *itself* repetitious. The advertising profession has been noticeably ambivalent about repetition in ads, periodically seeking, as in the historical vignette above, more "creative" ways to rise above the omnipresent media clutter. Ironically the high-water mark of such creativity, a veritable Creative Revolution (see below), coincided with the 1960s rise of repetitive music. But repetition *of* ads, based on the firm belief that a distracted consumer needed to be exposed over and over again to the producer's message, never went out of fashion. A long line of research into the psychology of memory had shown it to be absolutely essential. Without repetition of an advertisement, there would be no recall. Without recall of an advertisement, no matter how creative, there could be no reinforcement of the desire to buy.

Hermann Ebbinghaus first published the results of his pioneering experiments in learning and forgetting in 1885 — the same year that Thomas Smith proffered his famous hints — and the conclusions of German empirical psychology bestowed lasting scientific credibility on all such commonsense nostrums about advertising and repetition. His methodology would hardly pass muster today: the only experimental subject was Ebbinghaus himself, and the conditions under which he tested the effects of repetition on his recall of nonsense syllables in German were maximally artificial. In fact, a description of his additive procedure sounds more like experimental music than experimental psychology: using a metronome for precise timing, Ebbinghaus chanted strings of monosyllables to himself, reading and then repeating them aloud in a uniform tone, stopping every time he hesitated, until he could produce an entire series without error.[2] Not surprisingly, he found that the more repetitions, the more syllables longer retained.

Ebbinghaus's work provided a quasi-scientific rationale for immense amounts of repetition in advertising, crystallized in what quickly became reified by the literature as the "Ebbinghaus Curve" of forgetting: a rapid and exponential drop in the ability to recall followed by a slower decay over time. The function of repetition in advertising was obviously to straighten out the Ebbinghaus Curve, to keep the claims made on behalf of a product (or perhaps just its image) in the consumer's mind long enough so that desire for it could coalesce. Walter Dill Scott, a pioneer of twentieth-century advertising research and eventual president of North-western University, extrapolated from the Ebbinghaus Curve to declare in 1908 that if an advertiser could get people to remember his message for 20 minutes, they would then remember it for as long as a month. He recommended repeating an advertisement over and over "at frequent intervals," and warned against the common mistake of discontinuing advertising once consumers had begun to respond.[3] (As we shall see, the concepts of "frequency" and "continuity" have driven advertising media planning to this day.) Edward K. Strong, whose applied research at Columbia University was in large part underwritten by advertising indus-try associations, worked assiduously to quantify the precise number and frequency of repetitions necessary to maximize recall. A consensus began to emerge that even spacing of ads over time, a technique analogized musically by one researcher as the "rhythmic form of presentation," was most efficient. By the 1920s Strong, now a psychology professor at Stanford University, was declaring that "repetition — unending repeti-tion — is essential," and chiding advertising agencies and their clients for showing signs of battle fatigue: "The chief reason why there is not so much drill — repetition — as necessary is that the seller, not the buyer, gets tired of it. An advertiser lives with his copy and sees it for weeks before it appears in print. The reader may see it only once or twice."[4]

Even if four out of five professors of applied psychology agreed, the advertising community was always both a little ashamed and a little sus-picious of unadorned repetition as a sales technique; one path through advertising history would be to trace the periodic cycling between orgies of repetitive "hard" selling and self-conscious attempts to atone with something softer and more aesthetic. Claude Hopkins, in his 1923 classic *Scientific Advertising,* attempted to debunk ivory-tower theorizing about advertising; he decried brute repetition as a wasteful hangover from the days of the nineteenth-century "huckster," unworthy of a newly profes-sionalized industry and insulting to consumers' intelligence. The senti-ment was echoed in the 1950s by advertising legend David Ogilvy in his introduction to a new edition of Hopkins and, later, in his own writings; the urbane adman, "enraged by the barrage" of mass media advertising, attempted to absolve Hopkins and the agencies for media clutter, laying blame on the "profit motive of those who own the media."[5]

Repositioning Hopkins (his mentor), Ogilvy was taking direct aim at another Hopkins student, his greatest rival: Rosser Reeves, the implaca-ble 1950s champion of the "hard sell." Reeves's immensely influential campaigns for the Ted Bates Agency were based on identifying for any product what he called the Unique Selling Proposition, usually a vague, quasi-scientific claim to technological superiority. (It was Reeves, for instance, who discovered that Wonder Bread "helps build strong bodies twelve ways.") Once the USP was formulated, repetition was used to pound it into consumers' heads. In 1961 Reeves published a book called *Reality in Advertising,* and the reality he preached was that while creative ads often failed to sell, boring ones usually did, if they were pushed hard enough. He was unapologetic for flooding the media with advertising ("Certainly some of our clients use the brute force of money to move goods — but, oh, do they sell soap!"), even though the work coming out of Bates was notoriously and deliberately philistine. He didn't care that his campaign for the pain reliever Anacin — featuring endless repetition of a cartoon hammer pounding inside a skull followed by a hectoring insistence on the already repetitious slogan: "Fast! Fast! Fast Relief!" — was considered to have inflicted on viewers the "most hated commercials in the history of advertising."[6]

Reeves ran that same ad, substantially unchanged, for *seven years.* Anacin sales rose from $18 million to $54 million, but the campaign gave every adman a headache, as well as a bad reputation. By the early 1960s Reeves's brutal repetitious style was not only universally despised within the industry — it was on the way out, to be replaced, synchronicitously enough, by advertising's embrace of "minimalism" (Figure 3). "Think Small," the first of the famous Volkswagen ads created by the iconoclastic Doyle Dane Bernbach agency, appeared in 1959; the witty, understated campaign, which set black-and-white images of the Beetle swimming in oceans of white space, ushered in what would come to be known as advertising's Creative Revolution. At first glance, the timing of this revolution is strikingly inapposite: just as repetitious process was beginning to gain ground in art and music, advertising loudly swore off the repetitive hard sell forever. (And it truly did: the only place you can experience a USP these days is in the bottom-feeding world of the late-night infomercial.) Tempting as it is to link the repetitive, minimalist aesthetic of the 1966 VW ad reproduced here to the exactly contemporaneous composition of *Piano Phase,* by 1966 that ad, too, was out of date: "In the early years of the advertising revolution, creativity meant minimalism: sans-serif typefaces and simple uncluttered layouts. But in the mid-1960s, the look and language of creativity changed dramatically; the symbol for the 1966 Art Director's show is a color photograph of a woman nude and supine for the camera, her body painted from head to toe with elaborate Day-Glo flowers and rainbows. Creativity had merged

Figure 3 Minimalism in advertising, ca. 1966. Reproduced courtesy of
Volkswagen of America.

with counterculture."[7] Thomas Frank observed that when advertising *really* went countercultural, it dumped minimalism. The soundtrack for the 1960s Creative Revolution was folk rock, not Steve Reich.

Here is where the distinction between repetition in ads and repetition of ads becomes crucial. The advertising revolution may have begun as a brief flirtation with the surface features of minimalism, but it redefined creativity as *avoiding* the insistent repetition that is a key structural principle of most minimalist music. In the design of individual ads, the "engineering" approach of the 1950s was supplanted in the 1960s by the freewheeling hipness of what finally began to live up to its name as the Creative Department. But on the level of the ad campaign, repetition remained as central to mass market advertising as it had ever been. In fact, larger media trends were converging to spark an explosive, unprecedented growth in every parameter by which repetitive advertising might be measured: in the sheer number of ads, the amount of time they consumed, their intrusiveness in everyday life, and, last but not least, the increasingly rapid and regular rhythm of their nonstop barrage.

A Brief Commercial Interruption: Television, Spot Advertising, and the Timely Birth of "Flow"

> Why does the audience seek this [minimalist] music? The answer I have come up with owes much to a seventeen-year-old, prematurely knowing relative. I took him to the Brooklyn Academy last year to a performance of a Philip Glass work, *The Photographer*. . . . My young informant effortlessly explained it to me as we waited for a taxi to take us back to Manhattan. "It's very simple," he said. "This is what television should be."
>
> **Richard Sennett, "The Twilight of the Tenured Composer" (1984)**

The catalyst for this explosion of repetition was a dramatic shift in the way advertising was deployed within the newly dominant medium of broadcast television.[8] Television had been steadily gaining as an advertising vehicle all through the 1950s, surpassing radio in 1952, and by 1955 was absorbing more in billings than the entire output of the nation's print media.[9] The new medium was seen by many advertising executives as the single most powerful selling tool ever invented, visual and kinesthetic to a degree that almost made viewer discretion irrelevant. (NBC's researchers reported, "Television is the medium which depends least on consumer cooperation to develop a rich response to symbolic stimulation." Ad executives were more frank: "On TV, we've got you by the eyeballs.") It was a timely mass-media godsend for a business community scrambling to find new ways of mass-producing consumer needs on a scale commensurate with a new glut of mass-produced goods. Pat Weaver, president of NBC, hammered the point home in sociohistorical terms that oddly anticipate Jean Baudrillard: "[Television] advertising is to mass production what individual selling was to craft production."[10]

But the power of the new medium could not fully be unleashed until the correct economic linkage between advertising and programming was found. In its first decade television was financed by the same sponsorship model that had been central to radio. Corporate advertisers underwrote large, fixed chunks of broadcast time, filling them with branded programs *(The Voice of Firestone, Texaco Star Theater, Gillette Cavalcade of Sports)* often produced in-house under the supervision of their own advertising agencies. As television exploded in popularity, this system became increasingly unworkable. Big companies clung fiercely to aging shows and their "prime-time" slots, to the despair of network executives who wanted flexibility to respond to changing audience tastes. Even worse, as television's selling power became clear and ad rates skyrocketed, these few large corporations were the only ones able to pay top dollar for an entire hour of network airtime. (In the middle 1950s the aggregate number of advertisers steadily fell, even as total billings rose. By 1957 one conglomerate, Procter & Gamble, accounted for $1 out of every $11 spent on network television.)

There are only a finite number of hours in a broadcast day. The networks soon realized they could make much more money by auctioning off smaller slices of advertising time to a wide variety of sponsors at a very high rate — *if* they took back programming, delivered consistent ratings, and maximized audience share during prime viewing hours. The pretext for their assertion of control was the quiz show scandal of 1959. The public outcry after it became known that a corporate sponsor had rigged Charles Van Doren's dramatic winning streak on NBC's *Twenty-One* provided the cover, and all three networks did what smaller ad agencies had been begging them to do for years: they accelerated the switch to the "magazine concept" of broadcast advertising. As in print media, the networks would control all editorial content (programming); short advertising spots could then be sold and inserted periodically into the viewing schedule. The new model was flexible, it maximized the value of broadcast time (since the number of slices was, in theory at least, limited only by the speed with which a single product impression could be made), and it quickly came to dominate the medium: in 1955, three out of four shows had a single sponsor; a decade later, only one in eight did.[11] By the 1965–66 broadcast season — almost certainly *not* watched regularly by Steve Reich as he cut and spliced tape and developed the phasing techniques that would culminate in *Piano Phase* the next year — advertising on commercial network television had largely taken on the intermittent form that we know today. (The sponsorship model survives only in public television, where Texaco and GE are still sponsoring prestige programming, and on cable, where broadcasters turn over low-value hours wholesale to the producers of infomercials, a kind of "leased access" to the airwaves that was once the norm.)

The socioeconomic implications of this restructuring were profound, pervasive, and long lasting. Television immediately became a much bigger business, with tens of millions of dollars riding on each hour of programming — money that correlated not with the tastes of a single imperious sponsor, but with the fungible abstraction called "ratings," which made slices of time innately valuable to anybody willing to buy. In effect, television moved from selling big chunks of broadcast time to selling big chunks of broadcast audience. Thus entered the apparatus of Nielsen meters, sweeps, and ratings points that have dominated and homogenized TV content, causing media historians to anoint the early, sponsorship years as the medium's retrospective "golden age." But television did not just find its economic feet in the mid-1960s; the new reliance on spot advertising changed the entire phenomenology of the TV experience. When it combined the smooth temporal continuity of a performance medium with the staccato rhythms of the "magazine concept," television found its distinctive structure as a cultural form.

What were the phenomenological implications of the shift to magazine-style advertising on television? In the old days of single sponsorship, the rhythms of broadcast television were spontaneous, irregular, even improvisatory. Serious dramas were presented live, with few, if any, commercial interruptions from the sponsor, and those usually bunched at the beginning and end of an hour. The variety-style programs had more advertising in them, but the relationship between showmanship and salesmanship was designed to be unpredictable. A discrete, filmed "commercial" was only rarely dropped into the act: perhaps the camera would swing over, and the show's announcer — or, even better, the star — would break conversationally into the pitch ("And now, a word from our sponsor . . ."); often the sponsor's name was emblazoned on the set, or, on a few memorable occasions, worked into the comedy sketches or song-and-dance routines.

The magazine concept shattered this intricate dance of entertainment and selling, destroying the complex unity of the half-hour or hour "show," which, interrupted though it was by advertising messages, was at least filtered through a single theatrical sensibility and featured a single product. (The whole point of sponsorship was to fuse the product and the show into a single attractive package in the consumer mind.) Spot advertising, by its very logic, fractured the viewing experience. Scrutinized with proper attention to detail, as in this self-consciously phenomenological description by artist David Antin, a half hour of television discloses itself as a complex mélange of loosely related chunks, arbitrary slices of time that are themselves quite friable, liable, under pressure of money, to infinite fissuring and cracking:

> In half an hour you might see a succession of four complete, distinct and unrelated thirty-second presentations, followed by a twelve-minute half of a presentation, followed by a one-minute presentation, one thirty-second presentation and two ten-second presentations, followed by the second and concluding half presentation (twelve minutes long), followed by yet another four unrelated thirty-second presentations. But since this would lead to bunching of two two-minute commercials into a four-minute package of commercial at every hour ending, and since viewers are supposed to want mainly to look at the programs — or because program makers are rather possessive about their own commercials and want complete credit for them — the program makers have recently developed the habit of presenting a small segment of their own program as a kind of prologue before the opening commercial, to separate it from the tail end of the preceding program, while the program makers of the preceding program may attempt to tag onto the end of their own program a small epilogue at the end of their last commercial, to affix it more securely to their own program. Meanwhile the station may itself interject a small commercial promoting itself or its future presentations. All of these additional segments — prologues, epilogues, station promotions, and coming attractions — usually last no more than two minutes, are scaled to commercial time, and are in their functional nature promotions for either immediately succeeding or eventually succeeding transmissions. This means that you may see upward of fourteen distinct segments of presentation in any half hour, all but two of which will be scaled to commercial time.[12]

In fact, as Antin persuasively argues, *all* of network television is scaled in some sense to commercial time; determine the length of the shortest spot, and you can extrapolate the metrical structure of television: "The smallest salable piece turns out to be the ten-second spot, and all television is assembled from it."[13] Commercials and programming have the same basic syntax, and with the widespread acceptance of spot advertising, television came to be dominated by "the linear succession of logically independent units of nearly equal duration." These units pile up into complex additive blocks, small gears driving the larger ones: "The industry seems to mark the separation emphatically by assigning the two roles different time signatures. The commercial is built on a scale of the minute out of multiple ten-second units. It comes in four common sizes — 15, 30, 60, and 120 seconds — of which the thirty-second spot is by far the commonest. The program is built on the scale of the hour out of truncated and hinged fifteen-minutes units that are also commonly assembled in four sizes — 15, 30, 60, and 120 minutes — of which the half-hour program is the commonest."[14]

The alert reader will recognize in this double metrical structure the "wheels within wheels" of repetitive music, the same fast-yet-slow experience identified with the experience of consumer desire. Antin's borrowing of musical terminology is apt: from the structural point of view, thanks mostly to spot advertising, post-1965 television is a vast, pervasive, endless experiment in repetitive process. It has the regular pulse of minimalism in its very bones.

Further, the structural process of 1960s-style television has always been a gradual one. A videographer himself, Antin was sensitive to the many ways network television blurs the transitions between its constituent units: an extremely limited repertoire of shot types and lengths and a tendency to meld one shot into another with zooms or pans tend to make every moment of TV viewing more or less like every other.[15] The highly teleological forms that seem to structure television — *catch the criminal, bring the lovers together, determine the winner, resolve the debate* — are first pulverized by the insertion of unrelated ads into units about the same size as ads, then reassembled with subtle camerawork and editing into a new, much larger sequence of units in which no unit is allowed to be very different from any other. Raymond Williams called the result of this process *flow*, a new kind of media experience that he considered "the defining characteristic of broadcasting, simultaneously as a technology and as a cultural form." Flow is the actual not-really-teleological experience of television, and like minimalism in music, it tends toward the temporally expansive: "It is evident that what is now called 'an evening's viewing' is in some ways planned by providers and then by viewers *as a whole;* that it is in any event planned in discernible sequences which in this sense override particular program units."[16]

Perceiving flow, many critics of television jump to the conclusion that television is totally nonteleological, that it ushers viewers into a timeless trance state, an electronic drug trip, a simulacrum of the mindless circular routine of industrial production and the assembly line.[17] Conversely more than one commentator has seen this absence of *telos* as the fundamental source of viewing pleasure, epitomized in the endless serialized *jouissance* of the soap opera (the "dramatic" form most completely assimilated to TV flow), and apostrophized in terms all too familiar from the discourse around minimalist music: "Unlike all traditionally end-oriented fiction and drama, soap opera offers process without progression. Nothing grows or ripens in soap time and nothing is corroded or scattered. There is no future and no past but an eternal featureless present in which each day looks like the last or the one to come. Soap time is for and of pleasure, the time of consumption, of a collectivized and commercially induced American Dream."[18]

There is no doubt that television is a "low-involvement" medium, to use the term coined by media researcher Herbert Krugman in the previous chapter; but low involvement does not mean *no* involvement, a complete surrender to the hypnotic rhythms of the flickering flow. If that were true, then television would be nothing more or less than a diabolical form of "brainwashing or hypnosis or mind-zapping or something like it":

> For the entire four or more hours per day that the average person is watching television, the *repetitive process* of constructing images out of dots, following scans, and *vibrating with the beats* of the set and the *exigencies of electronic rhythm* goes on. It was this *repetitive, nonstop* requirement to reconstruct images that are consciously usable that caused McLuhan to call television "participatory." In fact, watching television is participatory only in the way the assembly line or a hypnotist's blinking flashlight is. Eventually, the conscious mind gives up noting the process and merges with the experience. *The body vibrates with the beat* and the mind gives itself over, opening up to whatever imagery is offered.[19]

Jerry Mander, advertising man turned cultural activist, considered this mind-destroying "hypnopaedic" effect the strongest of the four arguments for the total elimination of television he published in 1978. It will not have escaped the reader guided by my added emphases that Mander describes television in rhythmic terms that could interchangeably be applied to disco, techno, or minimalist process music; and yet, as with those musics, a view that simply assumes the absence of all teleology, and thus of agency and subjectivity, is not nuanced enough to capture the specifics of the cultural form. (We'll see below that Krugman, who had already by 1965 both referenced McLuhan and analogized low-involvement inter-action with television to a drug "trip," goes on to outline a much more complex, multiphase theory of consumer information processing and motivation.)

Mander may well have found fodder for his paranoid imaginings in an argument by Michael Novak that appeared in the 1977 collection *Mass Media Issues,* encapsulated in a short essay with the ominous title, "Television Shapes Our Souls." Novak was also appalled by television's global effects on viewer subjectivity, the way it acted as a "molder" of what he called "the soul's geography." But he was too acute an observer to sign on to a simplistic "TV-watching zombies" critique. Novak was interested in television, one assumes, for the same reason Susan McClary became interested in tonality: like music, commercial television socializes us, for better or worse, to a unique and specific experience of teleology. In Novak's precise formulation, television "builds up incrementally a psychic structure of expectations." One recognizes in his description of television a species of recombinant teleology, a "structure of expecta-tions," arising within post-1965 television as the direct consequence of spot advertising and the slightly choppy flow it inevitably generates: "For reasons of synchronized programming, the ordinary television show is neatly divided into segments of approximately equal length, and each of these segments normally has its own dramatic rhythm so as to build to dramatic climax or subclimax, with the appropriate degree of suspense or resolution. The timing of television shows tutors their audience to expect a certain rhythm of development."[20]

Television purports to broadcast a sequence of discrete dramatic pro-grams but, thanks to the constant interruptions of spot advertising, actu-ally bathes viewers in a gradually shifting, for the most part undifferenti-ated, flow. Still, as Novak understands — and this is absolutely crucial to understanding television as a cultural form — the experience of flow does *not* mean that television has no teleology, that the built-in climaxes of its formulaic programming simply evaporate. (If that were true, no one would be watching except zombies.) In fact, TV teleology undergoes the same mutation as does tonal teleology in minimalist process music: in neither case does the structural tension disappear. Rather, it is dispersed across a greatly extended time field; distributed across repetitious, gradually chang-ing cycles; and prolonged through interlocking polyrhythmic pulsation.

This is why Sennett, in the epigraph above, could argue (by proxy) that minimal music is "what television should be." He has already made the

Novakian case that television works according to minimalism's interrupt-driven "technique of repetitive accumulation":

> Certainly the mass media have prepared people for this new [minimalist] aesthetic. Radio and television programs are constantly being interrupted — by advertisements, station breaks, and filler. Interruption has its own logic, one that writers of TV scripts have to study carefully. The story that gets cut into pieces by commercial breaks cannot be so powerful in any one segment that the viewer will be furious when the break comes — an angry viewer is not a receptive buyer. A rhythm of content is established by the people who contrive mass entertainment: the "show" is broken into regular short segments, each of which terminates at a point at which the viewer (or listener) wants to see (or hear) more but isn't so overwhelmingly engaged as to resent the break.[21]

Post-1965 television, it turns out, has a precisely calibrated *telos*: just enough suspense in each segment to keep you watching, but not so much that the segmentation itself, the constant resetting, becomes annoying. Television is repetitive music's teleological double. Sennett's implied take on Glass's *The Photographer* is structurally similar to McClary's ("he repeatedly gives us a typical Mahlerian buildup-to-cadence, only to loop back at the point of promised climax to the beginning of the buildup");[22] but the looping that McClary interprets as immanent critique of tonality appears to Sennett as a cool, unwitting artistic simulacrum of network television.

Writing in 1984, Sennett found his generation's indiscriminate embrace of minimalist repetition rather sad; he was, at heart, more intellectually attuned to the asceticism of Pierre Boulez. But he refused to pigeonhole minimal music as "simply a phosphorescent reflection" of mass media; he hoped, in fact, that it could be something like a transcendent redemption, a glimpse of "what television should be." Sennett ended up making the classic minimalist argument that the flow of this music, even more effectively than television, could provide a necessary meditative respite from the onslaught of daily life. But it would be a respite — and this is Sennett's unique and useful observation — that the flow of television had prepared an entire culture to recognize. Glass, he remarked, was not a crossover artist; "mass culture prepared people to cross over to him."[23]

Fundamentals of Media Planning

The advent of magazine-style advertising did more than pulverize television into repetitious cycles; it also led to a quantum leap in the number of repetitions any given ad — regardless of media vehicle — would receive. Although spot advertising on television was originally understood as a transfer into the new medium of the way print advertising had always worked, conventional wisdom within the advertising profession was that TV watchers would stand for much more brute repetition of advertising than magazine readers ever had. As one executive hypothesized, "A television commercial is like a song. I can listen to a song a hundred times a week and enjoy it every time. But please don't make me read a short story over and over a hundred times in a week."[24] In the pre–remote-control era, it was easier to imagine readers quickly flipping the page to skip an ad already seen than viewers getting up from their sofas and disengaging from that seductive TV flow.

It was comforting to think that TV ads didn't wear out, because, of course, the cost of shooting each 30- or 60-second spot dwarfed that of typesetting a full-page glossy magazine ad. The tendency in 1960s and 1970s advertising was to follow, out of both conviction and convenience, Edward K. Strong's prescription for "repetition — unending repetition." Ironically, even as the much-vaunted Creative Revolution was gathering steam in the copywriters' bullpen, the true locus of creativity was shifting away from those who made individual ads (of which there were fewer) and toward those who "merely" placed iterations of them — of which there were, suddenly, a lot more. The discipline of *media planning* was born, integrating immense amounts of ratings and demographic data with theories of audience behavior to predict and then execute the most efficient purchase patterns of advertising time. The end of the sponsorship model of television made advertising a massively quantitative business, as agencies used punch cards and computers to track ratings for dozens of shows, and then place thousands of repetitious spots among those shows in any given week.

In the complex new era of spot television, the practice of advertising had become, in large part, high-stakes media buying — and, more than ever, efficient use of repetition in the mass media demanded a psychological approach left to specialists, dedicated research scientists who now studied nothing but advertising response. The first issue of the *Journal of Advertising Research* appeared in March 1961. It was an austere publication, so austere that no actual advertising sullied its pages until 1967. The *Journal* avoided the flash and gossip of trade papers like *Advertising Age* and *Ad Week*, adopting instead a stern, scientific tone. It was aimed not at the idea men and copywriters who actually made up ads, but at a new kind of advertising professional: the "quantitative men" who staffed newly created departments of advertising research and media planning. Their job was not to make ads, or even to decide which ads worked best, but to decide on the most effective way of deploying *any* advertising across an increasingly complex media spectrum. What was needed to justify those expensive computer models, and the orgy of media buying they triggered, was an ironclad, up-to-date theory of desire and repetition in advertising.

In the mid-1960s, advertising research had nothing to do with the huckster Freudianism of what Packard had called "the depth approach," or even the commonsense empiricism of Ebbinghaus and his followers; the "quants" were followers of Skinner, and their methodologies were taken directly from behaviorist — and later cognitive — psychology. They had little interest in whether an ad was "creative," or whether it would hook into consumers' primal emotional needs; they wanted to measure as precisely as possible how a distracted mass audience would register, remember, and ultimately react to an entire ad campaign — to repetitive iterations of (basically) arbitrary "stimuli" beamed at them indiscriminately over mass media. *The Hidden Persuaders* had gotten it both right and terribly wrong: right, in that modern psychological science and broadcast media were being harnessed to solve the crisis of desire by mass-producing it; wrong, because the last thing advertising research cared about was probing into any individual's unconscious drives and fixations. Nor did advertising researchers share the worry of creative types about whether repetition was uncool. In the early 1960s the only question for advertising research was, how much repetition is *enough?*

In media planning, advertising is intuitively understood as an extreme version of what Walter Benjamin, in a quite different context, called "post-auratic" art. Not only does mechanical reproduction strip individual ads of any aura of uniqueness, but to the inherent "distractedness" with which we consume mechanically reproduced images one must add the distinct possibility of total unawareness (never saw the ad) or even active disinterest (saw it, but turned the page or flipped channels). The advertising researcher and the media planner can never count on an audience, so they start by asking how many people will at least be *exposed* to an ad. The fundamental concepts of media planning are thus two measures of a given population's exposure to advertising: *reach* and *frequency*. Reach is the *percentage of a population* that is exposed to an advertising media vehicle (a TV show, say) at least once during a designated time period; frequency is the *number of times* the average prospect is exposed to the advertising vehicle during that time. (Frequency is thus only a fraction of the actual number of times the ad runs.) Multiply reach by frequency and you have a rough measure of the number of "hits," the number of chances to build desire, that your ad will have — what advertisers call *gross ratings points,* or GRPs. Divide that number into the total cost to you of advertising in the particular vehicle, and you have what the media planners, though their target populations now number tens of millions, persist in calling *cost-per-thousand (impressions),* or CPM.[25]

As a concept, frequency has the most suggestive implications for the analysis of minimalism as cultural practice; it shows how deeply the idea of desire creation through mass-mediated repetition has been embedded into advertising theory and practice. In fact, a paradigmatic assumption of 1960s advertising research was that at least some repetition was necessary if advertising was to have any effect at all; the holy grail of quantitative research was to determine precisely what this *effective frequency* was. Effective frequency is commonly defined as the number of times — that is, the amount of repetition — necessary for an advertisement not just to be noticed, but to do its work: to achieve brand awareness, attitude change, brand switching, or recall of messages. Researchers attempted to plot the "response function" to repeated advertising stimuli, and from about 1960 to the early 1980s, it was assumed that the curve of the advertising response function would be roughly S-shaped (Figure 4, *left*). There is an initial "threshold effect" (the beginning flatness of the curve); not enough frequency, and the ad makes no impression at all. At the effective frequency, the threshold is overcome, the curve turns sharply up, and consumers begin to display measurable influence. And, researchers assumed, after a certain point, increasing the number of impressions would no longer increase the response; thus the curve flattens out again. As one can imagine, actual experimental validation of the S-curve was not easy to achieve; but most advertisers took it on faith. After all, psychological research on learning going back to Ebbinghaus had shown that repetition of a stimulus not only increased the chance it would be noticed, but also improved retention and recall. In a seminal 1959 article, "The Remembering and Forgetting of Advertising," cited through the 1960s, researcher Hubert Zielske bombarded housewives with 13 repetitions of an ad for soap and showed that it was indeed possible to boost their recall to very high levels.[26] (He also discussed the most efficient way to do it, but more on that later.)

By the 1970s the S-curve was generally accepted as psychological fact. In 1972 Herbert Krugman, in another widely cited article, pegged effective frequency at three repetitions; by 1979 enough research had accu-

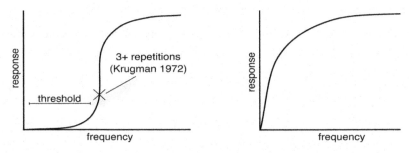

Figure 4 The "S-curve" *(left)* and concave curve *(right)* models of advertising response. The S-curve, with its implied "threshold effect," dominated theories of repetition in advertising from the late 1950s until about 1985.

mulated on this perennial problem to support an entire book on the subject, in which it was concluded that three to five repetitions was the most cost-effective frequency.[27] Any less, and you ran the risk of having your message ignored; any more, and you were spending money on impressions that did little to increase levels of response. Still, achieving an effective frequency of three worked out to a staggering level of actual repetition, since it might take as many as five actual placements of an ad to get a basic frequency of even one in a given population (not everybody watched everything), and, at minimum, two of those frequency hits were "wasted" just getting people's attention. Fifteen to 20 repetitions of an ad — and, on television at least, those repetitions would be exact — was thought barely enough to ensure that an acceptable percentage of the target audience got past the threshold effect and responded to your message at all.[28]

Thus 1960s and 1970s advertising research seemed to prove once and for all the scientific validity of Thomas Smith's 1885 piece of advertising folk wisdom. As Krugman pointed out, Smith's homespun parable of repetition includes a bona-fide threshold effect overcome by the requisite three to five repetitions. (The S-curve of the advertising response function "explained" why his distracted reader did not even notice the ad until he saw it for the third time.) Smith demands a slightly higher frequency than researchers thought cost effective by the 1970s, but he does make the same Baudrillardian assumption that they did (and I call your attention to line 14 in the epigraph that opens this chapter): given enough repetition, advertising could create invidious desires that would seem to the recipient both authentic and self-generated, as the hapless consumer "remembers," right on cue, "that he has wanted such a thing for a long time."

Let's jump ahead of the chronological narrative, and follow this quick survey of advertising theory to its end. The consensus on repetition and effective frequency collapsed in the 1980s, as the influence of Ebbinghaus and Skinner finally began to wane; new studies attacked the model at every point. Controlled experimental research seemed unable to replicate the threshold effect, and the S-curve was replaced with a simpler concave curve (Figure 4, *right*) that showed an immediate response to a "good" ad with a logarithmic falling off as repetitions piled up.[29] Studies also attacked the correlation between recall of advertisements and desire for products; it seemed that consumers decided to buy on their own, and the best repetition could do was ensure that your ad might be the one seen at the crucial moment. Finally, and most destructively, the very idea of a mass market reachable most efficiently through mass media began to pall; as one famous propaedeutic from the early 1990s put it, advertising faced a "one-to-one future."[30] In a world of 500 cable channels, increasingly careful market segmentation, narrowly targeted direct mail advertising, and infinite customization of products, the idea of "effective frequency" — paying skyrocketing prices for ads not seen or ignored by a mass of people, most of whom you didn't really want to reach anyway — seemed absurdly antiquated and wasteful.

Who was right? That is not really the issue. I have delved into the arcana of advertising research and pseudo-research not to determine how advertising actually works (still a mystery, even today), but rather to establish the rise and fall during the 1960s and 1970s of a cultural practice of advertising in sync with musical minimalism as a cultural practice, both correlated to a particular model of how repetition could be harnessed to create inauthentic desire. The model dominated advertising media planning for two decades, practically guaranteeing that all mass media, especially television, would be filled with the endless repetition — 15 to 20 ad placements to get an effective frequency of one! — that was thought necessary to mass-produce consumer demand. Is it any wonder that minimal music began to echo back this pervasive background hum of repetition? Is it so outlandish to assume that pulsed process music, like advertising, used those repetitions to construct its purely musical desires?

We are, finally, homing in on a possible hermeneutic framework for American minimal music. We saw in the last chapter how basic features of the minimal aesthetic — blankness, loss of affect, externalized relationships, collapse of depth — can be interpreted in terms of a crisis of subjectivity and authentic desire in postwar America. We have moved closer and seen how the dominant technical feature of pulsed process music, its pervasive repetition, can be read as a *zeitgeistliche* reflection of mass-media advertising strategies for reconstructing an (inauthentic) simulacrum of that lost desire. A brief history of TV shows that the historical correlation can be made with tolerable precision: the new combination of television and spot advertising unleashed a torrent of repetition on American audiences around 1965, the exact moment that the first repetitive music emerged in the hands of experimental composers like Terry Riley and Steve Reich.

That same year critic Barbara Rose led off her report on the new "A B C Art" for *Art in America* by quoting Marshall McLuhan, who, only months before, had unwittingly predicted the rise of something like repetitive music, arguing in *Understanding Media* that experimental art could act as an immunizing "counter-irritant" to the self-protective numbness of a society bombarded by the sensorium-remapping intensities of the new electronic media: "In the history of culture there is no example of a conscious adjustment to new [media] except in the puny and peripheral efforts of artists. The artist picks up the message of cultural and technological challenge decades before its transforming impact occurs. In experimental art, men are given the exact specifications of coming violence to their own psyches from their own technology."[31] It would take over a decade for Jerry Mander to grow so terrified by what he saw as the technological violence of commercial television that he would argue in print for the total abolition, on public health grounds, of its advertising-driven rhythms. But by then, as Richard Sennett's 17-year-old nephew testifies, repetitive music had been immunizing us all, helping us cross over to a new sensibility, preparing us, like all truly experimental art, to "ride with the punch," as McLuhan demotically put it.

From its very beginning, repetitive music has showed us not what television should be, but what, as a cultural form, it actually is. At the dawn of spot advertising on television, minimalism was already providing the exact specifications in sound of the coming repetitious orgy of desiring-production. It is now the twenty-first century, *Four Arguments for the Elimination of Television* has been on library shelves for over a quarter century, and television still has us all by the (eye)balls; reading Mander's screed again isn't going to help. Listening to minimalism, on the other hand, *does* help. Without hectoring us, it lets us feel how we might surf the repetitions, how we might achieve, in a phrase that spans the distance from Marshall McLuhan to La Monte Young and Donna Summer, an "understanding of the life of forms and structures created by electric technology."[32]

It is to those forms and structures that we now turn. Our understanding of process music's formal "specifications" can be made eerily exact. It is possible to correlate specific ways that repetition is organized in minimal music with specific technical features of advertising media planning — first at the local level of texture, and then at the global level of directed linear-harmonic structures.

HERMENEUTIC ANALYSIS:
MINIMAL MUSIC AS ADVERTISING CAMPAIGN

Flighting and Pulsing

Research in the 1960s told the media planner he needed to repeat ads over and over to create desire; it also had suggestions about the pacing of those repetitions. One of the first to test the effects of various rhythmic patterns was the aforementioned Hubert Zielske, during his 1959 investigation into the "remembering and forgetting" of advertisements. The real point of that article was not the simple fact that repetition improved recall of advertisements; Zielske had actually set out to test two quite different ways of deploying those repetitions in time. He exposed two sets of housewives to 13 repetitions of the same ad over a one-year period; one set saw all 13 in the first 13 weeks and then nothing, while the other set saw the 13 ads spread out evenly across the entire year. The two lines on the much-cited and reproduced graph in Figure 5 show the very different results. The quick burst of ads had the effect one might expect: a very high level of recall at the end of week 13, and then a precipitous decline to almost nothing by the end of the year. The same ads spread evenly across the year never achieved that high, but were able to maintain a steady, if lower, level of recall for the entire year.

The two media strategies tested by Zielske became codified as "flighting," that is, intensive bursts of advertising interspersed with media silence, and "steady state," which seeks to maintain a much lower level of advertising all the time.[33] Given limited resources, each strategy has drawbacks. Flighting maximizes reach and frequency in the short run, but it risks a total loss of product awareness during what can be extended fallow periods; steady-state advertising maintains continuity but risks being unable to sustain the level of repetition that can surmount the threshold effect. Extensive research in this area identified a compromise strategy that maximized resources: maintain a base level of advertising for product awareness, but add a series of less intensive flights to guarantee a periodic breakthrough to effective frequency. The

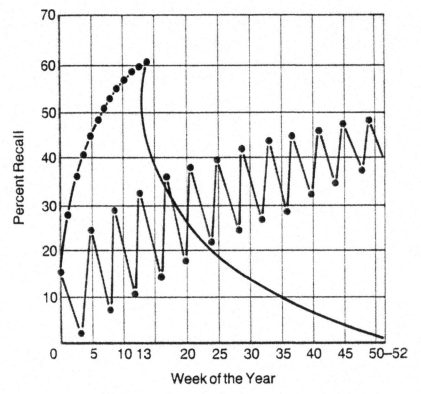

Figure 5 Zielske subjects housewives to 13 repetitions of a soap ad and demonstrates that "pulsed" repetition is the most effective way to maximize recall of advertising (1959). Reproduced by permission from Hubert A. Zielske, "The Remembering and Forgetting of Advertising," *Journal of Marketing* 13, no. 1 (January 1959): 239–43.

name for this common media-planning strategy will resonate with a strange familiarity to the student of minimalist process music: media planners call it "pulsing."

This hermeneutic window is the one we have been trying to pry open for the last few dozen pages: *Pulsed repetition turns out to be the key structural trope of both process music and modern advertising campaigns.*

The multilevel media plan of an advertising campaign is normally represented as a two-dimensional matrix, with various mixtures of media arranged vertically, and time proceeding, as in a musical score, from left to right. The pulsing and flighting take place polyphonically, different media "voices" moving in their own distinctive daily, weekly, or monthly rhythms. Sometimes the resemblance to visual representations of repetitive music is striking. Consider Figure 6, where a hypothetical media plan

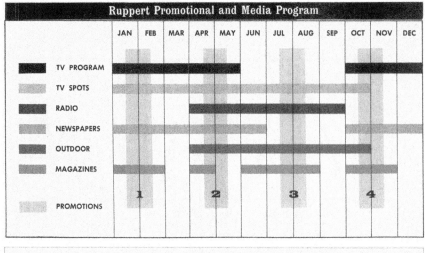

Figure 6 (top and bottom) A sample media plan from an advertising textbook, ca. 1964, compared with a characteristic graphic representation of repetitive ambient music, ca. 1978. Reproduced from Roger Barton, *Media in Advertising* (New York: McGraw-Hill, 1964), p. 423; Brian Eno, *Ambient 1: Music for Airports,* Editions EG EGS 201, 1978.

for "Ruppert Beer" from a 1964 advertising textbook by Roger Barton[34] is juxtaposed with Brian Eno's 1978 graphic representation of musical processes in *Ambient 1: Music for Airports*.

On a purely iconographic level, Eno's quasi score closely resembles Barton's media plan: both use staggered gray horizontal bars at different vertical levels to represent different "instruments" whose parts enter and exit contrapuntally but are "sustained" until they overlap. The sustenance is literal in Eno's case, since each rectangle represents an individual synthesized tone. In Barton's plan, however, the gray bars represent sustained bursts of advertising: they collapse a highly regular and repetitious pattern of pulsation into a single sign, much as the tremolo sign ($\not\equiv$) in music allows the composer to specify many evenly spaced repetitions of the same note with a single symbol. (We can ignore the vertical bars in Barton's plan, which represent special "promotions" outside the mass media, like in-store displays and holiday sales.) We understand that at a higher degree of media magnification, each gray blur would resolve itself into a more or less complex rhythmic dance of advertising placements.

For instance, the second bar from the top, extending through the entire year, representing spot advertising (still coexistent ca. 1964 with formal program sponsorship in this slightly outdated textbook account) stands in for what would probably be thousands of individual beer ads — in effect, an elaborate pulsation of beer ads — tossed into the larger pulsating flow of network television. On any given evening, the quick rhythm of the TV spots would interlock with similar placements on radio as drive time gave way to prime time, while the entire apparatus of print media — newspapers, magazines, and outdoor billboards — proceeded in its own polyphony of daily, weekly, and monthly patterns. (Billboards, which change only once or twice a season, form the sustained cantus firmus for this complex prolational canon.) If we could zoom in on Barton's media plan, the pulsed campaigns on television and radio might trace something like the overlapping, angular piano arpeggios that proliferate across the score of Steve Reich's 1979 *Octet/Eight Lines* (Example 11). But what of the sustained chord progression in the strings — a generational descendant of the ever-expanding organ part in *Music for Mallet Instruments, Voices, and Organ* — which provides the necessary temporal counterweight? One reading of these overlapping, decelerating lines would be as analogous to placements in media with slower cycles, so that the stratified texture gives the listener something like a three-dimensional sonic experience of the wheels within wheels that drive an advertising campaign.

Compare Reich's score with the actual media plan in Figure 7, drawn up by the Leo Burnett Agency in the early 1980s for Samsonite luggage,[35] and this rather harebrained notion gains at the very least a certain hermeneutic suggestiveness. Burnett's "what if" scenario, designed to show the client the kind of media saturation possible when budget is not an issue, maps pretty well onto the kind of textural layering on display in the *Octet*. One first notes, at bottom, intricate arpeggiated placements jumping among pricey general-circulation men's magazines, pulling polyrhythmically against the ticking backbeat of biweekly spots in two national newspapers. At the same time, sustained flights in cheaper, specialized publications — for a luggage manufacturer, Burnett will target airline in-flight magazines — advertise in a smooth *legato*, bathing the key demographic of business travelers with a sustained high frequency of exposure. These in-flight flights are designed to overlap with bursts of intense network TV coverage that can deliver both reach and frequency during the run-up to peak travel months. On paper Burnett's plan, laid out in blocks and horizontal bars on a regular time grid, resembles nothing so much as a short, repetitive piece of music in the "piano-roll"

Example 11 Steve Reich, *Octet/Eight Lines* (1979), opening.

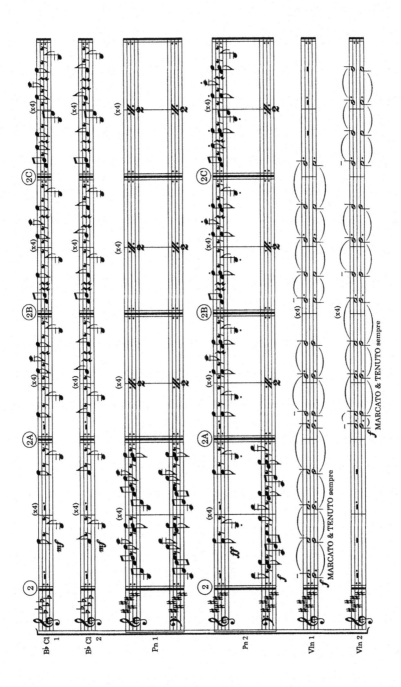

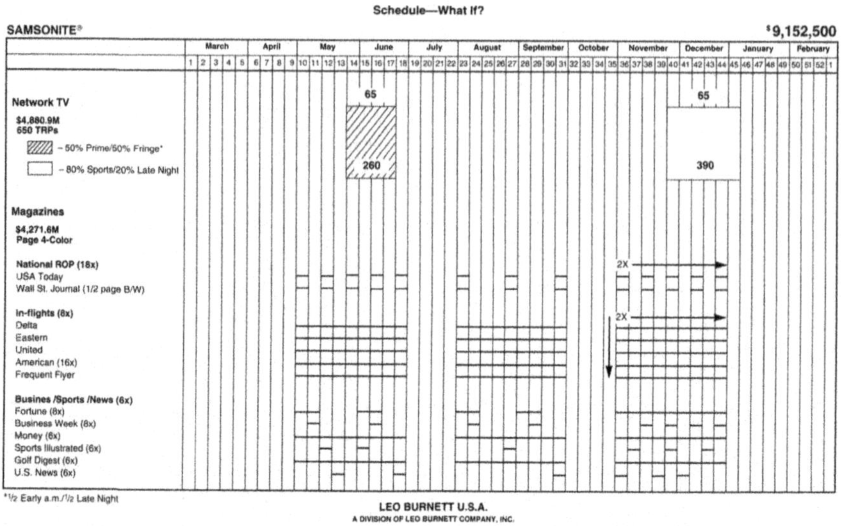

Schedule—What If?

SAMSONITE®   ʼ9,152,500

	March	April	May	June	July	August	September	October	November	December	January	February

Network TV
$4,880.9M
650 TRPs

▨ – 50% Prime/50% Fringe*

☐ – 80% Sports/20% Late Night

65   65

260   390

Magazines
$4,271.6M
Page 4-Color

National ROP (18x)
USA Today
Wall St. Journal (1/2 page B/W)

2X

In-flights (6x)
Delta
Eastern
United
American (16x)
Frequent Flyer

2X

Busines /Sports /News (6x)
Fortune (8x)
Business Week (8x)
Money (8x)
Sports Illustrated (6x)
Golf Digest (6x)
U.S. News (6x)

*1/2 Early a.m./1/2 Late Night

LEO BURNETT U.S.A.
A DIVISION OF LEO BURNETT COMPANY, INC.

Figure 7 An early 1980s media plan, created by the Leo Burnett Agency, for Samsonite luggage. Reproduced from Arnold Barban, Steven Cristol, and Frank Kopec, *Essentials of Media Planning,* 3rd ed. (Lincolnwood, Ill.: NTC Business Books, 1993).

notation favored by MIDI sequencing programs. Transcribed diplomatically into pitches, it would sound like pulse-pattern minimalism — of a rather brain-dead and square variety, no doubt. Our hypothetical advertising symphony becomes much more interesting, more like, say, Terry Riley's *In C,* if we remember that corporate advertisers are moving at different speeds through dozens, if not hundreds, of such media plans at any one time, plans whose various modules are synchronized not with each other, but with the relentless, metronomic pulse of mass-media commercial time. (Making the background pulse of *In C* audible, as you'll recall, was *quondam* percussionist Steve Reich's idea.)[36]

Mass-Producing Musical Desire:
Minimal Music as Advertising Campaign

Thus at every moment the pulsating, repetitious textures of minimalism loosely mirror the pulsed repetition of mass-media advertising. But we can't make the reductive assertion that everything that goes on in a piece like Reich's *Octet* is a simple "phosphorescent reflection" of this or that pattern of media buying. To correlate the large-scale structure of minimalist process music with that of the advertising campaign, we'll have to loosen up our hermeneutic enough to include the interpretive arguments of previous chapters. Minimalism is not just a species of program music for the consumer society, a sonic representation of the advertising-saturated media environment in the way Beethoven's Pastoral Symphony depicts birds in the woods outside Vienna; repetitive music enlists its form and process to make us *feel* the effects of that media barrage on the psyche. As any ad executive will tell you, an advertising campaign is not just orchestration of the media to create elaborately hypnotic pulsation; advertising has a clearly defined goal, which is to create desire in the consumer for its company's products. And if minimalism mirrors the day-to-day pulse of advertising in its texture and rhythm, it reflects the desire engendered by advertising campaigns in its long-range melodic structure. Using pitch structure to depict desire has been, since the seventeenth century, a central preoccupation of Western music; but this consumer desire is — to quote the advertising discourse that gave it birth — something fundamentally "new and improved." The trek through postwar sociology, advertising theory, and Baudrillard's system of objects has prepared us to recognize that, in the Affluent Society, desire-for-objects is the radical result of a planned mutation. Since the 1960s the mass-media environment has provided its denizens the everyday, collective experience of recombinant teleology, of the attempt, through pervasive, repetitive advertising, to engineer and disseminate desires with the methodical efficiency of industrial mass production.

Some of the most influential pieces of minimalist process music have incorporated that recombinant teleology into their long-range linear structure, transposing "artificial" consumer desires into equally artificial musical ones. This is, I believe, the larger historical and cultural context for the recombinant musical teleologies whose "discovery" and phenomenological description were the burden of Chapter 1. The reader will recall how 1970s popular reception portrayed disco and minimalism (the "higher disco") as two musical aspects of the same deviant cultural phenomenon. Both types of music were interpreted as enacting — with varying degrees of explicitness, to be sure — radically new teleological trajectories of physical desire. Musical analysis then uncovered in both a common structural trope: the *linear ascent* was a juxtaposition of long, static plateaus, each extended through gradual, systematic process until terminated by a sudden upward melodic shift, the whole series creating a terraced musical ascent that provided at least a section of the work with a coherent, if attenuated and mechanical-seeming, experience of goal-direction.

Never explored in the course of that discussion was *why* this particular extreme linear mutation of musical teleology should arise at all, or what forces in the larger culture might have given rise to it, might be represented by it, or at very least might correlate with it. The previous chapter's long sociological survey of the postwar affluent society, with its attendant crises of subjectivity and desiring-production, and the present chapter's elaborate history and phenomenology of mass-media advertising were necessary prolegomena to a reading of repetitive music that, unsupported by such stickling for detail, must sound dismissive or, at best, glib. The "sexy" moments of recombinant teleology trafficked in by 1970s minimalism and disco present the listener with a structure of feeling that has the same basic shape as the experience of desire and subjectivity crafted in the mid-1960s by mass-market advertising.

This is why the constructions of desire in repetitive minimalist music do not sound like those in *Poppea* or *Tristan*. The pioneering theoreticians of desire and its construction when Reich was composing his *Octet* were not Renaissance rhetoricians or nineteenth-century Romantics, but hardheaded advertising professionals. Musical minimalism works to create desire the way those advertisers then thought mass-media advertising worked; in other words, process music is a specific midcentury construction *of the construction* of desire. At some point during the endless repetitious pulsing, linear desires arise — not the Schenkerian *Tonwillen*, the authentic "inner" need of individual scale steps for resolution, but a mass-produced musical desire imposed on them (and us) en masse by relentlessly organized repetition. "How inauthentic!" critics cry; and they are correct. Only, as Baudrillard is always ready to remind us, in the consumer society there is probably no more authentic experience to be had.

Close Readings: Reich, Riley, Andriessen

Taken as a whole, the pitch structure of Steve Reich's *Octet/Eight Lines* consists of a series of extended plateaus formed by the operation of strict rhythmic process on static harmonic materials. Within these plateaus, as the additive and subtractive processes methodically work themselves out, the music does feel almost motionless, as if the pulsating, minimally teleological flow of television had been transposed into sound. But when Reich adds plateaus to one another, he must change the chord progressions; in the *Octet* he sometimes changes them in accordance with classical tonal teleology and its tried-and-true linear-harmonic means of achieving directional coherence. Example 12 extracts from the texture

Example 12 Analytical reduction of partial linear ascent in Steve Reich, *Octet/Eight Lines* (1979).

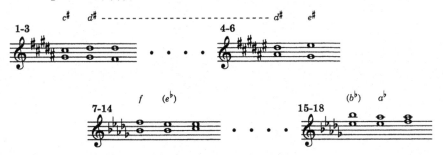

the pitch content of the sustained overlapping string figures that are subjected to expansion and contraction within each of the *Octet*'s five large composer-designated sections. The linkage between the first and second sections is particularly clear, as C♯ and D♯, the top notes of the violins' overlapping double-stops, stretch out over pulsating arpeggios, contract back to their original length, and then shift directly up to D♯ and E♯. The melodic rise is accompanied by a harmonic shift "up one sharp," from the Dorian collection on C♯ to one a fifth higher, on G♯. The third and fourth sections are shifted up another fifth, to D♯ Dorian, but the soprano pitches in the violins remain the same. (Reich notates this key area enharmonically as E♭, so these notes, spelled E♭–F, at least appear higher.) The fifth and final section remains (more or less) in E♭/D♯ Dorian, but the violins slide up one more time to alternate between B♭ and A♭.

One would not want to overstate the coherence of this ascent. Although the general trajectory of the oscillating string figures is clearly upwards, the only obvious stepwise ascending connection is between the first and second sections of the piece. It seems that Reich had no interest in creating a work that *as a whole* exhibited classical teleology, nor did he worry about articulating the work's five sections in any consistent manner. In fact, only between the first two sections is there a clear break and an obvious linear ascent; it is as if the rest of the work just collapses on the sofa and sinks back into the flow. (Reich, like a good 1970s TV producer, worked diligently to create that sense of flow, to smooth over the interruptions in his programming sequence: "The division between sections is as smooth as possible with some overlapping in the parts, so that it is sometimes hard to tell exactly when one section ends and the

Example 13 Terry Riley, *In C* (1964), "stochastic" ascent of Modules 1–6.

next begins.")[37] Still, this recombinant teleology has a distinctive bipartite structure of feeling: first, a long, static plateau, chopped into a teeming multitude of short repeating fragments, segments just differentiated enough by process-driven change to hold the attention, but across whose sequential flow "nothing really happens" harmonically or melodically; then, as if to release the energy stored up, a melodic event, a decisive shift upwards, often accompanied by a new pitch collection that increases the overall level of harmonic tension.

On the other hand, sometimes the pitch plateaus and melodic ascents of repetitive music interpenetrate in a seamless experience that melds gradually increasing linear tension with a feeling of unbroken flow, as in the famous opening of Terry Riley's *In C* (Example 13). While the ensemble is moving through the first six modules of the score, a fuzzy, gradual linear ascent from E to G takes shape in the listener's mind, one of many such acoustic effects arising within Riley's carefully controlled system of 53 musical objects calibrated to succeed each other in pitch content, contour, and rhythmic placement. These first six modules certainly seem minimal, like melodic primitives, evolving from a raw arpeggiation of the tonic triad (Module 1), through neighbor note motives (Modules 2–3) and passing tones (Modules 4–5), and back again to the unadorned tonic. But they work together quite subtly to evoke a stochastic melodic *Zug* (tension-span), filling in, with subliminal slowness, the minor third between scale degrees 3 and 5. Module 1 introduces E as a melodic tone; as the players move raggedly forward, E is gradually contaminated by the F above, which first appears only on weak beats (Module 2) and then, as the percentage of F in the texture increases, on strong beats too (Module 3). When G appears, it also is on the weak beat, while F mutates from accented neighbor note to accented passing tone (Module 4); by the time G has appeared on an accented beat, the most impatient performers have already begun to resolve its weakly implied dominant by leaping up to a sustained high C (Modules 5–6).

Riley executes several such linear ascents in the course of his work; one of the most dramatic, involving Modules 22–26, picks up the E and

Example 14 Terry Riley, *In C* (1964), Modules 22–30.

G of the opening, now sounding as scale degrees 1 and 3 in E minor, and uses systematic rhythmic variation of a simple ascending scale to extend the melodic center of gravity stepwise through the upper third, to B natural (Example 14). Aware, at some level, that the key center has shifted up one sharp to the mediant minor as substitute dominant, and that the melodic line is rising inexorably to hammer on the leading tone, the performers in almost every recording of *In C* treat this section as a powerful build-up of tension.[38] It is then possible, when the E–G–C of Module 29 resolves the leading tone and snaps the key center back to the tonic, to hear a dramatic release at what begins to sound suspiciously like a traditional "moment of recapitulation." (The effect is strengthened by the way Module 29 reproduces in a single melodic motive the complete E–G–C voice-leading trajectory of the opening "exposition.")

Riley's score, like Reich's, and unlike a traditional tonal piece "in C," does not display classical teleology, or even a consistent pattern of recombination. It is, for the most part, just a hypnotically pulsating flow, out of which, on occasion, when some perceptual threshold effect is surmounted, stirrings of old-fashioned linear-harmonic desire can be heard to coalesce. But there are, in fact, minimalist process pieces that use the musical equivalent of complex media planning to structure large chunks of musical time. Reich's later extended works can often be analyzed this way;[39] but there is a satisfying situational irony in concluding this analytical survey with an aggressively Marxist composer whose embrace of repetitive music was part of a polemical project to rescue it from the taint of advertising. Louis Andriessen's *Hoketus* does not sound anything like a soap commercial — its jagged asymmetrical rhythms and snarling dissonance make sure of that — but this first product of the 1975–76 minimal music project at The Hague shows that Andriessen had internalized the key structural trope underpinning American minimal music quite thoroughly.

As the title might imply, *Hoketus* is scored for two identical amplified groups of mongrel instruments (pan flute, piano, electric piano, electric bass, bongos), which turn Reich's process of rhythmic construction into a tricky, high-intensity game of irregular antiphonal attacks. Consider the synoptic Example 15, which is not precisely a "reduction" of Andriessen's score; the composer himself presented the harmonic material of each section of his piece in this condensed way. Since the pitches remain static in each plateau section, he need notate the cluster chord(s) only once, write out the rhythmic process in shorthand, and allow the performers to assign the notes to the rhythms more or less as they wish. Andriessen specifies only the outer parts: the basses are told always to play the lowest note of the chord together, and the pair of pan flutes are restricted, for most of the piece, to one or two notes circled by the composer on his score. Evidently Andriessen wanted to control the implied melodic progression of the two hocketing soprano instruments, and as even a cursory glance at Example 15 will show (the notation makes the analyst's task, well, minimal), the four long plateaus that comprise the first 15-odd minutes of the piece trace a clear ascending line in the soprano, the very uningratiating tritone from D to A♭.

Unlike Reich, Andriessen did absolutely nothing to soften the edges of his plateaus; each linear ascent arrives as an unexpected, grinding lurch upward. Rhythmically complex, fiercely dissonant, and unremittingly loud, *Hoketus* bears more than a passing surface resemblance to the most Dionysian and "primitive" moments of Stravinsky; insofar as its succession of dissonant, static harmonic blocks is tied together by a coherent, yet nonfunctional melodic ascent through a series of stacked pitch plateaus, it betrays an even more obvious structural debt to Stravinsky's "American" period and works like the *Symphony in Three Movements*.[40] Jonathan Cross, in his survey of Stravinsky's late-twentieth-century legacy, prefers Andriessen to the American minimalists — all equally indebted to Stravinskian *uproshcheniye,* or "simplification" — because Dutch minimalism sounds more directional, less hypnotic, more European, and less "commercial" than theirs.[41] Andriessen's dialectical reversal of minimalism has received mostly admiring reviews, and this author yields to no one in his admiration for the vitality and intellectual rigor of the New Hague School. But in transposing the American pattern of static, process-driven plateaus in ascending linear sequence into his overtly modernist idiom, Andriessen incorporated, willy-nilly, the entire cultural formation he sought to banish. *Hoketus* may not sound like an advertisement for dish-washing liquid — but its overall structure is that of a

Example 15 Analytical overview of pitch plateaus in Louis Andriessen, *Hoketus* (1975–77).

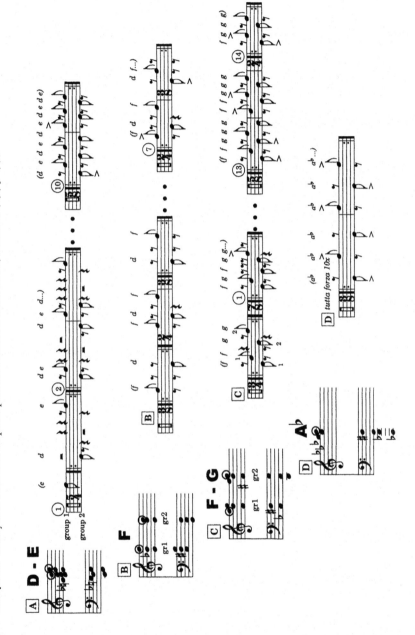

classic Procter & Gamble *(Sorry, Louis, but you're soaking in it!)* advertising campaign.

Actually it is Andriessen's pattern of clearly etched static plateaus separated by abrupt melodic jolts that most closely resembles the best working model ever proposed within the advertising world for how repetition actually motivates a consumer to buy. Herbert Krugman, last seen in 1970 attaching electrodes to the skull of a TV viewer to determine her delta-wave quotient, had first proposed his influential theory of "low-involvement learning" and advertising response in the bellwether year 1965.[42] Krugman became convinced that, unlike print advertising, which triggers the familiar "high-involvement" process of conscious mental processing that the writing culture uses to assimilate facts and evaluate truth claims, advertising on television was registered, if at all, in a new, "low-involvement" mode. When he characterized television in the previous chapter as primarily an experience of ambience, akin to sitting meditatively on a park bench watching a landscape go by, he helped make a very general connection between television's quasi-hypnotic flow and the "trippy" aspect of minimalist process music. But Krugman was not just interested in the fact that television provided a low-involvement experience within which one would neither demand conscious instruction or syllogistic logic; he had worked out, he thought, how low-involvement learning could influence consumer behavior, how something to which you paid almost no attention could ultimately get you to lay down your hard-earned cash at the point of sale.

Krugman's hypothesis was that television didn't try to argue with you or convince you, it simply proceeded to change, gradually and almost imperceptibly, the potential salience of certain ideas and images in your mental landscape. Only in the face of a purchasing decision would the "trap" snap shut; as it turned out, you would have learned quite a bit without realizing it: "The purchase situation is the catalyst that reassembles or brings out all the potentials for shifts in salience that have accumulated up to that point. The product or package is then suddenly seen in a new 'somehow different' light although nothing verbalizable may have changed up to that point."[43]

What better cultural analogue to the musical structures we have just been discussing? Listeners traverse extended pitch plateaus, stretches of repetitive musical flow where nothing much seems to be happening, no tonal arguments are being made, but where they are actually learning without involvement, having the salience of certain melodic possibilities raised through gradual process. Then, in a musical version of what

Krugman called the "behavior-choice situation," they encounter a quick rush of desiring-production, a sudden linear ascent that catalyzes accumulated melodic tensions they didn't even know they were feeling. The linear-harmonic implications of the plateau are retroactively remapped, "seen in a new 'somehow different' light," though one would be hard pressed, as with TV advertising, to explain in words why. This was the aspect of process music that dancer Lucinda Childs struggled to communicate to a *Time* reporter with a vague meteorological metaphor. "It takes you out like a mist," she said of *Einstein on the Beach,* in which she had performed for several years, "where you can see twenty miles, then you see nothing. It is an emotional experience to find you are in different places, but you don't know how you got there."[44]

Why Minimalism Now?

Krugman's hypothesis does more than provide a snug-fitting cultural template for minimal music's constructions of desire; his theory has an implied historical dimension. Although his experimental data directly contravened Marshall McLuhan's claim that television was a more involving and interactive — in McLuhan's terms, "cool" — medium than radio or film, Krugman would no doubt have agreed that the shift from a print-dominated culture (the "Gutenberg Galaxy") to one dominated by electronic broadcasting necessarily involved a historic remapping of subjectivity. Krugman was concerned, of course, mostly with advertising; but he contrasted the new and the old ways ads work on our psyches in terms that cry out for music-historical interpretation: "There is a difference in the change processes that are at work. Thus, with low involvement one might look for gradual shifts in perceptual structure, aided by repetition, activated by behavioral-choice situations, and followed at some time by attitude change. With high involvement one would look for the classic, more dramatic, and more familiar conflict of ideas at the level of conscious opinion and attitude that precedes changes in overt behavior."[45]

Gradual shifts in perceptual structure, aided by repetition — pulse-pattern minimalism is, in effect, a "low-involvement" style of music. Beethoven, on the other hand, exemplifies an older and more familiar high-involvement style, where the listener is invited to participate consciously in a staged dramatic conflict of musical ideas. Process music acts on us like the flow of electronic media, while traditional tonal music — a music more or less coeval with print culture — has tended not only to be disseminated in print, but to elicit the appropriate high-involvement response from its cultivated (i.e., literate) audience as well. Thus we are able to give a more detailed response to the historiographic question posed but not really answered by Claire Polin in her contribution to a 1989 collection of essays on music and the politics of culture: *Why Minimalism Now?* Polin could only echo Christopher Lasch's *The Minimal Self* in language of extreme generality, arguing that "minimalism today represents a critical reaction to the condition of humanity in a complex and uncontrolled society." In other words, she has no idea why minimalism now — or in 1965 — and not at any moment in the chaotic history of Western civilization over the last, say, 2,000 years.[46]

My argument that minimalism reflects back to us the endless repetition of mass-media advertising would not necessarily guarantee a better historical argument than Polin's; advertising has been around for centuries, and it has been repetitively bombarding us from mass-media vehicles for over 150 years. Even the affluent society and its crisis of desire are cultural formations that reach back decades before the birth of repetitive music. But Krugman's hypothesis gives us the key: *Minimal music appears at the precise moment when advertising, the dominant discourse of the consumer society, switches decisively over to the low-involvement model of desiring-production.* The critical year is 1965, around which cluster the first breakthroughs of Pop, optical process, and Minimalism in the visual arts and their criticism; the first performances by La Monte Young and the Theatre of Eternal Music of the key drone work *The Tortoise (His Dreams and Journeys);* the first performances of Terry Riley's *In C;* Steve Reich's first experiments with gradual phase shifting; and Philip Glass's first encounters with additive process in Indian music. The year 1965 is also the *annus mirabilis* during which spot advertising completed its transformation of television into pulsating flow — and during which ad researchers like Krugman first began to grasp that television had, in its turn, transformed advertising into a new avant-garde cultural practice, a kind of media-plan minimalism that used massive amounts of low-involvement stimulus to effect the gradual, but inexorable, mass production of desire.

It may be useful to conclude this line of argument by formally restating the music-historiographic implications of the complex linkages among sonic teleology, repetitive process, post-1965 media advertising, the industrial consumer society, and the creation of desire-for-objects. The president of NBC spoke truer than he knew when he argued that TV advertising was to mass production what individual selling had been to craft production. In their preindustrial state, our needs and desires were irredeemably incoherent; they were "fluid and contingent," linked to specific objects not easily compared, contrasted, or mass produced. In what Baudrillard calls the "stage of artisanal production," these needs were fulfilled by the equally incoherent multiplicity of custom-made objects. But with the advent of industrialization, production is rationalized, totalized, systematized. It becomes the job of advertising and the system of objects to make consumption follow suit: "At the stage of artisanal production objects reflect the contingent and singular character of needs, but since the beginning of the industrial era, manufactured goods have acquired coherence from technological organization and from the economic structure. The system of needs has become less integrated than the system of objects; the latter imposes its own coherence and thus acquires the capacity to fashion an entire society." The dubious triumph of consumer society is that desire for products, like the products themselves, can be *processed* — systematically produced and thus endowed with meaning thanks to the same kind of total control that governs industrial production: "the ultimate goal of consumer society (not through any technocratic Machiavellianism, but through the ordinary structural play of competition) is the functionalization of the consumer and the psychological monopolization of all needs — a unanimity in consumption which at last would harmoniously conform to the complete consolidation and control of production."[47]

In effect, the all-inclusive process at work in the music of Glass and Reich is to be understood as the same kind of totalizing and systematic evolution of earlier, less regimented and pervasive techniques of channeling *musical* desire: namely, the short, individualized rhythmic processes whose functioning I have elsewhere described during pitch plateaus in Stravinsky and Beethoven.[48] To control linear tension over huge spans of low-involvement musical flow, minimal composers must "mass produce" the rhythmic transformations that now appear in retrospect to have been "custom-made" one at a time by their predecessors. These previous disruptions of syntax gave the illusion of spontaneity, of embodying an unique and immediate compositional response (Baudrillard would have called it an "artisanal" response) to a particular linear-dramatic "need."

Minimalism's most characteristic rhythmic processes can be seen as systematic or exhaustive working out of the individual tricks of earlier practice. Beethoven and Stravinsky could keep our attention focused for 12 seconds on a repeated pitch or melodic fragment by shifting it between the beats of a steady metrical pulse; in a work like *Piano Phase,*

Reich systematizes and totalizes this process so as to last 12 *minutes*. The phase-shifting process causes the melodic pattern in the phasing piano part to occupy every possible position relative to the bar line implied by the stationary part. Starting on each successive one of its 12 sixteenth notes, the shifting pattern defines a new, "industrial-strength" system of exhaustive rhythmic reinterpretation.

At the same time the actual shifting between beats, once an instantaneous gesture, is now slowed down and broken into a seeming infinitude of incremental steps. In between the previously definitive binary states of "on" and "off" the beat, an entirely new level of process opens up — one that rivets the attention with extremely disruptive, yet perfectly rationalized rhythmic interference patterns. It is as if nineteenth-century rhythmic salesmanship has undergone the same rationalization by industrial techniques that Baudrillard saw in modern marketing. The unique, handcrafted stratagems of Beethoven have now been replaced by industrial machinery that works to a much finer tolerance; the task of creating desire has been analyzed (through "time and motion studies") and broken down into microtasks (the "phase-shifting process"). Or, to make a more explicit link to the system of consumer objects, the musical idea, a "product" that used to come in only two "models" or "brands" (on the beat; off the beat), now has achieved full brand differentiation — a virtual infinitude of rhythmic placements whose effect is to maximize and systematize our desire for that moment when the two piano parts in *Piano Phase* come back into sync.

Reich's favorite 1970s process of rhythmic construction, "substituting beats for rests," provides an even more uncanny double of industrial desiring-production. Instead of dividing the "precession" into micro-increments, Reich later rationalized the process by breaking the pattern itself down into individual beats ("interchangeable parts"), and building it up note by note in another voice, one or more beats out of phase. The effect of such a passage is inevitably one of assembly — and more significantly, the assembly line: the composer gradually, systematically assembles a duplicate of a given object out of a mass of simple, interchangeable units. Like any consumer product, this constructed pattern-object comes in many different models or brands, formally distinguished by their differing relations to the beat. The ultimate result is exactly the kind of "impoverished" signifying structure Baudrillard attributes to the system of industrially mass-produced objects. The relation between all the shifted patterns does not maintain the syntax of canon — it inevitably tends toward a blurry flow into which the high-involvement distinction between first and last, *dux* and *comes,* collapses. And yet . . . somewhere in this pulsating web of low-involvement *différance,* we are more or less guaranteed to discover our own musical desire. And when it arrives, we will remember, as Thomas Smith predicted over a century ago, that we really had wanted such a (musical) thing for a long, long time.

THE TERROR OF "ABSOLUTE FREQUENCY": FROM THE MERCANTILE TO THE MEDIA SUBLIME

> That movement, from wonder to the wonder that a country should be so big, to the wonder that a building could be so big, to the last, small wonder, that a market-place could be so big — that was the movement of history. Could there be wonder in that? The size of the con?
>
> **George W. S. Trow, *Within the Context of No Context* (1981)**

The climactic sequence of the movie *Koyaanisqatsi* (a Hopi word that, as the final credits inform us, means "life out of balance") is edited to the increasingly frenetic rhythms of a 21-minute minimalist crescendo, to which Philip Glass gave the menacing, slightly Luddite title "The Grid."[49] The sound of the piece, with its endlessly rocking two-chord progression and whirring synthesizer arpeggios, epitomizes what most people think of as "minimal music," and it was, arguably, this 1982 film soundtrack that launched both Glass and his version of repetitive music into the pop cultural mainstream. Glass's music was pitched with a heavy spin, for "The Grid" underscores one of the most ideological sections of the film, in which director Godfrey Reggio used time-lapse photography and super-telephoto lenses to emulsify the denizens of New York, Chicago, and Los Angeles into frothing, twitching swarms of dehumanized Brownian motion. As the speed and intensity of the repetitive musical cycling relentlessly grows, Reggio begins to make his point with a series of visual puns, cross-cutting between varied scenes of urban life in and on the grid. Commuters and rushing traffic pulse like blood through overcrowded streets and stores; repetitive, paper-pushing jobs crush the soul with what we assume must be mind-numbing boredom; assembly lines churn out endless rows of Twinkies, televisions, and Camaros. All the cyclic motion through technological systems starts to blur together. City traffic looks as chaotic and meaningless as a video game; the robotic production of fast food seems indistinguishable from its joyless consumption; finally, as we zoom into space, the gridlike structure of the megalopolis maps onto the artificial nano-grids of the semiconductor world.

None of this is, ultimately, as profound a critique of industrial society as Reggio seemed to think. *(Look, those hot dogs pouring through chutes at the meat-processing plant look just like commuters squeezing onto the escalators at Grand Central Station! Our life* is indeed *out of balance!)* In fact, both he and Glass later distanced themselves from the rather callow New Age environmentalism that the film espouses.[50] But the way Reggio chose to structure his indictment does convey something crucial about the subjective experience of late capitalism, an indelible image of what Baudrillard called the "functionalism of the consumer." As the tempo of Glass's music rises, we move from scenes of transportation and manufacturing to venues more familiar to consumers: a video arcade, a bowling alley, a movie, the mall, the supermarket. Images of repetitive consumption visually rhyme with, and are constantly intercut with, images of repetitive mass production, all sped up by time-lapse photography so that we can witness *much more* of these activities at a time than normal human perception would allow. The climactic moments of the sequence cross-cut between extreme time-lapse and extreme slow-motion cinematography, providing yet another experience almost exactly opposite and almost exactly identical to the experience of speed. The vertiginous tempo shifts approach a disorienting peak, and suddenly we are faced with a single woman, holding two small children, all three completely motionless.

They are gazing, transfixed, at a TV set.

We can't see what they are watching, but behind them, in what is clearly a department store showroom, an entire wall of televisions, accelerated 50-fold through time-lapse photography, spews forth its chaotic overload (Figure 8). Almost immediately — in the sublime negative climax of the film — the entire visual field is filled by a single TV screen, first showing a video game, and then, for what seems like an eternity but is only 30 seconds, a raging torrent of network programming. The shot seems longer, because stop-motion filming compresses hours of broadcast time, dozens of channels, literally hundreds of program segments and advertisements, into a few frenzied moments. In this culminating moment the overall trajectory of the film becomes clear. Monumental scenes of unspoiled nature have given way over the course of an hour to machines and industry that rip at the land; then to a completely manmade landscape of repetitive production and consumption; and, finally,

Figure 8 The "negative climax" of Godfrey Reggio's *Koyaanisqatsi* (1982).

to the utter alienation of televisual flow washing over us at the speed of media. As Reggio put it, "I just wanted to express an idea that has been in my mind, to show that we are in a society that is becoming overwhelmed by spectacle and to show how this has distanced us. I wanted to make the point that we have to make choices between beauty and the beast."[51]

Facing down the mass-media beast, alone, in real time, trying to achieve by sheer endurance the Olympian perspective Reggio could only suggest with trick photography, has been a persistent feat of public literary machismo over the last four decades, fodder for the tiny, exotic genre of daredevil narrative we might dub the "I looked into the many-channeled face of television and lived to tell the tale" memoir. New York writer Charles Sopkin was the first to attempt a Stakhanovite act of total media consumption. In 1967, just as television flow was taking shape, he immersed himself into all six (!) channels of it for an entire week and wrote up the experience in a blistering jeremiad with the sardonic title *Seven Glorious Days, Seven Fun-Filled Nights.*[52] Thirty-odd years later, independent film executive Jack Lechner set out to duplicate Sopkin's "experiment," but by 1999, faced with well over 100 channels, he required 12 TV sets to capture a significant fraction of the flow. Sopkin's book was less about himself than about the sheer volume of bad television; Lechner, a confirmed child of the television era, seemed more interested in documenting how too much of a mostly decent thing can drive even a media professional slowly insane.[53]

Pride of place, however, must go to the methodical approach of Bill McKibben, author of *The Age of Missing Information:*

> This account takes the form of an experiment — a contrast between two days. One day, May 3, 1990, lasted well more than a thousand hours — I collected on videotape nearly every minute of television that came across the enormous Fairfax cable system from one morning to the next, and then I watched it all. The other day, later that summer, lasted the conventional twenty-four hours. A mile from my house, camped on a mountaintop by a small pond, I awoke, took a day hike up a neighboring peak, returned to the pond for a swim, made supper, and watched the stars till I fell asleep. This book is about the results of that experiment — about the information that each day imparted.[54]

Forget about seven fun-filled nights — it took McKibben *several months* of eight-hour days to watch 93 iterations, one for each channel, of that single, average day of television. Unlike Sopkin and Lechner, McKibben is not interested in showing off his ability to tolerate mega-doses of television, which he compares to a comforting narcotic, always there for the depressed and aimless. He has to watch it all, because, he concludes, "TV is cumulative." Repetition, particularly the endless repetition of advertising, is for McKibben the key environmental impact of television: "What I'm talking about is what happens when you see an ad, over and over, for small Ritz crackers pre-smeared and pre-stuck together with peanut butter and sold under the slogan 'No assembly required.' What habits of mind does this, in concert with a hundred other similar messages, help produce? And how do those habits differ from the habits, the attitudes people got from the natural world?"[55]

McKibben, a nature writer and environmental activist, has the same agenda as Reggio in *Koyaanisqatsi:* by contrasting the slow, inevitable rhythms of the natural world (he begins and ends his book with the image of a duck on an Adirondack pond "just swimming back and forth") with the frenzied overload of mediated culture, to convince us that our lives are out of balance, that we have totally lost touch with the subjective experience — and thus the wisdom — of the "real world." (That is the "missing information" of McKibben's title.) But, paradoxically, the main aesthetic effect of McKibben's and Reggio's work is an uncanny evocation of the mathematical sublime, of the sheer immensity and power of mass media's surging flow. Glass himself eagerly assented to an interviewer's claim that the "disturbing" time-lapse imagery in *Koyaanisqatsi* — even the nightmarish Los Angeles freeway traffic — could, by 1987, be appreciated in terms of its "vitality, and a sense of beauty."[56] But Reggio and Glass's image of an industrialized, mass-mediated culture of repetition is not beautiful at all; it is, in the full Kantian sense, sublime.

The media sublime is a subset of the larger mercantile sublime, of George Trow's wonder at our wonder at the size of the con; it became a theoretical possibility only after 1965, when spot advertising transposed the logic of the consumer system of objects onto broadcast media. Like the Kantian sublime, it derives from the abstract mental encompassing of a huge, terrifying, unrepresentable force — in this case the total productive force of mass-media advertising as it generates the entire system of needs, wants, and desires. Most commentators have assumed that minimalism in music is like McKibben's day meditating on the mountaintop, communing deeply with the cycles of nature that Steve Reich evokes in his famous description of musical process as like "placing your feet in the sand by the ocean's edge and watching, feeling, and listening to the waves gradually bury them."[57] But minimal music is actually just as much akin to a day bombarded by the repetitious flow pouring out of every TV set in the industrialized world. Process music is thus pure media sublime: its incessant repetitions present the listener with the sublime experience of living through every last iteration of every piece of advertising in an entire media plan, missing nothing — as if one could sit in front of every television in every home in America for as long as the plan runs. This impossible experience is available to no one person in reality; after all, even the most devoted ad executive cannot actually *watch* all the spot buys in his media plan.

An appreciation for the media sublime, and the thousands of hours of TV purgatory necessary (in the absence of time-lapse photography) to perceive it, can help answer an obvious question: people don't normally sit down to watch hours of advertising; why are they willing to listen to hours of minimal music? The only people to sit down deliberately and watch hours of commercials have been media daredevils like Sopkin, Lechner, and McKibben, and minimal music provides the same kind of thrill that their books do. Like *Koyaanisqatsi* — inside *Koyaanisqatsi*, for that matter — repetitive music provides us with the sonic equivalent of time-lapse, video archiving, and multiple TV sets: a chance to experience, as an aesthetic effect, the entirety of the media flow, with its sublime excess of repetitive desiring-production.

The aesthetic is an extreme, genuinely experimental one, as radical as the Dada-Futurist insight that someday we might listen aesthetically to the sonic chaos of industrial production. A moment's introspection will remind us that, though we may perceive our media environment as annoyingly repetitious, we are almost never allowed to experience directly just how repetitious it really is. Even a tiny taste of the media sublime, say, being exposed to the same ad twice during a single commercial break, can be quite disturbing. Why is this? When you see two ads in the same commercial block, you are seeing something that is not meant for you. Or, rather, not meant for you *alone*. At that moment the fiction that TV programming takes note of you as an individual evaporates; clearly the ad is running more than once so that you, the average viewer, will see it at least once. See it twice in a row, and for a brief moment you peek behind the curtain; you see the media through the eyes of a media planner. Instead of frequency (the iterations of an ad someone like you might see) or effective frequency (the iterations you actually notice), there is an intimation of something huge that nobody is supposed to perceive directly, what we might call *absolute* frequency: all the iterations of a given ad that are bombarding all of us all the time.

Minimalism in music is the avant-garde sound of absolute frequency. Listening to pulsed minimal music, hearing every repetition, is like having the experience not of any one consumer, but of all consumers at once. *You* are the mass market, and you feel the entire pressure of the mass media's power to construct desire — in other words, in a consumer society, the irresistible power to construct subjectivity itself — directly on your consciousness. The impossible attempt to represent that pressure directly gives this music its teleology, its content — and ultimately its shock and awe. It is not necessarily an unpleasant sensation; it can be quite literally entrancing, as the shoppers floating down the aisles of the local supermarket right now could tell you. In minimal music, the message is the (direct perception of the power of the) media. Or, more pithily, after McLuhan:

In minimal music, the media (sublime) is the message.

PART II

THE CULTURE OF THANATOS

Repetition as Mood Regulation

FOUR

"A POX ON MANFREDINI"

*The Long-Playing Record, the Baroque Revival,
and the Birth of Ambient Music*

[Glass's] *Music with Changing Parts* . . . and its immediate
successors — *Music in Twelve Parts* (1971–74) and *Contrary
Motion* and *Two Pages* — might, in their incessant iteration
and underlining of patterns and progressions, strike a hostile
observer as what Bach would sound like to a tone-deaf
listener.

Samuel Lipman, "From Avant-Garde to Pop" (1979)

PRELUDE: *EINSTEIN ON THE FRITZ*

The piece is, one has to admit, quite funny.

Build up a minimalist string pulsation in C major, over which a pianist
begins playing the first bar of the first prelude from Bach's *Well-Tempered
Clavier* — very fast and mechanical. Repeat it eight times. Repeat the next
bar eight times. The next, eight times more. Continue at glacial pace
through the familiar chord progression, cueing in the whirring arpeggios,
the dit-dah-dah syncopated brass chords, and the portentous bass drum
strokes. Add in that wheezy violin étude figure that Jack Benny used to
play — and, for counterpoint, "Three Blind Mice," in case anybody isn't
getting the joke.

The Prelude to *Einstein on the Fritz* is a recipe for joke minimalism, of
course; it is at the same time a piece of ersatz "Baroque music," assigned
number $e = mt^2$ in Peter Schickele's catalog of the works of his alter ego

P. D. Q. Bach.[1] Schickele (egged on, as the liner notes hint, by musicologist Leo Treitler) is clearly having fun at the expense of Philip Glass, his old Juilliard classmate; but critic Andrew Porter quite seriously made the same imaginative leap as he tried to convey to his readers at *The New Yorker* the way Glass's *Satyagraha* was put together: "For a start, imagine the first prelude of Bach's 'Forty-eight' played in strict tempo with each measure repeated and a further repeat sign at every fourth bar; add in some extra sixteenth-notes here and there, to vary the meter but not the pace."[2]

Minimalism as the "New Baroque" music is a pervasive and variegated critical trope. Steve Reich never fails to remind interviewers that Bach was a formative influence, along with Perotin, Stravinsky, and bebop. (He told Analynn Swan that his favorite music at age 14 was Charlie Parker, the *Rite of Spring,* and the *Brandenburg* Concertos.)[3] The 1970s ensemble pieces of both Reich and Glass impressed sympathetic reviewers as akin to upbeat modern-day concerti grossi: "The loud textures [of *Music in Twelve Parts*] are extremely rich and sensual . . . it conveys a mood which is overwhelmingly joyous. Although the music does not resemble anything by Bach, it sometimes lifts me up the way a 'Brandenburg' Concerto does"; "the players [in *Music for Eighteen Musicians*] seem to fuse into one large instrument giving out a clean, impersonal, optimistic music, a bit like a large synthesizer playing the Brandenburg Concertos."[4] On the other hand, more than one newspaper critic, casting around for the explanation of an obscure Baroque contrapuntal exercise's stunning rise to popularity, hit upon the hypnagogic similarity between Pachelbel's Canon and the most popular style of contemporary classical music ca. 1984: "Examining the bass line all by itself might remind you of the music of Philip Glass or Steve Reich — and perhaps its resemblance to these popular modern composers is a key to the Canon's popularity with modern audiences. Glass spends long stretches of time (it can seem like hours) playing three or four notes over and over, with a hypnotic effect. The notes are usually those of a simple chord — a triad, stretched out into an arpeggio — and this is essentially what Pachelbel uses."[5]

An assumption that minimalism and Baroque are both basically musics of tightly patterned cyclic repetition — that, as Jonathan Scheffer claimed, "baroque and minimalist music *sound* alike; they belong together" — led the intellectually restless director of the Eos Ensemble to devise a concert program and accompanying collection of essays under the rubric *Perceptible Processes: Minimalism and the Baroque.*[6] Scheffer's belief in his ear's ability to forge transhistorical links is absolute: "Think of the Bach Suites for solo cello, and their long series of arpeggios through the circle of fifths. They are at once expansive in time and rigid in gesture — harmonic rhythm locked in a regular, marching pulse. Now think of Philip Glass, of ecstatic arpeggios and simple harmonic changes, and you may begin to hear a great unison sounding through the history of music."[7]

The concerts, during which Scheffer essayed the *Einstein on the Fritz* trick of orchestrating preludes from the *WTC* in the style of Glass, sounded this pure historical diapason with some success for New York audiences; but the accompanying book outlines a much more complex and dissonant relationship. In the only one of the essays to address the relation of minimal and Baroque music directly, Ben Yarmolinsky finds himself backtracking constantly. Yes, minimalism and Baroque music both begin as "reform" musics after a period of complexity — but Baroque composers were breaking with contrapuntal complexity in the service of individual emotional expression, not collective hypnotic trance. Isn't the basso continuo style that freed up soloists to explore musical depictions of the passions the exact opposite of minimalism's "democratic group activity"? Yes, the Pachelbel Canon is harmonically repetitive — but as in "Zefiro torna" and all the other Baroque ostinato pieces it resembles, isn't what transpires over the repeated bass pattern anything but minimal? (Circles of fifths may seem "simple" and "predictable" to us now, but they were fresh and unusual in 1700.) Most troubling of all, doesn't Baroque music's *seconda prattica* use music to heighten the expressive content of poetic language? Minimalist music is about sound, not words; it abstracts language into rhythm or grinds it into sonic mush.[8] How can a shared fondness for arpeggios paper over all this difference?

Yarmolinsky is too polite to say it explicitly, but in spite of some striking sonic coincidences on the surface, minimalism and the Baroque have little to do with each other, if by "the Baroque" we mean the wildly diverse music of composers between Monteverdi and Bach, considered in the historically contextualized fullness of its technical and hermeneutic complexity. But there may be another connection. Reich's personal link back to Bach is not based on some transhistorical affinity for motor rhythms and arpeggiated triads; he is interested in the way Bach's music worked in society: "Well, Western music, when it was tied to the church, had a real function. And that's part of Bach's greatness. He's an incredible artist, but really he was an employed craftsman. [laughs] He had a gig, and he had to have it ready by Sunday. We're not interested in your greatness, we're not interested in your inspiration, just have it ready by Sunday! In this rather pedestrian role, he writes what I think is the greatest music ever written in the West."[9]

"Bach the humble craftsman" is, of course, no more historical a reading than "Bach the protominimalist." But it does move us from the domain of technique to the domain of music's societal function. Perhaps the link between minimalist and Baroque music is not how they are produced, but how they are consumed. Reich's positioning of Bach is consistent with his general anti-Romanticism, hewing to the Stravinsky–Nabokov–Hindemith–Ortega y Gasset line in its materialist "defrocking" of artistic pretensions; but it also betrays him as a child of his own historical moment. Reich's "rather pedestrian" image of the Baroque composer as employed craftsman turning out functional music to order has its roots in the neoclassicism of Paris and Weimar;[10] but as an American growing up in the 1940s and 1950s, Reich's image of "functional" Baroque music (and the same goes for Riley, Glass, and others of their generation) would have been formed primarily by the flood of new "long-playing" recordings that sparked an unprecedented popular and commercial interest in Bach, Vivaldi, and their contemporaries.

It is within the context of this LP-mediated "Baroque revival" that I want to consider the relationship of musical minimalism and Baroque music. The link is not to Baroque music per se, but to a certain subset of late Baroque and pre-Classic music — the crisp, impersonal, concertante music that H. C. Robbins-Landon, at the height of its popularity, dismissively dubbed *barococo* — as it was revived and disseminated during the 1950s and 1960s. Seeing a link between minimalism and Baroque music does not mean casting back two centuries for some elusive tonal essence the two styles share; it means recognizing that the infancy of the former was saturated in the actual material sound of a commercially driven technological transformation of the latter. As the multistranded narrative of this and the following chapter will show, it was just as musical minimalism was taking shape that the postwar Baroque revival refracted the "repetitive patterns" of late-Baroque instrumental music through new recording technologies, performance practices, mass media, and mass production. The result was a radically new way of listening.

And performing: the influence of recordings and mass production had their influence on music pedagogy, as Americans hearkened for the first time to a strange hybrid of Occidental industrial technique and Oriental philosophy filtering back from Europe through our new ally in the

Pacific, Japan. Taken together, the Baroque revival (consumption) and the Suzuki Method (production) show recordings of eighteenth-century music functioning as newly abundant raw material for the construction of late-twentieth-century repetitive musical experiences — experiences that eerily prefigure and intertwine with minimalism's own developing culture of musical repetition. In a very real sense, barococo recordings of the 1950s *were* minimal music, at least culturally — and it is those recordings, not the Velvet Underground or disco, that, consumed in great bulk on the record changers of the period, represent the earliest popular embrace of "hypnotic" trance music in American mainstream culture.

The sociological connection between 1980s minimalism and the 1950s barococo revival has not escaped minimalism's detractors; even John Adams, whose music was prominently featured by the Eos Ensemble in the company of Bach, shied guiltily away from being compared to, say, Vivaldi: "Bach . . . is such a universe unto himself that I never think of him as a 'baroque' composer. . . . To be quite honest, I've often felt bored by much of this music, baroque and minimal . . . too often the silly chatter of baroque sequences and the stupefying repetitions of minimalist pieces are all that we are offered."[11]

When minimalism is under discussion, "the Baroque" becomes such degraded historical territory that Bach himself must be airlifted out. Or hadn't we rather say, when minimalism is under *attack*? The patterned repetition of eighteenth-century music is hardly ever trotted out to link minimalism with the canonical composers of the Baroque; it is more usually adduced to link minimalism to the canonical consumers of barococo, the Yuppies and proto-Yuppies who since the 1950s stand accused of using large, uncut swaths of eighteenth-century music as an inexpensive method of interior decoration:

> The current rage for such minimal exercises [as Steve Reich's *Tehillim*] reminds me of the baroque concerto grosso craze of the 1950s, when the most simplistic wallpaper products of the era chugged out of hi-fi sets in college dorms all over the country and soothed a generation of adolescents.[12]

> Bach and Handel excepted, most baroque music is, like Minimalism, music of pattern. Your typical Corelli, Vivaldi, Locatelli, or Geminiani concerto grosso is virtually devoid of personality or imagination. It moves in a purely sequential pattern, its harmonies circumscribed largely to tonic, dominant, and subdominant chords. Everything in this kind of music is predictable. . . .
>
> As such, it is wallpaper music. Perhaps that accounted for its tremendous fad in the early 1950's. This, too, was a fad largely promulgated by the young. Part of the attraction of baroque music was that one did not have to *think* while listening to it. Its excuse for being was that it wrapped the

listener in innocuous sound, the busy patterns moving up and down without ever really saying anything. Diddle diddle diddle, diddle diddle diddle . . . what was there to dislike in this enormous bland field of nothingness?

Thus it is with Minimalism.[13]

Wallpaper Music. An epithet that, passing over the avant-garde composers who clamored for it (Satie, Cage, Eno), has come to characterize one repertory of music above all: the Italianate Baroque concerto, especially when consumed in doses larger than, say, three in a row. On the day I write these words, *San Francisco Chronicle* music critic Joshua Kosman has chided a San Francisco early music ensemble for programming six concerti grossi at a single concert, giving the proceedings a "wallpapery, FM-radio flavor."[14] Sensitized to the negative cultural implications that have piled up around the act of listening to multiple Baroque concerti, Kosman finds that the experience strips the aura from what was, after all, a live performance with considerable period-instrument flair.

But is FM really to blame? Classical music radio is now a conveniently endless source of Baroque instrumental music, to be sure, but that is a recent (and much lamented) phenomenon. Classical radio weaves its seamless Baroque tapestries out of discrete recordings played in sequence, and this method of consuming Baroque music was *not* pioneered by the captains of cultural industry, or by the program directors at major classical radio networks. During the 1950s and 1960s, this kind of listening was the underground practice of classical music consumers newly empowered by technological innovations within the recording industry. One hesitates to valorize this mode of listening as "resistant," but it was (as we shall see) certainly unauthorized by the major record manufacturers, record reviewers, and high-fidelity experts. Many, then as now, railed against the hanging of musical wallpaper even as they benefited financially from it.

But the new culture of repetitive listening was not so easily eradicated and, in fact, has come to dominate the way classical music is disseminated and consumed. The repetitive music of Young, Riley, Reich, and Glass was incubated in this wallpaper-lined environment — and shows it. Whether celebration, capitulation, or critique, minimal music is classical music that incorporates repetitive listening into its very fabric. As so often in this study, we must admit that hostile critics who compare minimalism to Baroque wallpaper music are on to something, a kind of long-and-yet-fuzzy-attention-span listening environment that the two experiences take for granted. A cultural history of minimalism must move beyond the sneer and engage directly with this "degrading" practice. Where did it come from? And what were the illicit pleasures it offered to classical music consumers?

The Joys of Wallpaper Music (LPs, Record Changers, and the New Culture of Repetitive Listening)

Though it is impossible to know how listeners of the time heard the less distinguished music of the eighteenth century, it now seems to many music lovers attractive precisely because of its availability in large quantities, its moment-to-moment predictability, its relative lack of contrast and of specific memorability.

Samuel Lipman, "From Avant-Garde to Pop" (1979)

HERE'S HOW RECORDS GIVE YOU MORE OF WHAT YOU WANT: THEY'LL GIVE YOU HOURS OF CONTINUOUS AND UNINTERRUPTED LISTENING PLEASURE.

Just stack them up on your automatic changer and relax . . .

Columbia record sleeve, late 1960s

References to the concerto grosso "craze" or "fad" not only betray a desire to rewrite subsequent history (barococo music, like rock and roll, is here to stay); they also mystify the clear technological impetus behind the rise of repetitive listening.[15] Comforting though it may be to classify the barococo revival under "Popular Delusions and the Madness of Crowds," there is nothing irrational or inexplicable about the growing market for Baroque concertos in the 1950s and 1960s. Baroque music was an inadvertent beneficiary of what I would argue was a logical and understandable consumer appropriation of the new listening experience inherent in the concept of the "long-playing" record.

This experience really *was* new — the possibility of "hours of continuous and uninterrupted listening pleasure" simply did not exist for the average consumer before 1950. Of course, you could turn on the radio (and contemporary sociological data suggest Americans had gotten into that habit as early as the 1930s), but no radio station was then broadcasting a continuous stream of "canned music." It was not until slightly *after* the barococo revival, and during the rise of television, that radio stations shifted from a format based on news, entertainment, drama, comedy — and, of course, music, usually "live" concert broadcasts — to the much cheaper expedient of simply playing records one after another.[16] ("Classic-FM" programming, with its long stretches of completely un-modulated barococo, did not begin to emerge until the late 1980s, when deregulation threw the radio industry into a frantic scramble of leveraged buyouts, consolidations, and staff cuts.) The phonograph, of course, was of little help: the standard 12-inch 78 rpm disc held a maximum of just under four and a half minutes of music. Bulky machinery for playing records in sequence had been in use since the 1920s, but trusting the heavy, fragile shellac records to the clumsy manipulations of these devices was hardly an invitation to relax and enjoy.

The LP was supposed to eliminate all that. It was the continual inter-ruption of symphonies as the records flipped on his father's old phono-graph that inspired inventor Peter Goldmark to push for a "long-playing" record at CBS. On June 20, 1948, company president Edward Wallerstein stood between an eight-foot stack of 78's and a 15-inch pile of the new LPs and announced its arrival. He probably gave little thought to the pos-sibility that stacks of LPs would actually materialize on consumer turnta-bles, although one early demonstration already shows the temptation to use the new long-playing capability as, well, sonic wallpaper: "At our annual sales convention a little later in Atlantic City, Paul Southard, our sales manager, had a rather clever idea: He designed his speech so that it ran exactly the length of *The Nutcracker Suite*, which was on one side of an LP. When Paul began to speak the stylus was placed on the record, which continued playing very softly in the background. When the speech ended and Paul removed the stylus, the distributors went wild."[17]

Marketing stunts aside, the LP was designed for serious classical music, its 22 minutes per side carefully chosen to allow uninterrupted playback of single movements within the standard concert repertoire.[18] The assumption was that classical record listeners were so intent on the progress of their favorite sonata movement that the elimination of clunky interruptions would allow an even deeper engagement with symphonic logic. That LPs would be used to create an endless aural tapestry out of dozens of homogenous movements, over which the listener's loosely focused attention could waver and dart, was no part of the strenuously high-minded efforts at Columbia Masterworks.

The new repetitive listening was an unintended consequence of the fact that RCA-Victor, Columbia's major competitor, was not prepared to take the LP lying down. CBS offered to license the technology to any and all comers, but by 1949 RCA had decided to develop its own 45 rpm microgroove format. The small vinyl discs were light, convenient, and their fidelity was equal to Columbia's LP — but the playing time of a seven-inch 45 rpm record was no longer than one of the old 78's. To compensate, RCA developed and marketed with fierce intensity what it accurately touted as "the world's fastest record changer" — a standalone device that, when hooked into an existing television or radio, would allow its owner to stack 10 45 rpm records on its thick central spindle and thus match the 50-minute playing time of the LP.

The years 1949–50 saw a destructive "battle of the speeds" — CBS's long-playing records versus RCA's super-fast record changer — during which both companies saw their sales sag. Standard histories of the recording industry have read the eventual outcome as a truce and partition: both majors began to manufacture both speeds, with the LP and the 45 taking up their familiar positions as album and single format, respectively. But a history of repetitive listening should focus on an unplanned but not unforeseeable *fusion* of the two heavily marketed innovations. With both companies releasing music in both formats, consumers needed record players that combined the speed and efficiency of RCA's changer with the ability to play the larger and heavier LPs. RCA's name for its standalone player stuck and was generically applied to any device that played records. In the 1950s, the appliance that had been called variously "gramophone," "Victrola," and "radio-phonograph," and that would eventually be known either as the "hi-fi" or simply the "stereo," was popularly referred to as a "record changer," as in "Put some records on the changer, would you, dear?"

> When word got out, people from all over the neighborhood clamored to see the wonderful gadget. Such a major advance in technology! Imagine how much easier life will be! Douglas Rigsby remembers how everyone crowded into his family's home in Brooklyn to marvel at this thing called a "record changer." "People used to come from all around the neighborhood just to see the records drop," he recalled. "They'd say, 'Oh my God, look at that!'"[19]

By the 1960s the record changer was no longer a novelty; a glance at the pages of any audio magazine from the period shows that to buy a record player *without* a changer was next to impossible. American consumers had rejected RCA's 45's as a format for classical music; but they had taken the record changer, and its power to make life easier, to heart.

It was actually repetitive listening that record changers made easier — so much easier that an entire genre of music, Easy Listening, was created to fill a need that had never existed before 1950. Audiophiles like Roland Gelatt, editor of *High Fidelity,* winced at the rise of Mantovani, the Ray Conniff Singers, Hugo Winterhalter, and their compatriots, blaming the new format for a "conspicuous decline in attention": "The four-minute [78 rpm] side did, however, prevent dozing. It was the LP that spawned the recorded sleeping pill — 'Reveries for Languid Lovers,' 'Melodies for a Lazy Afternoon,' and the like."[20] The Easy Listening phenomenon per se is out of the scope of our investigations (interested readers are referred to Joseph Lanza's factoid-filled *Elevator Music* for more information);[21] but let this jacket copy, from one of the classics of the genre, the Melachrino Strings' 1958 *Music for Relaxation,* stand as testimony to a new way of marketing and consuming recorded sound:

> In some far-off countries, people relax by standing stiff as ramrods, or by easing themselves onto a bed of nails, or by hanging from trees by their bent knees. Listening to Melachrino's superb essays on familiar themes certainly seems much more civilized . . .
>
> *And, if your phonograph can play it over and over again,* you will be as loose as ashes by dinnertime . . .
>
> This recording is an excellent one for children. Its purpose with young-sters is two-fold: by listening, they are exposed to excellent music, stirringly played; and they are soothed into a lulling sense of security and rest . . .
>
> But the best part of it all is, *it's a record you'll want to play over and over* for the music as well as the therapy.[22]

Note the permission to listen "over and over" to the same recording, only possible thanks to the new durability of vinyl records tracked by diamond styli on lightweight tonearms.[23] By linking repetitive listening to the education and happiness of children, RCA provides a strange cross-cultural echo of the Suzuki Method, about to burst on the American scene (see the next chapter) — but the native cultural soil within which American minimal music sprang to life and popularity was already rich with these exhortations to listen "over and over."

The first track on *Music for Relaxation* is an arrangement for string orchestra of a famous classical chestnut: the "Berceuse" from Benjamin Godard's 1888 opera *Jocelyn.* For those familiar with the flashy spatial-ized "exotica" of the early stereo era (Esquivel, Enoch Light), the first minute of *Music for Relaxation* is disorientingly flat and chaste: violins and violas intertwine in an austere, expressionless, quasi-contrapuntal passage that sounds quite . . . old-fashioned (Example 16). One might

Example 16 "Music for relaxation." Benjamin Godard, "Berceuse" from *Jocelyn* (1888).

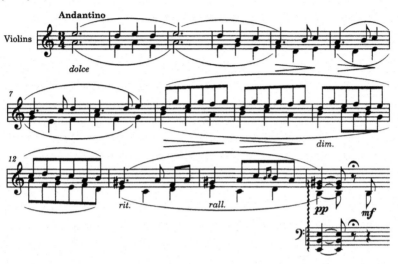

almost be listening to the orchestration of a barococo two-part invention. Melachrino's strings eventually warm up into the Romanticism of Godard's aria, and the album proceeds into lusher orchestrations of movie themes and Broadway tunes. But the sound remains "pure": neither backbeat, vocals, echoing reverbs, nor "high-fidelity" explorations of the recording spectrum are allowed to interfere with the continual plangent river of string sound.

Listen in turn to any of the early barococo LP recordings, with their close-miked performances by biggish string orchestras of conservatory students and aging opera-pit veterans — I Musici, the Virtuosi di Roma, the Chamber Orchestra of the Saar, the New York Sinfonietta, the Orchestra of the Vienna State Opera, the Academy of the Conservatory of Bologna. You will hear the same dark, heavy, dull sound — and the same plodding beat — that issues from the easy-listening strings of Melachrino and Mantovani. Of course the repertoire was totally different . . . or was it? There are moments when the liner notes of barococo recordings seem to offer the listener a relaxing and strangely *easy* listening experience: "Hoffman is a good craftsman who expresses himself in the common musical language of his period in a pleasant manner. . . . Well constructed and devoid of contrapuntal and harmonic complexities, [his Mandolin Quartet] is written in a light vein and is free of disturbing platitudes. . . . It is a piece of fresh and pleasant music, with a dose of

Viennese *Gemütlichkeit* to which many, after a day's hard work, are easily receptive."[24]

Classical music for relaxation? Dr. Joseph Braunstein of Syracuse University, the annotator of Turnabout TV 34016S, certainly never suggests that purchasers listen to its four relatively similar works for mandolin and strings "over and over." Barococo record labels like Nonesuch, Vox, and Westminster studiously avoided the very mention of automatic record changers. Most of the evidence for repetitive listening to Baroque music is negative, as we shall see when we survey the increasingly horrified reaction of performers, critics, and musicologists to the torrent of barococo washing over the classical recording market.

And yet . . . the discs themselves provide the most compelling positive evidence that consumers actually consumed whole the newly popular sets that spread massive volumes of concertos over multiple LPs: all *Four Seasons*, all six *Brandenburgs;* the round dozens that make up Vivaldi's *L'estro harmonico* and *La cetra;* even, visionarily, every one of Vivaldi's 500+ (with scores!) in Max Goberman's never-finished subscription "Library of Recorded Masterpieces." It is right there to see for anybody who actually looks at the records: many of these sets from the 1950s and 1960s, especially as distributed by cheaper American labels, put out their sides in "automatic sequence." To take the most scandalous example first: RCA-Victor VICS-6023, the 1965 American release of the Collegium Aureum's *Brandenburg* Concertos — the first-ever recording played on "authentic period instruments" — comes on two discs with the sides ordered 1–4, 2–3, and *not* 1–2, 3–4! Whatever the intentions of Gustav Leonhardt and Harmonia Mundi, RCA clearly assumed that its customers would want to put Bach on the record changer and sit back for two 50-minute stretches of "continuous and uninterrupted listening pleasure." The instrumental music of Bach, interpreted by internationally famous artists, was in fact a staple of the barococo record changer: other automatically sequenced sets include Yehudi Menuhin's 1960 *Brandenburg* set (Capitol SGBR 7217), Pablo Casals's Marlboro Festival performances of the *Brandenburgs* and the orchestral suites (Columbia D3-S816), and the complete harpsichord concertos performed by Igor Kipnis and Neville Marriner (Columbia M4-30540).

Even when multiple sets of barococo concertos appear in manual sequence, we can find hints that they usually ended up stacked on the turntable. Vanguard BG540–42, Felix Prohaska's three-record set of the *Brandenburg* Concertos, is manually sequenced. But in the recording engineer's technical note, after the obligatory celebration of the professional quality microphones used to capture the performance, and an admonition to owners of "high-fidelity" sets to follow the RIAA equalization curve, a suspicious anxiety betrays itself: "To realize the extraordinary dynamic range of this recording it is advised to play it at full room volume." Presumably many listeners were in the habit of piling sets like this on the changer, turning the sound way down, and taking in the concerto movements just as they came. (Ambient pioneer Brian Eno would undoubtedly have approved; see below.)

One kind of set invariably published in automatic sequence was the "introduction to Baroque music" samplers made ubiquitous by groups like the Musical Heritage Society (see the *History of Baroque Music*, Orpheus OR331–33). There was some slight justification for assuming that purchasers, having stacked two or three of these discs on the changer, would follow the "lesson" attentively, program notes in hand. But record companies were most indulgent when dealing with these beginners; witness this remarkably lenient passage from Jacques Barzun, in an essay, "The Art, and Pleasure, of Listening," that accompanied *The Story of Great Music: The Baroque Era*:

> The great secret is immersion in the medium. . . . If you come wholly un-prepared, what you may experience on a first hearing of classical music is confusion, or something so close to it that the experience is only the more irritating. But don't get irritated: play the piece over again — or part of it. One of the great advantages of the phonograph is that it permits immediate repetition. Play the piece two or three times running; then play it again twice the next day, and continue (it can't hurt you) until soon some parts of it begin to stick in your memory. Naturally, sense and pleasure will come faster if you concentrate. And of course you can't concentrate wholly on music if conversation is going on or if the rhythm of the dishwasher interferes with that of Beethoven, but it's for you to set your own pace.[25]

We will encounter other critics, not in the direct pay of the record industry, much less tolerant of half-listening to Baroque music while washing the dishes — but what is extraordinary is Barzun's explicit exhortation to repetitive listening as self-indoctrination, reminiscent of Cage ("In Zen they say: If something is boring after two minutes, try it for four. If still boring, try it for eight, sixteen, thirty-two, and so on")[26] and the Suzuki Method. One senses a rare, tolerant hope that repeated listening might be a path to greater (or at least different) awareness of music, not simply indulgence in homegrown Muzak. But again we face the law of unintended consequences: subsequent history shows us that long stretches of repetitive, loosely focused listening to barococo did not develop an awareness of musical structure and thus impel consumers toward what Barzun hoped would be a more "active" listening; rather, the repetitive patterns of Baroque concertos helped develop a taste for repetitive patterns per se, and thus for ever more expansive bouts of loosely focused, repetitive listening. Barococo was not training listeners for Beethoven; it was training them for minimalism.

We are thus faced with a new kind of antistructural hearing, dialectically opposite to the "atomized" listening anathematized in Adorno's attacks on the culture industry, attacks that reveal his anxieties and prejudices to be those of the pre-LP era. Adorno feared the 78 rpm attention span of the man who "listens to Beethoven's Fifth as if it were a potpourri of themes from Beethoven's Fifth" — and, indeed, early recordings of symphonic literature often presented this chimera as a nightmarish material reality, slicing and dicing works like the third *Leonora* Overture or the "Unfinished" Symphony so that their famous themes, if not their symphonic logic, could be traversed within the limits of one or two four-minute sides. (Until the mid-1920s, the accolade *Partiturgetreu* (true to the score) on a Polydor recording did not imply musicological delving for an authentic performance practice; it simply meant that the work had been played without debilitating cuts.)[27] But the LP and the record changer encouraged home listeners to "err" in the other direction, to run separate works together into a kind of faux-unity where dozens of similarly textured movements fused into a single *Überwerk*: "I rather suspect that to listeners for whom the physical coherence of an 'album' is a more vivid reality than the concept of a 'piece of music,' a recorded sequence of unrelated short pieces may well take on a kind of inevitability that is almost always musically irrelevant. (At the same time that the LP record restored the desirable continuity of pieces that the 78 had sundered, it imposed spurious continuities on shorter ones.)"[28]

In fact — to pick up the thread of an earlier argument — the relation of a stack of barococo recordings to an actual classical concert featuring the same works is precisely the relation that an evening of television has to the live, theatrical, journalistic, and cinematic works it incorporates: a series of discrete, dramatically structured forms is pulverized and then recombined into a uninterrupted, evenly pulsating flow. The record changer is an instrument of flow, and in this it is the opposite of the channel changer, an integrator rather than a disintegrator. The rise of soi-disant "postmodernism" — the aesthetics of zapping, 500 channels, and Plunderphonics — has pushed some critics to reevaluate Adorno's rejection of atomized, "substructural" hearing: today's listeners can negotiate the most radical disjunctions imaginable, following multiple strands of coherence through instantaneous shifts of tone, language, and even medium. So what if we can't listen to a single symphony all the way through? In light of minimalism's rise to cultural power, perhaps sympathetic critics can also reclaim the diffuse, repetitive, "superstructural" listening strategies of the barococo revival. Barzun's passive listeners seem to have found a kind of diffused attention that gave pleasure even in the face of long stretches of stripped-down, austere, "boring" music. Maybe they *liked* the way the pulsations of the dishwasher motor went in and out of phase with the steady beat of the basso continuo. That is how La Monte Young and Steve Reich listened; it may be that wallpaper music has had something to teach us after all.

Stripped-Down Bach (Barococo as Minimalism)

Barococo recordings did more than incubate a new kind of listening; in their densely packed liner notes, apologists for the style disseminated a new reductive image of "the Baroque" — an image that rings significant changes on the "modernistic" Bach reception of the 1920s so ably dissected by Richard Taruskin, even as it strangely anticipates elements of the 1960s minimalist aesthetic.[29] Consider, for instance, this utterly characteristic program note: "The beginning of this work gives the impression that the music has been underway for some time — as though you opened the door to an auditorium where a performance is already in progress. There are no prefatory remarks or fanfares: the music simply begins, and from then on continues its lilting, inexorable beat without pause. It is a brilliant piece of rhythmic manipulation. The rhythm constantly shifts from strong beats to weak ones and back again. It is rhythm that defies listeners not to tap their feet."

Aside from a few false notes ("lilting," "fanfares") the preceding might be a description of Steve Reich's *Drumming* or Terry Riley's *In C:* a steady pulse, a constant rhythmic process, pervasive syncopation, the absence of classical teleology. Of course, it isn't — the piece in question is actually a concerto for three oboes and three violins by Georg Philipp Telemann, as presented in the program booklet that accompanies *The Story of Great Music: The Baroque Era.* Like many other barococo recordings, this Time-Life set seems predisposed toward concertos for multiple instruments; the Telemann concerto *à six* is followed closely by the Bach-Vivaldi concerto for four harpsichords. Is it unreasonable to see the 1960s barococo predilection for Vivaldi's multiple violin concertos —

and, later, for the three identical violin lines of the Pachelbel Canon —
aiming at the same undifferentiated field of sound favored by contemporaneous minimalists? Witness Steve Reich: "[Before 1971 and *Drumming*, I avoided] mixed timbres. All these pieces were for four organs,
four violins, two pianos, sets of tuned drums and so on. If you want to
have that field of interlocking patterns, and you're playing piano and I'm
playing marimba, they won't coalesce."[30] Time-Life's commentary on
the Bach-Vivaldi traffics in just these interlocking patterns, inflected by
older clockwork metaphors ("The first harpsichord runs up and down
the keyboard while the other three hammer home their own patterns. . . .
[T]here is something superbly machine-like in this music, and the overall
effect sounds somewhat like four harmonious watchmakers, keeping perfect time"); while Edward Tatnall Canby encouraged consumers of the
Nonesuch recording (H71079) to listen to it as pure (protominimalist)
texture music: "through recording mikes at close range, the purring vel-
vety touch of many fingers, the plucking of dozens of quills upon hundreds of silvery wires produces a curiously even sheen of sound, a tapes-
tried effect that is immeasurably rich yet utterly luminescent."

In a very influential take, Canby saw Vivaldi as a "a kind of skeletal
Bach, stripped down." His music was not really Baroque, if by "Baroque"
one meant the ostentatious, even overwrought splendor of North German
religious music rather than the "original Italian *concerto grosso,* [which]
was a lean, spare form, pared to the essential," achieving "splendor
through artistic economy." Such reductive genius made Vivaldi's concertos uniquely suited for transcription and elaboration: "Bach understood
that to support the extraordinary contrapuntal complications he could
devise for four skillful keyboard artists playing at once, a structure of the
Vivaldi sort — lean, rock-like in harmony and rhythm, stark and almost
bare — was absolutely essential." This minimalist Vivaldi appeared most
clearly if the record listener followed Canby's quasi-Schenkerian advice on
the jacket, bypassing the exciting solo parts of concertos in favor of the
tonal scaffolding underneath: "Paradoxically, it is in the *tutti* music, the
supporting background, that one must look for the basic musical 'meat' in
these works, even though the entire forward interest centers in the solo
part. For it is in the background that the structure of the concerto finds its
strength." Listen as Canby demands, and Vivaldi becomes the Mies van
der Rohe of music — or its Richard Serra:

> In a sheer virtuoso concerto, this sturdy support must be both minimal and
> at the same time immensely strong. Perhaps the toughest problem for unac-
> customed ears is to sense that strength in the peculiarly bare, sparse frame-

work that Vivaldi devised for the purpose, written largely in open octave-unisons, unharmonized, built on the simplest tonic and dominant harmonic base plus those repetitive sequences of moving chords which lead us, like fate, from one level to the next. We look for some deep "meaning" in this spare background and find instead only structure. The fault is ours; we should be attending to the soloist. If the harmonies seem conventionalized and rigid, they are precisely that, as is the steel frame of a modern building. No other composer of the day — as Bach knew — could provide such an admirably sound and durable musical skeleton.[31]

We look for some deep "meaning" and find only the simplest, minimal structure: one can almost see Frank Stella ("In the black paintings I was interested in creating a kind of painting that couldn't be read") and Steve Reich ("I am not interested in hidden structures . . . all the cards are on the table") nodding their heads. Obviously Canby's reading is bad music history and even incoherent on its own terms (should we listen to the soloist or not?); but it is echoed from every side. Nathan Broder in *High Fidelity* saw Vivaldi as the perfect "Music for the Age of Calorie Counters," because "the best of his music fits so well the requirements of the plain listener seeking respite from the clichés and excesses of the romantic style."[32] Annotating one of the first complete recordings of *L'estro harmonico* (Vanguard SRV 143) Abraham Veinus agreed: "the clean, muscular energy so characteristic of these concertos seems singularly appealing to the modern musical temperament; the confidence and unencumbered directness of this music a welcome tonic to the 20th-century ear."[33]

Examples could be multiplied almost without limit: the old modernist-structuralist reception of Baroque music, all terraces and tensile strength, had to change when the focus shifted from Bach to Vivaldi. Suddenly "Baroque" signified the exact opposite of what it had traditionally meant, now a synonym for "simple and predictable" rather than "surprising and (perhaps overly) complex." Annotators began to toss off generalizations like "the busy-ness of the *Allegro* consistently involves characteristically baroque textures and formulae," and to allow themselves damaging phrases like "*merely* Baroque."[34] Adorno once thundered at the early music movement, "They say Bach, mean Telemann"; when critics actually said Telemann and meant it, justifications of eighteenth-century music worked overtime to turn barococo's putative simplicity and predictability into cardinal musical virtues. Geometric Bach and motoric Handel may have gone with the cubist dynamism of Stravinsky and Picasso, but Vivaldi and Telemann, at least as they appear on 1960s record jackets, seem to harmonize better with the directionless asceticism of pinstripe paintings and Philip Glass. How else are we to interpret R. D. Darrell's back-handed praise? "Personally, I'm reminded immediately of my private, not entirely joking, criteria for the pure baroque style: 'Music that keeps going; knows exactly where it's going; and when it gets there, promptly stops.' And perhaps its very lack of surprising features makes this particular work even more representative of the fascinating mystery of the baroque-era concerto-in-general."[35]

The mystery of the "merely" Baroque sometimes defeated even the most determinedly upbeat sales pitch; Canby finds himself spluttering, "Here, we can suppose, is a fine example of the famed 'superficial' Telemann, laid out in all clarity for our hearing! We can only suppose that it had a purpose." Darrell, on the other hand, backed up by the full power of the culture industry and the full force of new media technologies, used the "concerto-in-general" as a weapon to twit music scholars and other guardians of musical greatness: "The astonishing current renaissance of interest in baroque-era music — an interest apparently spontaneously generated by recordings and broadcasts — already has had ironical, perhaps revolutionary consequences: It has exposed the fatal weakness of musical aesthetics — while scholars can convincingly 'prove' that the mighty Bach Mass in B minor, say, is indeed a masterpiece, they somehow always fail miserably to account for the literally irresistible charm of such 'little,' supposedly routine *divertissements* as the concertos of Vivaldi, Telemann, et al."[36]

Defenders of the "difficult" masterwork canon were initially slow to respond. But by the 1960s a barococo backlash was taking shape, rehearsing many of the same arguments that would be deployed against the rise of minimalism two decades later.

Baroque at Flood Tide
(Barococo Backlash and *l'Affaire Manfredini*)

Anxiety had been building all through the 1950s. At first, classical tastemakers like Jacques Barzun hailed the LP as an unalloyed miracle, freeing the dissemination of music from the dictates of "fashion," the caprices of taste that would "bury the whole musical past except a few dozen works arbitrarily selected." Barzun saw the LP *preserving* the canon, not undermining it; his analogy was to "the Renaissance rediscovering the ancient classics and holding them fast by means of the printing press."[37] In the first issue of *High Fidelity*, C. G. Burke made a more straightforward technological argument under the celebratory title

"Repertory Unlimited": in his view the LP and magnetic tape had freed music from the stranglehold of the professional symphony orchestra, with its need to guarantee full employment to 100-plus instrumentalists by recycling late-Romantic warhorses. The main beneficiaries would be inhabitants of the "hidden realms" of eighteenth-century music: Bach, Handel, Gluck, Haydn, and Mozart.[38]

But by 1958, the tenth anniversary of the LP, *High Fidelity* had become a little more circumspect. Editor Roland Gelatt, in an article entitled "The Pangs of Progress," began to note a downside to the new abundance. A "glut of merchandise" had stripped any lingering aura from the record as commodity, and "omnivorous listening" was becoming more passive. (It was this article that inveighed against the LP as a "recorded sleeping pill.") Performance standards were slipping, too: "the LP record has assailed our ears with a disproportionate number of indifferent performances. The kind of aimless interpretation that comes off the top of a musician's head is more prevalent on records than it was twenty years ago."[39] (We'll take this complaint up in more detail at the beginning of the next chapter.) Gelatt does not yet link the general slackening to the widening of the canon, or the new focus on eighteenth-century music as predicted by Burke. Ironically enough, the alarm was raised three years later by a critic who is perhaps the most energetic scholarly advocate eighteenth-century music has ever had.

H. C. Robbins Landon's take-no-prisoners attack on the barococo revival was entitled "A Pox on Manfredini," and it burst like a bombshell on readers of *High Fidelity* in June 1961. It is, to be frank, an intemperate screed, and it raised such a ruckus that the *Letters* column of the magazine was still buzzing two years later, when musicologist Paul Henry Lang weighed in with "A Second Look at Manfredini," which in turn set off another round of letters, recriminations, and cancellations of subscriptions. Clearly what Lang called *l'affaire Manfredini* struck a deep nerve with record buyers. (By way of contrast, the reader response to Milton Babbitt's equally incendiary 1958 "Who Cares if You Listen?" was precisely — nothing. Not one letter. Call the readers of *High Fidelity* stupid, exile them from contemporary music concerts, fine — but don't *ever* disrespect their attachment to Vivaldi!)[40] I am going to analyze Robbins Landon's diatribe at length, because it was both an unusually influential take on repetitive listening and an unusually indiscreet one. The cultural anxieties on display fairly beg for diagnosis, and they provide valuable historical perspective on the equally intemperate reactions to minimalism — the new barococo — in its own heyday.

Robbins Landon's opening rhetorical gambit puts his argument against barococo and repetitive listening squarely in the realm of the sociological; he goes to great lengths to skewer, with witty and aristocratic condescension, the musical pretensions of a certain sector of the professional upper-middle class:

> I should have seen it coming when, in 1952, I returned from Vienna to New York and was invited, one hot summer evening, to the chic apartment of a couple in the (you guessed it) advertising business. The rooms were just right — two or three well-chosen abstracts on the wall, the furniture and drapes worked out in rhythmic color designs (red-gray-red-black-gray — a few years back they would have called it "our Mozart Rondo room"), Kafka and Auden on the table, filter cigarettes in the Japanese boxes. And as the martinis were served, I noticed that you didn't use gin to make martinis anymore, you used vodka; and you didn't play Mozart quartets on the phonograph, you stacked a pile of LPs on the changer — Albinoni, Geminiani, Corelli, Locatelli, and, of course, the father-figure of barococo music: Antonio Vivaldi.[41]

Robbins Landon works this rich vein of Madison Avenue satire throughout the article, envisioning a four-color magazine ad featuring the perfect Westchester couple (he with imported vodka in hand, she in "tapered slacks with the right foot toed outward") exchanging overpriced barococo recordings for Christmas ("Darling! It's Manfredini!"). He sees barococo music as the anodyne of "Highbrows" who are not, after all, so highbrow: the well-educated yet shallow, rootless, and cosmopolitan type of professionals who populate the advertising, media, public relations, and culture industries. Robbins Landon's barococo status-seekers, with their thin veneer of fashionable culture, are recognizable as early Yuppies (who, we later learn from *Stereo Review*, enjoy Pachelbel, but only on original instruments);[42] they are also the forerunners of what neoconservative intellectuals of the 1980s would dub the "New Class," the clever yet empty "liberal elite" with self-serving hands on the levers of cultural and political power. Samuel Lipman, who saw minimalism as the 1980s equivalent of barococo music, also saw it as the characteristic music of the New Class:

> The social characteristics of the audience for *Einstein* are, I think, quite clear. Affluent, relatively educated, moderately successful in the professions, old enough to know about the 1960s, too young to know that the events of the 1960s had a historical context beyond personal concerns. . . . If this analysis of the audience is correct, one can understand why the *New York Times*, Gotham's mission to (and trading post for) the Yuppies, is in the forefront of the publicity wave for the "Next Wave" festival. . . .

Whether one calls *Einstein on the Beach* performance art or multimedia, there can be little doubt that it symbolizes the nearest we have yet come in this country to an art form crafted to the tastes of what has been called the new class, that group which, we are told, alone possesses the skills to run our society. The new class certainly will have its progeny; will its art?[43]

Shallow pretentious music for shallow pretentious people. Lipman actually imagined *Einstein* taking the place of barococo, nothing more than good cocktail party music: "As music heard apart from the stage spectacle (and at low volume on one's home phonograph) Glass's score seems not only harmless but even appealing." The sociological argument was as tendentious in 1984 as in 1961, but putting Robbins Landon and Lipman side by side helps us see how attacks on minimalism, like attacks on the Baroque revival, are at root class-based defenses of the master-works canon — in particular, the power of a narrowly defined canon to adjudicate nasty spats *within* the professional upper-middle class between original proprietors and technologically enabled *arrivistes* of culture.

But Robbins Landon is just warming up. He introduces an anony-mous authorial surrogate — one of the "left-wing crowd in Britain (of the *New Statesman* type)" — and gives him center stage for a Savonarola-style rant of well-nigh incredible offensiveness:

> "Listen, Robbie," he began firmly, "let's get our bloody values straight. We've just had the whole of Vivaldi's Op. 3 on the BBC Third Programme. Mind you: I was much struck with its originality, and how much difference there is between the various works. They are brilliantly written. But, look here: it's completely *un*intellectual, small-boned music. It's not *thinking* music like Mozart. . . . And that's the whole secret of this great fuss nowadays about Vivaldi. It's easy music. It's precisely the right music for half-intellectuals and snobs; moreover, you'll notice it's the homosexuals' delight — bright, brittle, fast-moving, surface glitter."
>
> He got up and walked to the piano and, standing over the keyboard, began to play *Art of Fugue*.
>
> "I'm sorry," he said dreamily, as he worked into the fourth voice and the room began to be filled with the somber D-minor peace that only Bach knows how to write; "all this Vivaldi business — the five hundred concertos on 292 LPs — is just nonsense. Degenerate. it's another symptom of our civilization's sickness; five minutes before twelve; how Spengler would have laughed."[44]

Listen to Vivaldi and have your class, intelligence, *and* sexual orientation impugned: is it any wonder several readers of *High Fidelity* were outraged enough to cancel their subscriptions publicly in Letters to the Editor?

Record magazines rarely provide such a florid spectacle of cultural hysteria. (The musicological one-upsmanship is priceless: evidently this radical British politician can "dreamily" realize Bach's *Art of Fugue* from open score while diagnosing Goberman's Vivaldi project as the Decline of Western Civilization. Why not go all the way and have him finish the six-part *Ricercare* extemporaneously with one hand tied behind his back?) And though the attacker is presented as a voice from the cultural left, the anxiety he expresses is traditionally bourgeois. The key phrase here is "surface glitter": linking materialism, cultural degeneration, sexual perversion, mechanically mediated mass culture, and the erasure of musical depth, Robbins Landon drops us squarely into a traditional defense of nineteenth-century bourgeois subjectivity in music: "The masses, however, lack the soul of genius. They are not aware of background, they have no feeling for the future. Their lives are merely an eternally disordered foreground, a continuous present without connection, unwinding chaotically in empty, animal fashion. It is always the individual who creates and transmits connection and coherence."[45]

I have argued elsewhere that virulent quotes like the above, from Heinrich Schenker's 1935 compositional treatise *Der freie Satz,* index the degree to which the depth and interiority ascribed to musical masterworks — depth that mirrored the depth and interiority of the bourgeois ego — were perceived as under assault by industrialized, egalitarian "mass" culture.[46] It is unlikely that Schenker would have had much sympathy with the "left-wing crowd in Britain"; but he might well have nodded approvingly at Spenglerian attacks on massified and commodified musical culture to the accompaniment of Bach fugues. Schenker's anxieties during the Weimar Republic resonate strangely with those experienced by Robbins Landon on Madison Avenue and broadcast in the pages of *High Fidelity* during the 1950s and 1960s: in both cases the critic resorts to a rhetoric of perversion and apocalyptic proclamations of cultural degeneration as a defense of the "deep" masterwork canon, which is in turn a defense of the depths of the bourgeois ego, in mortal danger of being overwhelmed by the "surface glitter" of the mass and its mass-produced musical pleasures.

This is precisely the matrix within which many anxieties about minimalism have been voiced; witness Andrew Porter, by no means a detractor of the style, worrying in 1978 about the effect of Reich's *Music for Eighteen Musicians:* "Was it indecently promiscuous to surrender so soon and so readily to simple harmonies and a steady beat, even if they were enlivened by rhythmic intricacies and pretty timbres? [The] music has a joyful, very attractive surface; it may be that some of his admirers do not get beyond it." *The New Republic* was more forthright in 1983: "To a certain extent, Glass's music is anti-intellectual. It is emotion-first, feel-good music that depends, at least for part of its effect, on high amplification and a glittery, glassy surface."[47]

Many musical critics, faced with what Roland Gelatt characteristically referred to in 1954 as "the prevailing currents of the LP flood,"[48] sought rhetorical higher (and dryer) ground: psychoanalytically suggestive imagery of engulfment, even in discussions that were meant to celebrate the new abundance of recordings, recurs over and over. Burke, whose "Repertory Unlimited" gloried in a new "wealth of Eighteenth-Century Music," was one of the first to use it: "This LP torrent, whose velocity and volume rise as the months pass, is establishing a musical reservoir immediately at hand, and vast beyond the [most] optimistic expectations."[49] By 1958 Gelatt was showing signs of anxiety: whereas once two opera recordings would make an entire season, they are now "pebbles in an avalanche," swept up in "the current deluge of records"; the reviewer is liable to be "swamped with new releases."[50] Lang, replying to Robbins Landon in April 1963, was unimpressed by his historical determinism ("Why should we assume that because more recent music is of a different kind it is superior and more highly developed?"), but he did agree that barococo record labels had "watered down" the Baroque musical canon: "they take us into their confidence, though they have little to confide, pouring into our ears a copious flow of thin music."[51] By 1965, when Igor Kipnis, a notable beneficiary of the barococo revival, submitted an article to *HiFi/Stereo Review* commenting on the "inundation" of the classical market by Nonesuch, Turnabout, and their competitors, it was completely natural for the editors to title the essay simply, "Baroque at Flood Tide."[52]

Is it fanciful to interpret this "flood tide" imagery in terms of a fear of drowning (subjectivity) in a new abundance of (presubjective) music? The narrow masterwork canon of "*thinking* music" appears to have been buttressing critics' view of themselves as thinking *people*, as musical subjects with enough taste to hold themselves aloof from the mass of "snobs and musically semiliterate" (Robbins Landon). The collapse of that canon — the hierarchical "rule" by which the musical world used to be disciplined — unleashes a recorded torrent of soothing barococo trash. In a particularly disastrous example of repressive desublimation, "easy" listening threatens to sweep away both external class boundaries and the inner development of musically trained cultural professionals:[53]

> Minimalism's reception has, at times, dabbled in equally Baroque images
> of liquids — and bodies — in flux. Minimal music can sometimes take the
> part of that irresistible external flow that unleashes the ego-destroying flow
> within: The pulse, that's the main thing. It hums, it thrums, surging, tidal,
> as blind, libidinous, and basic as a heartbeat. . . . [In *Harmonium*] the
> music is gut, vast, viscous; you can float on it or smother, depending on
> your mood. A single chord becomes an ocean here. . . . And always there
> is that pulse, galvanic, relentless, almost shockingly intimate, like something
> turned inside out: this is music of the blood.[54]

To be fair, this sweaty passage, from a 1984 appreciation of John
Adams, is hardly typical of minimalist reception in general. (It appeared,
interestingly enough, in the pages of *Esquire*, a literary space almost as
toxically hetero-normative, it seems, as that carved out by the *New
Statesman*.) Even during what might plausibly have been seen as the
"high tide" of minimalist music (1981–85), there was little tendency to
analogize the spread of the style hydraulically, no spate of articles about
a "flood" or "torrent" of minimalist performances and recordings to
match the "Baroque at Flood Tide" trope of the 1960s. The actual relation between minimalist and barococo reception is quite a bit more complex. For it was precisely during this brief minimalist high tide that the
music itself — not its pattern of commodified dissemination — was consistently compared to fluid in violent motion. Analynn Swan made the
hermeneutic connection explicit in 1983 when she remarked that
"Glass's sea-of-sound music seems everywhere these days," as repetitive
listeners enjoyed "the experience of sitting back and letting a music carry
you along on a shimmering wave of sound." She went on to praise
Glass's ballet *The Photographer*, whose third act climaxes with "one
huge amplified wave of sound that builds and builds while the audience,
caught up in the tidal force, waits breathlessly for the climax."[55] Michael
Walsh had noticed the same climax a year earlier, evoking its sublime
aspects in language that could have come right out of Kristeva or Deleuze
and Guattari: "By Act III, the piece has become a raging cataract of
sound that evokes the spirit of Wagner's *Rheingold* Prelude: a mighty
river at flood tide, frightening in its intensity."[56] Tim Page, searching for
a summary image in 1981, asked unfamiliar listeners to imagine that
"Minimalist composers are framing the river."[57]

This metaphoric register had always been available: had not Reich, in
his 1969 "Music as a Gradual Process," likened gradual musical process
to (among other things) "placing your feet in the sand by the ocean's edge
and watching, feeling, and listening to the waves gradually bury them"?[58]

It may be that by the 1980s, minimalism's new sonic lushness and increasingly overt climax mechanisms made analogies to weaving patterns and transistor circuitry seem a little . . . *dry.* But I would argue further: the minimalism-as-violent-flood trope is a *transference* into the construction of the musical experience itself of anxiety/anticipation about the sociological situation "outside" — a situation in which a new, seductively "easy" style was spreading quickly and irresistibly over the musical landscape, washing away modernist redoubts and breaching canonical dikes. The inexorable power ascribed to minimalist musical "flows" represents both the outer (main)stream of commercial success — and the inner stream of libidinal response evoked in listeners.

Ironically Robbins Landon himself doesn't actually use the "flood" metaphor. He doesn't need to, because the climax of his article actually stages the author's own attempted immolation-by-concerto. Heading off to the record shop to buy $100 worth of barococo recordings, the intrepid critic sits himself down for two full weeks of repetitive listening. Determined to defend the canon of musical taste whatever the personal cost, he plunges headlong into the barococo torrent.

Like the daredevil authors of *Seven Glorious Days, Seven Fun-Filled Nights; Can't Take My Eyes Off of You;* and *The Age of Missing Information,* Robbins Landon tries to look with sustained attention into the abyss, to confront the media sublime directly with an act of heroic consumption. Bill McKibben attempted to watch every single television program broadcast over almost 100 channels during a 24-hour day; Robbins Landon tried to listen, score in hand, to 208 concerti grossi in a row. The risk of drowning, of losing all musical ego boundaries, was not inconsiderable: before announcing the result, Robbins Landon affirms that he loves music, that he could easily imagine listening to Beethoven or Mozart every night "as long as they last"; in fact, he testifies somewhat ingenuously that he "approached [this] barococo marathon . . . with curiosity and with the expectation of much pleasure." But the critic is not swamped, he does not end up, like the flabby consumers of *Music for Relaxation,* "as loose as ashes by dinnertime." On the contrary: he tenses up; he stands firm, rigid, aloof; the wave breaks on him with no (overt) effect. Robbins Landon determinedly submits to *no* pleasure, night after night: instead, he experiences "the absolute negation of music . . . the dreary horror of an evening with Signor Manfredini!" Completely changing the ground of his earlier argument, he rises to a rhetorical climax in which the absent-minded hedonism of the penthouse gives way before something joyless, grim, even obsessive-compulsive:

I simply cannot for the life of me comprehend what ghastly perversion has brought us to the pitch where we sit around the phonograph, deadly serious and intent, listening to fourth-rate concerti grossi which never should have left that dusty archive shelf. To me this is the absolute negation of music; it is the point where musicologists (most of whom don't like music anyway) have triumphed. Groaning under their Teutonic footnotes — and often expressing themselves in a language only faintly resembling that generally conceded to be English — they have elbowed their way into our musical culture; talked record companies into recording hundreds of LPs of endless, jogging, pre-classical trash; persuaded all the snobs and musically semiliterate to buy these records and fill up concert halls whenever these touring Italian chamber orchestras come to play two and one-half hours of music whose original function must have been *Tafelmusik.*[59]

Leave aside the anti-intellectual attacks on musicology, and the sour class *ressentiment;* amazingly, Robbins Landon seems to have forgotten that by his own previous accusation the only one sitting around the record changer, "deadly serious and intent," is himself. Staring at the Medusa's head, he finds himself turned to stone. (How and why did people actually listen to barococo? Stay tuned.) In this moment of what we might call the *barococo sublime,* the sheer abundance of preclassical music on records is experienced as an awe-inspiring, overwhelming, even soul-destroying force ("the absolute negation of music"). The cultural analogy with critiques of advertising and television is quite exact: in both cases there is a terror of too much, a sense that by actually paying attention to the cultural overproduction that is addressed not to the individual (ego) but to the mass (market), one can uncover something terrible and even anti-aesthetic.

Thus the link between minimalism and the Baroque revival goes far beyond the unsatisfying transhistorical style resemblances, and even past the fact that Baroque music on record in the 1950s and 1960s both trained ears for and prefigured the reception of minimal music in the 1970s and 1980s. On the deepest cultural level, minimalist repetition bears the same expressive relation to the "torrent" of indistinguishable barococo recordings as it does to the "pulsing" of advertising campaigns and the "flow" of television broadcasting: the structure of these media, their repetitious overload, is immanent in the repetitious structure of minimal music. This is undoubtedly why enemies of minimalism constantly bring up the Baroque revival. Repetitive music must seem to them a nightmare come true, a "bland field of nothingness" that actualizes every fear of the slackening (of attention, of canonic standards) that barococo seemed to portend. But maybe it's not so important, as

Robbins Landon's mandarin British friend so peremptorily demanded, that we "get our bloody values straight." Perhaps by mastering the repetitious structure, by listening repetitively to minimalism, we train ourselves to surf the flood tide, to accept and survive the "ghastly perversion" that Robbins Landon could only reject. We need not then fear Manfredini's pox; we are already inoculated.

Who Cares if You (Don't) Listen?
(Toward a Defense of Repetitive Listening)

Minimalism draws not so much on the folk art of our day as on what could be called the folk art of listening. The new music connects to how people hear.

Richard Sennett, "The Twilight of the Tenured Composer" (1984)

I must admit I am bemused to find Robbins Landon unintentionally filling in a serious sociological gap in my analysis of minimalism and advertising culture (Chapters 2–3).[60] More than one reader must have wondered whether there was a link between the actual musical culture of 1960s advertising executives and the repetitive rhythmic campaigns they designed. Clearly they weren't listening to minimalism! But they *were* listening to barococo, and listening repetitively, which we now recognize as the 1960s equivalent of listening to repetitive music. Still, Robbins Landon's attack on Madison Avenue barococo consumers obscures the connection while making it; he is not really interested in how these people listen, because he is too interested in convincing us that they don't really listen at all: "As the guests move about, balancing their glasses and cigarettes and canapés, chatting brightly with each other, Manfredini floats from the corner, barely heard above the party uproar, obligingly made welcome." This sardonic description of what actually happens when barococo is on the adman's record changer leads us right back to the Vivaldi as wallpaper music argument — and it's worth pointing out at this juncture just how class-specific such arguments really are. That "flood" of Baroque recordings so threatening just a few paragraphs ago? Compared to the mighty mainstream of popular music — or even just the smaller tributary called Easy Listening — the barococo "torrent" was really more like a trickle. And yet Robbins Landon doesn't mention Bobby Darin or George Melachrino. Evidently he had little interest in what the proles and middlebrows were (not) listening to.

But . . . putting Manfredini instead of Mantovani on the record changer threatens to break one of the most powerful taboos of art music culture: the taboo against *not listening,* against using any kind of "classical" music as background music. (Rock has its own taboos against "elevator music," but that is a different, more overtly antiauthoritarian story.) Attacks on background music in stores and restaurants — a musical practice that UNESCO, an organization not normally associated with artistic censorship, has tried hard to have banned by law — are one of the few satisfyingly elitist gestures left to classical musicians. In the pages of popular guides to Western art music, "classical" music is often defined simply as nonambient music, "the music you listen to," and the first step toward musical literacy and the pleasures of high musical culture is to stop letting music wash over you without concentrating on it, to stop treating Mozart as if it were Muzak. In fact, critiques of Muzak by serious musicians (not just "classical" musicians, either) usually focus not on the manipulative aspects of Muzak itself, or even the political implications of using subliminal music to reconcile workers to otherwise intolerably dull and repetitive working environments. Their rather self-interested complaint is that Muzak inculcates bad listening habits and spoils people for serious music: "For me, the essential distinction that needs to be made is the one between the active experience of listening and making discriminations, and the passive experience of hearing indiscriminately. I must say that I've had the thrilling and rare experience this morning of being *certain* about something: I am certain that Muzak is the single most reprehensible and destructive phenomenon in the history of music, precisely because it conditions the lack of discrimination, the lack of listening, in favor of the passive acceptance of hearing."[61]

Thus Roger Reynolds, joining in the general baiting of a representative from the Muzak Corporation after her presentation at the 1977 centenary conference on *The Phonograph and Our Musical Life.* One can sense something of the same rare thrill running through Robbins Landon's attack on barococo (and by extension many later attacks on minimalism): comparing any classical music to "wallpapery" background music instantly strips it of all respectability, and strips the consumers of such music of any claim to cultural respect. This is important — because there could be nothing more destructive to hierarchies of taste than a listening practice that masquerades as active though it is totally passive, no worse Trojan horse inside the classical music establishment than "music you listen to" *that you don't actually have to listen to.* One must remain vigilant against a "pseudo-classical music written for listeners who think they are now being exposed to classical music" (minimalism); against "the Muzak of the intelligentsia" (barococo); against "a pop music for intellectuals, an easy-to-listen-to music" (minimalism); against a "music sufficiently old to be respectable, and sufficiently boring not to need listening to" (barococo).[62]

This might be why Robbins Landon harps so incessantly on the elite economic and social status of barococo mass-consumers: they are aesthetic traitors to their class. The emergence of pliant new "easy listening" genres of music specifically designed for stacking on the record changer and background listening was fine, as long you didn't call the resulting music "classical," and as long as only the booboisie listened to it. The fact that even the most serious classical music is always susceptible to being played in the background unattended (as more than one reader wrote in to *High Fidelity* to point out) could be finessed by assuming that "even faintly musical people on Fifth Avenue felt there was something about Mozart that, unless you turned the volume down to near-inaudibility, kept on intruding into that third martini."[63] Mozart *resisted* repetitive listening, especially with the help of primitive recording technology that kept the host pinned to within a four-and-a-half minute radius of the 78 rpm turntable. But barococo on LP, like minimalism on CD, was uniquely reprehensible because it conferred the social prestige of difficult (i.e., classical) music even as it unresistingly submitted to repetitive background listening.

Isn't this a respectably anticorporate position? Jacques Attali's leftwing condemnation of background music is just as violent and absolute: "The music of channelization toward consumption. The music of worldwide repetition. Music for silencing." But Attali sees Muzak taking up the sonic space that might be occupied by spontaneous musical creation available to all: he thinks we should move forward from not listening to music (repetition) to making music (composition). Defenders of the classical canon simply want to replace not listening with listening (representation), to reinscribe the society of the spectacle, to force people to pay attention to "good" music and its message of hierarchy and order once again.[64]

Meet the *old* boss, same as the new boss.

So, at last, we have fully unpacked the cultural implications of comparing minimalism to the Baroque revival. Expressed syllogistically, the argument might go something like this: (1) Barococo music is resurrected *Tafelmusik*, popular in the 1950s because, unlike Mozart, it easily slipped into the background at parties; in the background at parties it was not listened to; thus it is more like Muzak than Mozart. *First corollary of (1):* the Muzak you don't listen to displaces the music you do; thus barococo, like Muzak, spoils people for Mozart. *Second corollary of (1):* Muzak you don't listen to isn't really classical; thus barococo music is classical Muzak that isn't really classical; thus it is the perfect music for shallow social climbers who want the prestige of classical music without the effort. (2) For both these reasons, barococo undermines the classical canon of great music from within; it represents a slackening of boundaries, both inside and outside the middle-class ego; thus its illicit pleasures are especially dangerous and must be shunned. (3) They must be shunned like those of 1980s minimalism, which shares with barococo not just "moment to moment predictability," but the same Yuppie/New Class clientele, the same traitorous "pseudo-classical" status, and the same wallpapery pattern of nonattentive consumption.

I have already attempted to problematize this chain of reasoning at several key points. Multivolume sets of Baroque concertos were not just mid-twentieth-century *Tafelmusik,* but something genuinely different, classical music's adaptation to the aggressively marketed new pleasures of long-playing records and automatic changers. The "minimalism" of Vivaldi appears to be an artifact of 1960s record-jacket reception. Stern critical attempts to dam(n) the barococo flood have always had more to do with defending a narrow definition of musical subjectivity than with altruistic worries about the listening habits of the masses, or disinterested notions of aesthetic quality. But I have left unchallenged, so far, the single most damaging assumption: that minimalism and barococo are essentially "classical Muzak" — background music designed to function (for good or ill) in the complete absence of listening attention. Is there any difference between repetitive listening and *non*-listening?

I would argue that consumers of barococo were in fact "paying attention" to the music on their record changers — just not the kind of narrativized, continual attention that upholders of canonic propriety assume as the only adequate mode of musical response. Obviously there are many gradations of musical response between rapt attention and complete unawareness, and many possible rewards for intermediate states of musical attention other than transcendent awareness of musical structure and value. But this complex perceptual field is obscured by Robbins Landon's tendentious choice of the cocktail party as exemplary barococo venue. Even the most peripatetic denizens of Madison Avenue couldn't host or attend social events every night; it is hardly likely that they bought expensive record changers and barococo sets, like chrome-plated cocktail shakers and imported vodkas, simply to impress their guests. Why assume that Vivaldi was played only at parties?

Because "cocktail party" is a convenient shorthand for "worst possible listening environment." Placed at the scene, chatting, smoking, and drinking away, our subjects are already half-convicted, circumstantially, of not listening in the first degree. How *could* they be listening, when a trained musicologist can't seem to keep his own mind from wandering?

> As I sipped the first new-style martini, I listened with delight to the crisp patterns of a concerto grosso; as the evening wore on and the figurations in the violins (over that nice, springy, "walking" bass-line) went on and on, conversation, smoke, and vodka soon surrounded the phonograph in an indistinct haze. The music became scarcely audible, and I found myself barely listening as the record changed, every twenty minutes or so, and a new concerto grosso doodle-deedled its barococo way from groove to groove.[65]

At the party Robbins Landon describes a quick decay of listening attention, during which he loses his original focused awareness of the music's "crisp patterns," and during which his listening pleasure quickly wanes. Distracted, intoxicated, he loses track of the music altogether. His wandering attention is periodically reengaged, but only slightly, and only when the orderly progression through the recorded grooves is disrupted — that is, when the flow of music stops.

This is undoubtedly a precise phenomenological description of the way *Tafelmusik* functions, whether in a Venetian palazzo or a Manhattan penthouse. But let's imagine a different listening experience, where the music is just as patterned and repetitive, the ambience is less distractingly convivial, and where pattern, attention, and groove are placed in a quite different relation: "A listener to [Glass's] music usually reaches a point, quite early on, of rebellion at the needle-stuck-in-the-groove quality, but a minute or two later he realizes that the needle has not stuck: something has happened. Once that point is passed, Glass's music — or so I find — becomes easy to listen to for hours on end."[66] For Andrew Porter, the perception of pattern and the decay of traditional structural listening proceed *in tandem* — or rather, it is the perception of pattern, achieved only by relaxing into the haze of figuration, that then enables a shift in listening strategy. The music then becomes "easy to listen to," ultimately allowing for a much less focused — and much more extended — perception of musical structure. What Robbins Landon identifies as the *end* of social listening to barococo, the moment of "relaxing into," is in fact the *beginning* of listening to minimalism. It is when the needle is most firmly "in the groove" that the pleasure and the attention are unlimbered. Porter describes the resulting perceptual state precisely and evocatively: "The mind may wander now and then, but it wanders in a new sound world that the composer has created."

Why assume that barococo, minimalism — or even Easy Listening, for that matter — can be dismissed as nothing more than the twentieth-century incarnations of pure *Tafelmusik?* Yes, the first album by the Melachrino Strings was in fact entitled *Music for Dining* (Victor LPM-1000), and the second was the aforementioned *Music for Relaxation* (LPM-1001) — but their third release was *Music for Reading* (LPM-1002), followed in due course by *Music for Courage and Confidence* (LPM-1005), *Music for Daydreaming* (LPM-1028), and (surprise!) *Music to Work or Study By* (LPM-1029). Evidently the LP and the record changer were not just used to provide a pleasant, subliminal tinkle under dinner conversation; they helped to create all kinds of musical *ambience,* which we might define, after Brian Eno, as "an atmosphere, or a surrounding influence, a tint." Eno's ambient music is not for parties; it "is intended to induce calm and a space to think." Eno, Porter, and Melachrino seem to be on the same wavelength, and it is at the other end of the dial from Robbins Landon: the collective goal is to create musical "space" within which our minds can wander, by crafting a sonic experience that is somewhere between all-consumingly intense and alienatingly dull. (Eno: "Ambient Music must be able to accommodate many levels of listening attention without enforcing one in particular; it must be as ignorable as it is interesting.")[67] The musical attention must be held, *but lightly;* if the record does its job, the mind is protected from outside distraction, but left free to work, study, daydream — or even draft an essay on minimalism and Baroque music. (In the spirit of McKibben et al., most of this chapter was written while listening to an endless feed of Baroque instrumental music over Internet radio.)

I can't resist reminding the reader that Eno first used the word "ambience" in describing the effect of a barococo recording (he identifies it as eighteenth-century harp music), played "almost inaudibly" at his bedside after an immobilizing bicycle accident; the resulting inspiration led to his 1975 *Discreet Music* album, which intentionally sets out to reduce a barococo staple, the Pachelbel Canon, to an ambient wash.[68] It would be rhetorically effective to introduce here a midcentury riposte to Robbins Landon along these lines: an account where stacking Baroque instrumental music on the record changer creates an ambient aural space for recuperation, silent concentration, and serious work, not the frivolous and pretentious cocktail-party chatter he so effectively mocks. Unfortunately I have not been able to find one. This may well signal a weakness in my research (or my argument); but one might also hypothesize that, in the face of the LP glut and the "not-listening" taboo, an album called *Great Music to Work or Study By* would have been, at least in the 1950s and '60s, impossible to market openly. *High Fidelity* listeners who wrote in to defend barococo from Robbins Landon's attack denied that they used it as party music; but they also denied that they ever gave Baroque concertos, in small doses of no more than three at a time, anything less than their full musical attention. For first-hand accounts of repetitive listening to classical music and its effect on mental concentration, we'll have to move both backward and forward in time: backward to the 1920s, when the gramophone was so exotic that the strange listening habits of its devotees did not threaten the classical canon; and forward to the present day, now that the complete ascendance of repetitive listening has left that canon — and its associated listening taboos — in tatters.

In 1925 Scottish novelist Compton Mackenzie, the founder and editor of *The Gramophone,* was asked to contribute an article to W. W. Cobbett's *Cyclopaedic Survey of Chamber Music.*[69] Mackenzie's magazine had only been in existence two years, and barely a handful of chamber music recordings existed — but he came out enthusiastically for the gramophone, which allowed for a kind of intimacy and privacy in musical reception that the famously reclusive collector found lacking in concert-hall performance ("I find the contact of strangers repulsive when I am listening to chamber music"). An inveterate night-worker, he confessed openly that on his private island he played recordings of classical chamber music all night, night after night, as "music to work or study by":

> The privilege of putting one's mind in order by what surely at its best is the most orderly medium of art in existence — a string quartet — [is] of inestimable value. [That is] why I have made a habit of working to the accompaniment of chamber music. . . . Every writer, whatever his capacity for concentration, is peculiarly exposed to attacks of the irrelevant and trivial when he is most fain to be free of them. And these petty assaults are somehow warded off much more successfully when the background of my mind is occupied by great music. . . . It is the background of the conscious mind for which I crave an occupation. The music is playing the same part as the beads of a rosary. Usually, in spite of working I am able to follow the music intelligently enough to know when the wrong side of a disc has been placed on the turntable, but there are times, rare alas, but all the more

wonderful for their rarity — when the determination to hammer some sentence into shape is so tremendous that a long quartet can be played beginning to end without my being consciously aware of it.[70]

Mackenzie's horror at the idea of playing his chamber music records at a dinner party (let alone his horror at the party itself) can be imagined; but is the listening practice he describes any different from the one Robbins Landon, equally horrified, finds himself falling into after a couple of martinis? Thirty years later, the 72-year-old Mackenzie was using the new long-playing records to create a musical space within which, "when the invention flags," a piece of music "welcomes my attention to itself but declines to allow it to wander anywhere else."[71] (Compare this testimony with Porter on Glass: "The mind may wander now and then, but it wanders in a new sound world that the composer has created.") If Mackenzie is to be believed, the result is not heedless incomprehension of the piece, but the kind of *Gestalt* perception that we normally ascribe only to composers: "I shall have heard the essence of his inspiration as he must have heard it in a moment of time."

Compton Mackenzie had quite definite ideas about what kind of music could stand up to the "extensive reiteration" that his repetitive listening practice demanded. Obviously opera and song were out; so was symphonic music, especially if it came encumbered with a distracting program. Not all instrumental chamber music worked, and exceptional profundity was actually a drawback: early and middle Beethoven, for instance, were preferred to the intensity of the late quartets. The perfect ambience for concentration seemed to come from Haydn and Mozart, listened to as the purveyors of a bustling, upbeat, rather impersonal string music — what Mackenzie felicitously termed "mirth set out in a pattern." This happy music, dismissed by critics as too "external" and "lacking in depth" (sound familiar?), could accompany two months at a stretch of working nights.

How far is such late-eighteenth-century music from the early-eighteenth-century music that eventually displaced it? (Remember, it was precisely these "Mozart quartets on the phonograph" that preceded Vivaldi on the record changer in Robbins Landon's account.) There *were* no recordings of Baroque concerti grossi when Mackenzie formed his listening habits, but the music he did choose to work by is as close in effect to Manfredini as *rococo* is to *barocco*. The movements must be severely abstract and patterned, repetitious, perhaps even a little boring: order in music to engender order in thought; constant figuration so the mind finds something to hold onto whenever concentration wanes; no lyrics, no programs, no strong emotional eruptions, for these would be distracting connections to feelings, memories, and the life outside.

Jumping to the present day: Sociologist Tia DeNora's research into *Music in Everyday Life* provides abundant evidence that Mackenzie's is often the only way "classical music" figures in the lives of contemporary listeners. They choose it specifically when they are studying or need to concentrate, when they need to, as DeNora puts it, "reproduce an aesthetic environment of 'working' and to circumscribe within that environment 'where the mind can go'":

> *Diana:* When I was studying I would on the whole listen to something which I didn't have to think about, so I would be listening to Schubert, or Beethoven or um — a lot of Bach choral things. What else have I got up there? Quite a lot of Schubert, Sibelius — Mozart piano concertos, Mozart quartets, quintets, that sort of thing.
>
> *Q:* You mentioned things with words, are there any other styles of music that you wouldn't listen to when you were working?
>
> *Diana:* I could listen to jazz — but when I'm studying if it's something that, if you like, pulls at your heartstrings, or conjures up memories then I won't listen to it when I am studying.[72]

DeNora points out that for these representative college students, classical music is chosen not because of its social prestige or cultural associations; it is favored precisely for its pure abstraction, its lack of associations, its marginality within their musical lives. The most useful style appears to be the most abstract, the least individualized: "For the respondents who hailed 'classical music' as a 'focuser,' this was usually because such was least likely to be associated with aspects of their lives outside the realm of work or study — that is, music not strongly associated with specific aspects of their social or emotional lives or memories. (Indeed, they often did not know the actual composers or works they used for this purpose but rather made use of compilation CDs, such as Baroque highlights and so forth.)[73]

DeNora is specifically not interested in postulating a direct link between musical structures and psychological states; for her it is axiomatic that "Music is not a 'stimulus': semiotic force does not reside within its forms alone."[74] Thus she would be quite skeptical of the claim that either Vivaldi or minimalism is uniquely, intrinsically suited for use as a "focuser," even though the CDs of "Baroque highlights" she mentions are hotbeds of the barococo style. In fact, her research shows that, except for the oldest members of society, *any* kind of music is today susceptible to incorporation in a general project of what DeNora calls "self-regulation": the appropriation of recorded sound to constitute a virtual space within which moods can be deepened or discharged, energy channeled or worked off, and ultimately a private or public self constructed.

The clear patterning and predictable cycles of minimalism can have a mood-regulating effect that goes far beyond the simple warding off of distraction; often there is a strong positive emotional charge. Remember: Tom Johnson reported in 1972 that Glass's *Music in Twelve Parts* "conveys a mood which is overwhelmingly joyous. Although the music does not resemble anything by Bach, it sometimes lifts me up the way a 'Brandenburg' Concerto does."[75] (The explicit connection he makes back to barococo is a hermeneutic bonus.) For Susan McClary, the "minimalist 'clockwork'" in Janika Vandervelde's *Genesis II* does more than help her focus: "the completion of each cycle yields a sense of satisfaction and security."[76] (In this she echoes Porter's review of *Einstein on the Beach*: "The simple harmonic foundations induce a feeling of security.")[77]

Security can lead to strength: Elisabeth Le Guin describes minimalist mood regulation as a kind of empowerment in "Uneasy Listening," her solitary and courageous defense of New Age relaxation music. For Le Guin, the music of artists like Kenny G, Andreas Vollenweider, David Arkenstone, and Constance Demby works to create "a sense of comfort and safety": "The music establishes an environment, and assures me that that environment will not be disrupted. . . . With the sense of safety can come pleasure, of the mild diffuse variety — intense pleasure being just as disruptive as fear — and relaxation of mental focus. . . . Actual physical relaxation can follow exposure — at least, willing exposure — to this kind of programming, too: I often feel my breathing slow in response to it. So: a safe 'place' to be; a 'place' where one is pleasantly relieved of the necessity of having to focus."[78]

Repetition equals security, strength; ultimately, defense. Robbins Landon stumbles close to what is actually going on near the end of his jeremiad, when he blames reversion to barococo on "our neurotic civilization." In his context *neurotic* really just means *neurasthenic,* as a synonym for decadent. It's a putdown, not a diagnosis. But if we take his attack literally, clinically, we are impelled toward some basic lay-Freudian questions: if neurosis is a defense mechanism against anxiety, and anxiety is a symptom of repression, then what is it that is being repressed here? And how, precisely, does the defense mechanism work?

Answers to the first of these questions ('what is being repressed?'), ranging as widely as the annihilating H-bomb and the 12-tone music of Arnold Schoenberg, might be pursued at book length. At least once, they have been: the argument that minimalism in toto is a cultural defense against unbearable anxiety, a regression into narcissistic asthenia ("a radical reduction of the field of vision, a 'socially approved solipsism,' a refusal to feel anything, whether pain or pleasure") is the burden of Christopher Lasch's *The Minimal Self* (1984).[79] But it is the second, more specific question that we will attempt to answer here. Lasch's analysis, as we saw above, is extremely suggestive in the way it relates minimalist reduction and emptiness dialectically to the ever-increasing pressure and density of mass-mediated consumer culture. But it fails to take into account the possibility that some kinds of minimalist repetition might promise escape, not through narcissistic regression, but through co-optation. Music can drown out the omnipresent barrage of commodity culture with a barrage of its own. Music can even place that barrage under the control of the listener, and encourage her to toy with it, dominate it, experience it as an alternate, equally "full" space where she is free to pay attention or not, a space within which the mind can "wander" without anxiety.

So used, any music turns into an example of what media scholar Annahid Kassabian calls "ubiquitous" music, a meta-genre pioneered by the Muzak Corporation, but that can theoretically embrace all musical styles. (Muzak's patented "stimulus progressions" were simply crude attempts to mass-regulate what microelectronics now let us regulate for ourselves.) Kassabian is fascinated by the prospect that the systematic ubiquity of music is constructing a new, *ubiquitous subjectivity*: decentered, permeable, more background than foreground, more akin to a node in a complex distributed network than the proud, isolated monad of traditional bourgeois self-regard. (DeNora's concept of musical *co-subjectivity*, which she defines as "the result of isolated individually reflexive alignments to an environment and its materials," is a related sociological formulation.)[80]

The 1950s "craze" for barococo thus had little to do with semiliterate musical snobbery, Spenglerian cultural exhaustion, or a sudden eruption of musicological pedantry. It was an early harbinger of the way most music is consumed now, which in turn is a constituent of the way most people *are* now. Barococo subjectivity has become the norm. Who could have imagined in 1961 that "serious," "difficult," classical music, the antithesis of background music, would become known to its self-regulating consumers as "soothing," "relaxing" mood music? Yet that is precisely how college students now use it. They collect the Melachrino Strings and other Easy Listening as fetish objects; they listen intently to Martin Denny and Esquivel. But when they want to study, they surround themselves with the faceless ambience called "classical music" — which, more often than not, means (nothing but) Vivaldi & Co.

DeNora reports that only two groups of informants consistently reject both public and private use of ubiquitous music as ambient mood regulator. Professional musicians like Robbins Landon continue to abhor the idea of background music absolutely. The other crucial correlation is not social class, or educational attainment, but *age:* respondents over the age of 70 had little interest in music except as something "one stops and listens to with intent." DeNora sees this as a crucial historical shift within what we might call the 'technology of the self':

> [Older listeners] were not so overtly objects of knowledge to themselves, less likely to speak of what they might "need" to hear and less likely to be "influenced" by music. . . . They were also most likely to do nothing but *listen* when they put music on the stereo, whether or not they had musical training. These age-linked uses of music in private life . . . therefore should be explored in relation to the history of consciousness. Are they in line with what some have suggested is an historical transformation of the relations of production and self-production of social agency?[81]

Subjects who were over 70 in the late 1990s would have already been young adults in 1948; they were thus the last generation to grow up in the 78 rpm era. This is, ironically, the same generation first diagnosed by David Riesman as exhibiting a predominantly "other-directed" personality structure; but in the consumption of music most of them seem to have retained the inner-direction of older generations.

The arrival of the LP and the record changer provided the technological means for transferring other-directedness into mainstream listening practice. (Born in 1926, Robbins Landon was both a professional musician and a member of this transitional generation; it's no wonder he was so upset.) Repetitive listening to eighteenth-century instrumental music in the 1950s and '60s may well be the first documented instance of the widespread appropriation of "classical" music for ambient self-regulation of mood — but it was certainly not the last. Soon a composed music would arise that incorporated repetitive listening, mood regulation, and ubiquitous subjectivity into its very structure. It is not possible to "listen with intent" to truly minimal music (that is probably why most 70-year-old ears are closed to it); the closer one pays attention to its process, the less one's inner-direction ("intent") is reinforced. On the other hand, minimalism can facilitate a transcendent form of "other-direction," a regulation of mood so powerful that only meditative trance can provide Steve Reich with a suitable metaphor: "While performing and listening to gradual musical processes one can participate in a particular liberating and impersonal kind of ritual. Focusing in on the musical process makes possible that shift of attention away from *he* and *she* and *you* and *me* outwards towards *it*."[82]

It may be that other-directed consumption of mediated music makes us susceptible to domination; dropping a stack of Vivaldi LPs on the record changer may have been just another step in (to use Adorno's unforgettable image) "the process that hammers the machinery into men's consciousness."[83] But Joseph Lanza may also be correct when he provocatively asserts that "Muzak and mood music are, in many respects, aesthetically superior to all other musical forms: they emit music the way the twentieth century is equipped to receive it."[84] Could not the same be said of barococo — and minimalism?

FIVE

"I DID THIS EXERCISE 100,000 TIMES"

Zen, Minimalism, and the Suzuki Method

Create inner strength by daily listening to the recordings.
Have the child listen daily to the recordings of the pieces
he/she is and will be studying — the more frequently the
better. . . . Wake the child with the record. This is the first
listening of the day. Play it again at breakfast. Fine to play
it again while the child is at play. Once again at supper. Why
not play it again when the child goes to sleep in place of a
lullaby?

Shinichi Suzuki, "Inner Strength" (1983)

Our Soto way puts an emphasis on *shikan tazu,* or "just
sitting." Actually we do not have any particular name for
our practice; when we practice zazen we just practice it, and
whether we find joy in our practice or not, we just do it. Even
though we are sleepy, and we are tired of practicing zazen, of
repeating the same thing day after day; even so, we continue
our practice.

Shunryu Suzuki, *Zen Mind, Beginner's Mind* (1970)

PRELUDE: "I SOLISTI DI HOOPLE"

The one thing that H. C. Robbins Landon's "A Pox on Manfredini" did *not* complain about in its savaging of the barococo revival was, surprisingly enough, the quality of performance enshrined on those multiple-disc sets. This may be because his attack was primarily on the consumption habits of musical "snobs," and thus the collections he reviewed are "models of luxurious presentation . . . with pages of illustrations, facsimiles, and engraved musical examples." But as anyone who has sampled these 1950s and 1960s sets can attest, the playing and "interpretation" (or lack of it) on the cheaper ones is, side for side, some of the most hypnotically mechanical on record. It may be hard to think of Vivaldi as a "minimalist" or "ambient" composer if your mind's ear is filled with the quicksilver intensity of Il Giardino Armonico's 1993 recording of *The Four Seasons;* but in the 1950s, actual recordings of Baroque instrumental music were as often as repetitive and impersonal as the most extreme experiments in contemporaneous trance music.[1] This influential (if unintentional) wave of "minimalist" playing was a direct result of the same technological forces that unleashed the barococo flood. Thanks to LPs and cheap, editable magnetic tape, Vivaldi was ground zero for the repetitive Taylorization of musical performance.

A certain fly-by-night aura characterized many of the new, small labels (Vanguard, Westminster, Vox) that exploded into the classical recording market in the early LP era; their entire business model was predicated on carpetbagging and keeping overhead low: "For an investment of a few thousand dollars one could buy a first-class tape recorder, take it to Europe (where musicians were plentiful and low-salaried), and record great amounts of music." The big labels had all the big stars, so these new competitors concentrated on nonstandard repertoire and obscure musicians. The eighteenth century, with its simpler textures and smaller, conductorless ensembles, was especially attractive — but as Roland Gelatt, quoted earlier, admitted as early as 1954, "Not all of this rediscovered music was imaginatively or even adequately performed. The very ease and cheapness of tape recording had brought about a certain lowering of standards."[2]

Three factors conspired to make postwar barococo recordings some of the most "ambient" performances of early music ever captured. First was the aforementioned obscurity of the performers. When Peter Schickele invented the bumbling "Solisti di Hoople" to give the lesser-known works of P. D. Q. Bach a run-through, he knew what he was satirizing. The apocryphal band from the "University of Southern North Dakota" was standing in for the faceless, hungry conservatory students rounded up as *musici* and *solisti* to play *ripieno* in cities like Bologna, Venice, and Rome. More experienced players, like those in Vienna's world-class ensembles, were brutally overworked and underpaid; how else could Robbins Landon's own Haydn Society have wrung symphonies out of them for $50 a movement? (Perhaps it was his own bad conscience that kept him from caviling at lackluster barococo performers!) Work schedules in postwar Vienna hardly left time or energy for interpretive niceties; Herman Scherchen's description of the conditions under which some 1950 Bach recordings were made is sadly typical: "The orchestra worked from 8:00 to 11:00, 11:15 to 12:15, and 1:15 to 3:15 with me, from 3:30 to 6:30 with Clemens Krauss for a trip to Yugoslavia, and from 8:00 to 11:00 with Karajan."[3] Finally, the problem was compounded by the sheer mass of unfamiliar repertoire these orchestral *maquiladoras* were expected to churn out: there were no performing traditions, no interpretive routines to fall back on. Much the easiest thing to do was just to pound through the endless sixteenth-note passagework as evenly and cleanly as possible. As *High Fidelity* complained in 1958, "The kind of aimless interpretation that comes off the top of a musician's head is more prevalent on records now than it was twenty years ago."[4] That the recordings produced were polished-sounding enough to be commercially successful was mostly due to the regenerative power of tape splicing. For the first time, classical recording, which had always meant facing "the challenge of the unpatchable wax blank,"[5] was *more* forgiving of errors than live performance. But there was an interpretive price to be paid.

The advent of recording and broadcasts of classical music had already caused some historians of performance to talk about a "standardization of interpretation"; as Frederic Dorian observed in 1942 (well before the LP-tape era), the exigencies of radio favored those performers lucky enough to have been born with "absolute tempo" (analogous to absolute pitch), the ability to perform a piece in exactly the same amount of time, night after night.[6] Tape recording provided the impetus for a full-scale "Taylorization" of classical musical performance. The idiosyncratic skill of the virtuoso performer would be deemphasized in favor of an ability to play in precisely the same way over and over again, so that a perfect performance could be assembled from edits. In barococo recordings of the 1960s, artisanal production gave way to the precision of the assembly line; the orchestra, so often analogized to a factory, actually began to work like one. Neville Marriner, whose Academy of St. Martin-in-the-Fields was one of the great beneficiaries of the Baroque revival, has always prided himself on his sense of absolute tempo; in the studio no interpretive whims or deviations from strict pulse would ever interfere with a recording engineer's need to crosscut between multiple takes.[7] Jindrich Rohan was a specialist in twentieth-century music; but thanks to his 1960s work for Supraphon (the Czech budget label) he prized — and taught — exactly the same robotic recording technique:

> In Czechoslovakia in the 1960s and 1970s . . . an orchestra would rarely have given a recent live performance of the work to be recorded before the studio sessions, and so would often be learning the piece, or an interpretation. . . . Rohan found it essential to teach his students at the Prague Conservatoire the special disciplines and techniques that would enable such work to be undertaken efficiently, to develop a "perfect sense of tempo," to be able to wake up in the middle of the night and be shown a score open at page 32, bar 4, and to know without hesitation exactly what speed you as conductor habitually took this passage; his aim was to teach his pupils to make music "in a 100 percent professional way."[8]

Classical music recording no longer demanded nerves of steel, the ability to get it all right in one punishing take; what was now required was extreme consistency, an almost Zen-like tolerance for exact repetition. It does not seem too fanciful to imagine barococo conductors and performers engaged in a series of involuntary, poorly paid attempts at one of minimalism's seminal musical challenges: La Monte Young's 1960 *arabic number (any integer) to Henry Flynt,* in which the performer attempts to repeat *exactly* a given sound an arbitrarily large number of times. (We'll follow up the "Zen connection" between midcentury Baroque performance and minimalism at great length below.)

A brisk, uninflected performing style and an unvarying, metronomic pulse could minimize intonation and ensemble problems, while guaranteeing that successive takes could be spliced and intercut at will to fix whatever mistakes did occur. As an added bonus, this style of playing was already ideologically attractive to the most forward-thinking performers of the Baroque revival: to them it sounded "historically authentic." Richard Taruskin has argued convincingly that what the twentieth century has considered "historical" in performance practice is actually a form of modernism, a "geometric" antidote to the flexible "vitalism" of nineteenth-century aesthetics and performance. For Taruskin the seeds of this geometric performance are planted early in the century and emerge full blown in the 1920s with the recordings and pronouncements of musicians as diverse as Virgil Thomson, Arturo Toscanini, and (above all) Igor Stravinsky.[9] But the postwar American triumph of modernist performance practice — like the "International Style" in modernist architecture — may have had as much to do with the economic and technological imperatives of modernity as with its aesthetic ideologies. This is not to say that the needs of the record industry (more product) and the new capabilities of recording technology (interchangeable takes) simply *determined* performance style; one imagines, rather, that this changed environment encouraged a kind of natural selection, favoring those musicians whose ideas about the "correct" performance of Baroque music happened to make them quick and efficient producers in the recording studio.

The barococo environment was extreme, and it gave rise to an extreme mutation of European performing practice: a complete suppression of individuality and expression in the service of the repeated take. On records this culture of repetitive performance might well seem to justify Robbins Landon's dismissal as "the absolute negation of music." But even as they were being fed a steady diet of "low-calorie" Baroque music to (sort of) listen to, Americans were becoming aware that, in Japan, repetitive listening and repetitive performance were at the spiritual heart of a revolutionary new pedagogical method for Western music. The 1960s were not only the heyday of Vivaldi concertos in masses on the record changers of America. The same years found Americans gazing with bemused fascination at the spectacle of those concertos played in dogged unison by dozens, even hundreds, of Japanese children as young as five years old, arrayed in geometric patterns on the stages of conservatories and the floors of high-school gymnasiums. Their mentor, Shinichi Suzuki, a saintly old man already in his sixties, said that the young students who followed his "Talent Education" Method were "Nurtured by Love" — but, as details of the Suzuki Method became known, it became clear that these child prodigies were nurtured by — and ready to nurture in America — a Zen-like culture of repetitive listening and performance so intense that it had no analogue within the world of European art music.

Except, perhaps, the exactly contemporaneous rise of minimalism.

"NURTURED BY LOVE" (AND REPETITIVE LISTENING):
SHINICHI SUZUKI AND HIS METHOD

> Whenever a student finishes a movement [of Beethoven's
> Violin Concerto] in my lesson I have him play with
> Kreisler's record, paying attention to the tone and
> expression. The student doesn't pass if Kreisler can
> be heard over the student. The student's music becomes
> one with the record, and his sensitivity grows before he
> knows it.

Shinichi Suzuki, *Where Love Is Deep* (1982)

Shinichi Suzuki (1898–1998) lived through almost the entire twentieth
century — he was undoubtedly its most influential and innovative musical
pedagogue — and his life story is eerily shadowed by the economic and
technological aspects of modernity that gave rise to a culture of musical
repetition.[10] Much would later be made allegorically of the fact that
Suzuki, the mass-producer of violinists, grew up playing in and around
his father's string instrument factory. By 1910 the Suzuki Violin Factory
in Nagoya, Japan, was the largest in the world, producing 65,800 violins
a year.[11] Surrounded by machine-made violins, Suzuki was not a musical
child; he later confessed that he and his brothers thought of the instruments as toys, good only for hitting each other with and for crude games
of stickball. But a perquisite of the Suzuki family fortune was an expensive gramophone, one of the first in Japan, and it was through repetitive
listening that Suzuki found his way into music:

> The first record I bought was Schubert's "Ave Maria" played by Mischa
> Elman. The sweetness of the sound of Elman's violin utterly enthralled
> me. . . . To think that the violin, which I had considered a toy, could produce
> such beauty of tone! I brought a violin home from the factory, and listening
> to Elman playing a Haydn minuet, I tried to imitate him. I had no score,
> and simply moved the bow, trying to play what I heard. Day after day I
> did this, trying to master the piece . . . somehow I finally got so I could
> play the piece. Eventually I got so I derived great comfort from playing
> the violin, and became very fond of the instrument as well as developing
> a deep love for music.[12]

Suzuki's machine-made musicality was nurtured in Tokyo, and after
1920, in Berlin, through lessons with Karl Klingler, a chamber-music
specialist and pupil of Joseph Joachim. (One of Suzuki's Berlin acquain-
tances was another enthusiastic amateur violinist named Albert Einstein.)

By the early 1930s the Suzuki fortune was lost to the Great Depression; while his father struggled to keep the factory going, Shinichi supplemented his salary as an instructor at the Imperial School of Music by giving private violin lessons to young adults. As Suzuki tells it, when a father brought his four-year-old son in for lessons, his initial response was, "No — too young!" There was no accepted way to teach violin to a toddler, but Suzuki, in the tradition of the Zen antinomianism he had studied at Senshu University ("Read not 10,000 volumes; explore the logic of the heavens"), resolved to start from scratch.

Like most Japanese educators, Suzuki did not believe in innate talent. He reasoned that since young children picked up the intricate complexities of their native language effortlessly, simply by listening to their parents' speech, one ought to be able to induce them to play the violin the same way. But this "mother tongue" approach required that very young children be surrounded by violin playing the way they were immersed in language. Suzuki's solution was to prescribe for all students his own path into musicality: repetitive listening to phonograph recordings. As he later described, the first step in the Suzuki Method is setting prospective infants on an extended regimen of barococo listening: "There are some babies that have been brought up listening to a concerto (one movement only) by Bach or Vivaldi and have learned the music well. After about five months, another selection is added. The baby hears two selections every day. In this way, any baby will grow into a child with a rich musical sense. In other words, the environment develops a person's ability."[13]

In the formal Suzuki Method a child who is ready to begin lessons does not even touch a violin until a systematic progression of repetitive stimuli has inculcated a desire to play. The parents are instructed to play a recording of the beginning piece ("Twinkle, Twinkle Little Star") five or six times a day; parents and children attend the violin class together; the child is taken to concerts where other children are playing the beginning pieces; the mother, who is expected to learn at least enough rudimentary technique to supervise her child's home practice, begins to practice at home herself while the child watches. Eventually desire to join in arises; lessons start when the child tries to grab the violin out of the mother's hands.[14] This preliminary period of "learning through watching" *(minarai kikan)* is a feature of most traditional Japanese apprenticeship systems, from martial arts to calligraphy. It is also, in the way it marshals repetitious stimuli to channel (artificial) desire, a pedagogical analogue to the advertising campaign: like the hapless consumer in Thomas Smith's 1885 "Hints to Advertisers," the little student sees his mother enjoying herself with a violin for the fourteenth time — or the one-hundred-and-fourteenth time — and "remembers that he has wanted such a thing for a long time." (Suzuki puts it nicely: "We have caused him to acquire this desire.")[15]

There are some "tricks" to Suzuki's Method — special one-tenth–size violins, a paper template on the floor to ensure a grounded stance, "tonalization" exercises to solve the physical problems of crossing strings and producing secure tone — but the fundamental emphasis is on what Rohlen and LeTendre, in their survey of *Teaching and Learning in Japan,* translate as "entering through form *(katachi de hairu)*": "In all the learning situations we review, we see a consistent emphasis on mastery of the basics (i.e. the training forms) through repetition. Mastery of basics *(kihon, moto)* is the motto of every middle-school math teacher, potter, and line supervisor."[16] When lessons start, the intensity of repetitive listening increases, so that the beginning student hears the pieces she is working on as many as 40 times a day. The actual teaching proceeds with little explanation and extreme formal precision, as complex technical skills are "overlearned" through repetition and additive process:

> For instance, let us suppose that the pupil has become able to play piece A well. At that time I will add piece B. We will then work on piece B while still continuing to work on piece A. As soon as the pupil can play piece B quite well, I will add piece C to pieces A and B. When finally piece D has been added to the lessons, the emphasis on piece A will be reduced, and the lessons will consist of pieces B, C, and D. In this way, regular sequence is followed. . . . As the abilities are developed gradually in this way, the skills accumulated will add up to an ever-increasing store of basic ability making possible further great advances in ability.[17]

I quote Suzuki's homely description at length because in its repetitive rhythms it mirrors the student's progress through the Method; both are structured like minimalist process music. Long plateaus of repetition (Suzuki's own term)[18] lead to sudden phase changes, sudden leaps up in pitch, in ability. ("This step by step approach, which clearly parallels language learning, leads to a 'leap in ability,' a situation where the pupil accumulates the strength to suddenly advance more and more quickly.")[19] Shinichi Suzuki always claimed that repetitive listening and playing would lead to a direct, intuitive understanding *(kan* in Japanese) of the language of music. But in breaking that language down into its tiniest bits and dwelling on them at such great repetitive length, Suzuki's Talent Education *(Saino-Kyoiku)* Method seems more akin to the austerity of 1960s minimal music than the exuberant recordings by Casals and Kreisler to whose exact copying advanced students could eventually aspire. How different was the Suzuki Method from the obsessively methodical listening and playing it took to create and perform early minimalism?

> For the first month I played one drone note, then adding an open fifth for the next month or so. This made Young ecstatic. . . . After a month or two, I suggested that I might also sometimes play another note. What should it be? —And so began our extended discourse on the advisability of each of the various scale degrees.

> Teaching the singing parts to the chorus took place over the next four months. . . . I used a method I had learned from Alla Rakha when I had been studying *tabla* with him some eight years before. Very simply, we began at the beginning, memorizing a small amount of music. The next day we reviewed the previous day's work and added a new section. We continued this way, each day beginning with a review of the accumulated learned material and adding new material at the end. Ultimately we were able to do full run-throughs of the work entirely by memory.[20]

The first witness here is violinist Tony Conrad, recounting his part in the trial-and-error genesis of La Monte Young's *The Tortoise, His Dreams and Journeys;* the second is Philip Glass, describing how he devised his own version of "entering through form" while teaching untrained singer-dancers the intricate, barely notated music of *Einstein on the Beach*.

"FIDDLING LEGIONS" AND PEANUT-BUTTER SANDWICHES: SUZUKI IN AMERICA

Arthur C. Clarke once postulated that any sufficiently advanced technology is indistinguishable from magic. The reception of Suzuki's Method in midcentury America bears out Clarke's Law: early reports from Japan that dozens of tiny children were being taught to play Bach and Vivaldi perfectly in unison — even an audio tape brought back from the first Talent Education Institute group graduation concert in 1952 — were dismissed as impossible. It was not until 1958 that stunned educators at the Ohio String Teachers Conference sat and watched what would become the signature image of the Suzuki Method in America: a film of 1,200 children, ages five to 13, dressed all alike, standing in military formation on the floor of Tokyo's National Gymnasium and playing from memory violin repertoire up to the level of Bach and Vivaldi.

The spectacle of the mass concert — the endless *over-and-over* of the Method transformed into a living minimalist sculpture, an indelible stage picture of *more-and-more* — had been a polemical feature of *Saino-*

Kyoiku from the very beginning. Disappointed that journalists had hailed three-year-old Koji Toyoda as a "genius" and a "prodigy" after a public concert in 1934, Suzuki developed the expedient of having all his students play in unison to make the point: "Genius is an honorific name given to those who are brought up and trained to high ability." The import to a Japanese audience, schooled in the discourses of group solidarity, was clear; but for American string teachers the mass concerts represented a completely unprecedented experience. (Words like "sensational" and "fascinated" recur frequently in descriptions of early encounters with the Method.)

After 1958 (the year of La Monte Young's *String Trio*, lest we forget), pedagogical interest in Talent Education quickened; several Midwestern schools sent teachers to Japan, and many were in attendance when Shinichi Suzuki addressed the 1963 gathering of the International Society for Music Education in Tokyo. By 1964 (the year of Riley's *In C*), the groundwork had been laid for Suzuki's first visit to the United States. His 10 students created a growing sensation as they crossed the country from Seattle to Boston and New York; they played at the United Nations, the New England Conservatory, and the Juilliard School. The climax of the tour was a spectacular concert to over 5,000 delegates at the Music Educator's National Conference in Philadelphia, which garnered national media coverage. In the next five years Suzuki would give annual summer workshops in the United States, American teachers would flock to the newly constructed *Saino-Kyoiku* Building in Matsumoto, and by 1971 (the year Reich finished *Drumming* and Glass began *Music in Twelve Parts),* there would be a formal Suzuki Association of America (SAA) to supervise the rapid expansion of Talent Education in the United States.

Ironically enough, Suzuki's star was on the wane in his native Japan by 1970; the public novelty of his achievements had worn off, and the idiosyncrasies of Talent Education never made much headway in the tight-knit world of the Japanese music-educational establishment. In America, on the other hand, the early proselytizers for Suzuki were influential string pedagogues at the major conservatories, and Talent Education caught on immediately, if haphazardly, with public-school music teachers. (Any method that promised swift success with elementary-school children through efficient group lessons was an administrator's godsend.) But, as Suzuki and the SAA insistently pointed out, neither the American media nor teachers nor parents seemed to "get" Talent Education; stripped of its distinctively Japanese social and spiritual aspects, *Saino-Kyoiku* became simply another method.[21]

As it was received and practiced in 1960s America, the Method seemed to have little connection with what Suzuki, directly referencing Zen monastic training, called *ongaku-do,* "the spiritual way of music."[22] Mainstream media reports of U.S. tours by Talent Education students were filled with bemused, uncomprehending, and quite literal "Orientalism": *Time* actually headlined a November 1967 piece on the Suzuki phenomenon "Invasion from the Orient." The article, filled with condescending and casually racist clichés, reads like a tract written 100 years earlier: the idea of "migrant Orientals," whose ears are attuned to the "whining microtones of Oriental music," playing Western music on the violin may seem "freakish," but, as it happens, "the stringed instruments were physically ideal for Orientals: their nimble fingers, so proficient in delicate calligraphy and other crafts, adapted easily to the demands of the fingerboard."[23] Three weeks later *Look* ended a photo-essay on Suzuki filled with images of gravely bowing toddlers by wondering if "methods so gracefully Oriental" could survive "the chrome distractions of American life."[24]

Of course, as the diagnosis of Orientalism implies, it was precisely "American life" that was at issue: the intersection of Japanese culture and European music was being used to explore pervasive anxieties within postwar American culture. These anxieties — and this is the primary reason a discussion of the Suzuki Method appears in a book on minimalism — are the very same fears about modernity versus subjectivity that have tended to crop up around reductionist repetition in art: fears of mass production, other-directedness, advertising, conformity, Marcusian one-dimensionality. Americans have constantly misread Suzuki in order to indulge their darkest suspicions about the effects of his intense culture of repetition. Symptomatic is the way *Look* distorts one of Suzuki's perfectly reasonable assertions about developmental psychology ("A child's strongest ability is to conform to his environment") into a sensationalist pull-quote: "A child's proudest talent: conformity." The familiar 1950s buzzword appears in large type underneath one of *Look*'s trademark pieces of dramatic photojournalism (Figure 9), an image of three young Japanese performers shot with a telephoto lens at such an acute angle that their body parts appear to fuse. In case the reader is still not worried, a smaller photo caption informs us that these "cool perfectionists" have been attacked for their other-directed "lack of emotional intensity."

Though Suzuki always disavowed any plan to (as he himself put it in a 1959 *Time* profile) "mass-produce" professional musicians, even the most appreciative accounts of his U.S. tours tended to be filled with

Figure 9 "A child's proudest talent: conformity." Suzuki violinists in *Look* magazine, November 28, 1967.

vaguely ominous imagery of automation, overproduction, and the assembly line. *Newsweek* titled its 1964 report on the first Talent Education tour "Fiddling Legions," and felt it necessary to assure readers that the 150,000 students Suzuki had already trained were "far from robots."[25] *Time*'s "Invasion from the Orient" depicted Shinichi Suzuki as a shadowy industrialist shifting the international balance of trade in string players: the existing European models, mostly handmade in conservatories from Odessa to New York, were becoming too expensive and scarce, driving up prices ($12,480 a year, plus vacation and benefits!). But Japan had discovered a way to *(yes)* mass-produce cheap violinists, like transistor radios, thanks to Suzuki, whose "home-grown [method of] instruction has turned into a near industry." The "competent and eager" Orientals, available in bulk for "less than $100 per month," could cheaply fill gaps in the expanding ranks of U.S. symphony orchestras — at least until the first wave of graduates emerged from Suzuki programs at Eastman and Oberlin.

Even those most committed to the success of Talent Education in

America, the parents and teachers of Suzuki students, resisted aspects of the Method that made it seem, in American eyes, a little too close to assembly-line production and a little too cavalier about cherished Western artistic constructs like genius, individuality, inspiration, and creativity. American parents were never comfortable with the other-directed "period of watching and learning" that the Japanese use to set *Saino-Kyoiku* in motion; as one commentator put it, Americans begin with a very different "folk theory" of innate artistic motivation: "Training in the arts . . . is believed to be properly the product of the child's individual choice, rather than the result of a carefully orchestrated parental attempt to arouse the child's interest. Spending several months calculatedly stimulating a small child's desire to play the violin struck many American parents as overly manipulative."[26] As manipulative, perhaps, as spending several months (and millions of dollars) stimulating the desire for consumer goods in the child's parents. In this respect at least, Talent Education may have seemed, not strange, but uncomfortably familiar to an advertising-saturated public already worried about "hidden persuaders."

On the other hand, Suzuki teachers continually complained that American musical pedagogy was too much concerned with individual ego and competition. In a country that institutionalizes musical competition by having secondary-school wind players "challenge" each other as they duel for high-status positions in marching bands, Talent Education and its dogged insistence on group solidarity ("Social interaction and the opportunity to play as a group are important features that make lessons productive and satisfying — Cooperation is fostered — Great care is taken to avoid competition and its negative effects") seemed like the recipe for a world full of gray-flannel organization kids. Suzuki himself made the equation between musicality and Riesman-style other-directedness completely explicit: "In Suzuki's view, one of the most important virtues [that music can help foster] is sensitivity to other people. . . . True sophistication is to be sensitive to another person's feelings and have respect for their point of view."[27] (The contrast is total with currently popular American folk wisdom, where musical study is touted as a surefire method for producing smarter and more disciplined competitors in the zero-sum game of life.)

Perhaps even less congenial to American parents was the Method's reliance on the imitation of recordings to channel budding musicianship. American commentators were consistently bemused by this practice ("We heard of a young violinist with a small tape recorder strapped on his back, playing an endless tape constantly. . . . Would you believe, he made remarkable progress in one week!") and made the inevitable comparison with Muzak ("Recordings are played as 'background music,' for hours each day and at low volume levels").[28] It was one thing to have their children submit to a teacher, or blend into a group of classmates — but it strained American beliefs to the breaking point to have their children's other-direction directed at the "mindless" reproduction of a mechanical reproduction. Many parents (and teachers!) flatly rejected this as a surefire way to create musical automatons. American Suzuki parents have thus tended to skimp on the recommended repetitive listening, complaining that it is "boring."[29] In fact, the machine-like repetition involved in all aspects of the Method has consistently repelled American parents, but "repetition" is such a crucial trope for the intersection of Suzuki, barococo, Zen, and minimalism that I want to single it out for treatment at greater length below.

Why did American parents, enthusiastic consumers of recorded Baroque music themselves, bridle at its repetitive use as a teaching tool? For Suzuki, imitating recordings was merely the technological enhancement of a time-honored Japanese way of learning: imitation and rote repetition assured an incremental approach to perfection, at the same time as they inculcated rigid and hierarchical structures of group discipline. Whether the *sensei* was there in the flesh, or through the mediation of a mechanical device, was of little consequence.[30] But Klaus Theweleit has observed that, in the West, *consciously* submitting one's will to any machine, especially if that subordination is in the service of turning out masses of similarly skilled individuals, is antithetical to the idealized bourgeois subjectivity supposedly embodied by art music: "To the bourgeois mind, this conception of self accords precisely with the notion that we cannot be anything like 'machines,' 'mechanically' produced or producing, or even 'products of mass production.'"[31] Suzuki's new way into music was fundamentally foreign to classical music's traditional ideals of artistic creativity and performance — as foreign, to take an exactly contemporaneous example, as the even newer way exemplified by Steve Reich's *Piano Phase:* "Finally, late in 1966, I recorded a short repeating melodic pattern played on the piano, made a tape loop of that pattern, *and then tried to play against the loop myself, exactly as if I were a tape recorder.* I found, to my surprise, that while I lacked the perfection of the machine, I could give a fair approximation of it while enjoying a new and extremely satisfying way of playing."[32]

But why single out early minimalism as an American musical analogue to Suzuki's desire to "become one" with a phonograph record? After all, in the later 1960s most musically inclined American teenagers were working hard, through repetitive listening, to merge themselves with the recorded guitar solos of George Harrison, Keith Richards, and Eric Clapton — and these rock *sensei* had themselves learned to play by repeated listening to old rhythm 'n' blues 78's. American musicians have always taken Suzuki's "nontraditional" path into the profession, copping riffs off Armstrong recordings, playing along with Parker and Coltrane until they have the solos down, mimicking every vocal inflection of Marvin Gaye or Patsy Cline, without ever seeming to worry that the practice put their innate creativity as musicians at risk.

One might recall here the Mantovani versus Manfredini distinction: like relaxation, rote learning through repetitive listening was fine for popular music, but it trespassed on a vestigial taboo when "art" music was on the curriculum. More crucially the twentieth-century musical styles that make imitation of recordings a central pedagogical method idealize spontaneous improvisation in performance, while Western classical musicians must work within a much narrower range of interpretation, constrained by the opposing ideal of "fidelity to the work." The pop musician uses recordings to learn a fluid musical language, the Suzuki student to learn a series of fixed musical texts. Set aside this confusion of language with text, and Suzuki's Method seems perfectly logical: assuming one has chosen an authoritative performance that realizes the composer's intentions (as Suzuki's soberly Germanic training would demand), then, through repetitive listening and imitation, students will simply absorb *Werktreue* by osmosis. But, as many Western parents and pedagogues realized intuitively, the use of recordings shifts Suzuki's naturalized "mother tongue" instruction toward something much more rigidly mechanical. (Our mother tongue is nothing other than the language within which we can most fluently improvise.) In the absence of freely creating native speakers, one can hardly imagine a child learning to speak idiomatic English through phonetic drill and repeated viewings of *Hamlet* on videotape, no matter how definitive the recorded performance. Of course, she might be able to recite, perfectly yet uncomprehendingly, the part of Ophelia — even at age four.

Remember the record changer? Once more we encounter an inducement to repetitive musicking as the unintended consequence of technological (or, in this case, techno-pedagogical) "progress." Suzuki training turned its tiny charges not into fluent improvisers, or budding interpreters of the canon (as advertised), but into young protominimalists: inured to repetition, estranged from interpretation, precisely calibrating their own moving in and out of phase with a sound recording; like Steve Reich, doing their best, while playing along with a machine, to give a fair approximation of its perfection. Furthermore: in American Suzuki, as in the contemporaneous minimalism of the barococo revival, it was specifically LP recordings of early-eighteenth-century music that formed the training ground. American Suzuki was thus not only protominimalist; it also dovetailed nicely with the reigning authenticist performing style so economically and ideologically attractive to 1960s producers of barococo.

To be fair, Shinichi Suzuki himself never tied his Method to any one style: he began with folk songs and children's repertoire by nineteenth-century composers (Schumann, Brahms, Weber, even Paganini), and his tenth and final book of exercises consisted of two complete Mozart violin concertos (K. 218 in D and K. 219 in A). Ultimately, as the epigraph to this section reminds us, he had his most advanced students play the Beethoven concerto in unison with the famous 1926 recording by Fritz Kreisler. But the meat and potatoes of the Method was barococo: short pieces by Martini, Dittersdorf, Pugnani, Eccles, and Rameau; sonatas by Veracini, Corelli, Handel, and Bach; and concerto movements by Seitz, Bach, and the inevitable Vivaldi.

In fact, a familiar concerto from *L'estro armonico* (Op. 3, no. 6, in A minor) became Talent Education's signature piece, played en masse at almost every group concert and on every tour; in *The Suzuki Violinist*, William Starr singles it out as "one of the most frequently programmed selections in the Suzuki repertoire."[33] It is unlikely that Suzuki set out to highlight this piece (he actually preferred to have mature students show off with Romantic warhorses like the Mendelssohn concerto or Chausson's *Poème*), but various aspects of his pedagogical structure conspired to place this motoric "concerto-in-general" at the emblematic center of American Suzuki reception. The quick outer movements of Vivaldi's Op. 3, no. 6, occur at the end of Suzuki's Book IV, precisely one-third of the way through the Method. They are at the same time the first recognizable pieces of extended concert music in the books, and the last pieces begun before students start on the difficult tasks of learning to read music and master left-hand vibrato. Vivaldi's allegros are thus perfectly placed for journalistic hyperbole: enough like "great music" to catch a critic's attention, but early and unchallenging enough in the Suzuki canon to be playable by very large groups of still uncannily young toddlers. (The fast concerto movements in Book IV are considered playable by four- to six-year-olds, since they don't absolutely require the student to read music, use vibrato, or add expressive nuances.)

A Vivaldi concerto is not only the first "real" music Suzuki students encounter; for many it is also the last—at least as a Suzuki student. In general, few pupils on either side of the Pacific make it all the way to Book X. The Japanese start earlier and work harder, but they face intense pressure to abandon the violin as they begin to cram for college entrance exams in their early teens; Americans are more likely to keep playing the violin through high school, but the very youth orchestra infrastructure that keeps them interested demands they stop playing by ear and learn sight-reading and ensemble playing. For most students, parents, and audiences, the promise of Talent Education per se is fulfilled with solo and massed performances of popular barococo concertos.

Suzuki thus flooded American high-school auditoriums (and gymnasiums) with Vivaldi Allegros—and the style of performance he promulgated was perfectly congruent with the minimalism of the postwar barococo flood. Suzuki couldn't expose his young charges to Kreisler or Heifetz playing Vivaldi's Op. 3, no. 6 (they hadn't), so, as with all of the repertoire in the first eight books, he made demonstration recordings for them to absorb. As disciples tell it, Suzuki was moved to make practice recordings after listening to thousands of graduation tapes of his students and noting a disturbingly "wide variation in tempi and interpretation." He experimented with commercial records, but they often featured "a certain flair or interpretation" that seemed too much for young students to model.[34] The solution was a set of specialized recordings, played by Suzuki himself, deliberately designed to police and standardize interpretation.

What kind of performances did Suzuki model and demand? He played with the full, rich vibrato of a violinist trained in the 1920s—but, at the level of the Vivaldi and Bach concertos, did not expect young students to apply any themselves. What they *were* supposed to imitate was Suzuki's rhythmic drive and precision. Western visitors to the *Saino-Kyoiku* Institute used to refer jokingly to *tempo di Matsumoto,* by which they meant the crisp, unyielding tempos that Suzuki demanded of even the youngest players. ("Educate to tempo, the teacher must not go to the child's tempo.")[35] Talent Education focuses intensely on motor rhythm from its very first exercises. Suzuki did not begin his Method with long tones, partly because they are more difficult than short notes for novices with the bow, but also because, unlike his fellow music educator Zoltán Kodály, he believed that repeated rhythmic patterns, not sustained vocalization, should be the fundamental building blocks of musicality. Thus the beginning exercise infamous in American Suzuki as "peanut-butter sandwich," an onomatopoetic way to encourage toddlers to play four sixteenth notes and two eighth notes with crisp short bows. (It is customarily done first on all four open strings, and then on the pitches of "Twinkle, Twinkle Little Star.") The path from peanut-butter sandwich to the violin part of Vivaldi's Op. 3, no. 6, is not long for a diligent student: the entire thrust of the Method has been to get her comfortable playing extended strings of sixteenths and eighths in a steady, unwavering allegro. Vibrato, rubato, expression, phrasing — these come much later, if at all.

They certainly were never possible during Talent Education's mass concerts, where up to 1,200 students would play the opening Allegro in unison, demonstrating a ne plus ultra of repetitive, mass-produced performance that was received by ambivalent Western critics as simultaneously seductive and terrifying. Circus-like demonstrations of interchangeability on stage sometimes reached an eerie, dehumanized extreme ("at once impressive and absurd," as the 1964 *Newsweek* report put it), which, by an analogy now well worn in this text, we might call the "Suzuki sublime." Sometimes two students would be asked to switch back and forth between parts in the Bach Double Concerto on command — or, having lined up five or six identically dressed toddlers and begun a familiar piece, Suzuki would point randomly to each student in turn, swinging them in and out of the musical flow like interchangeable parts on a many-limbed musical automaton.[36] To rephrase Theweleit: these little barococo minimalists demonstrated the antithesis of bourgeois musical subjectivity, by being both perfect musical products of mass production and machines mass-producing perfect music.[37] For all the 1960s testimonials from Casals, Oistrakh, and Grumiaux, there was little real comfort for the individualistic, virtuosic traditions of Western classical music in the Suzuki sublime. But perhaps, somewhere near the back of the gymnasium, a classical record producer was smiling.

ICHI-MAN: REPETITIVE PRACTICE IN MINIMALISM, SUZUKI, AND ZEN

> If you lose the spirit of repetition, your practice will become quite difficult.
>
> **Shunryu Suzuki, *Zen Mind, Beginner's Mind* (1970)**

As this chapter draws to a close, I will undertake to gather together the multiple threads — recording technology, American minimalism, European Baroque music, Japanese culture — spun into what has turned out to be a complex, nonlinear cultural narrative.[38] Let us begin by exploring another, less-traveled path from the endlessly repeated rhythmic patterns of Suzuki's Book I. "Peanut-butter sandwich" prepares one to play Vivaldi Allegros, true; but, refracted through the repetitious mental discipline of the Method, it is an even better preparation for a pioneering piece of minimalism like Philip Glass's *1 + 1* (1968), perhaps the only piece of contemporary American art music that one could imagine succeeding (in transcription) at the hands of Talent Education four-year-olds.

1 + 1 is composed of nothing other than two short peanut-buttery rhythmic figures (♪♪♪ and ♪), hammered out on an amplified tabletop in fast, unrelenting *tempo di Matsumoto*. The piece, of arbitrary length, "is realized by combining the above two units in continuous, regular arithmetic progressions." (Glass's score provides several sample realizations but does not limit performers to them; see Example 17 for a few of mine.) Talent Education students of the 1960s might even have recognized Glass's expanding and contracting rhythmic processes as a special case of what an American string teacher once called "Matsumoto mathematics": "Suzuki tells a child to play a spot 10 times while he counts. The counting goes '11111 222222 3333333,' etc."[39]

Matsumoto math is, of course, a way to turn massive amounts of repetition into a game for young children. The crucial phenomenon that American minimal music, the Suzuki Method, and Zen Buddhism all share is an emphasis on *practice,* the raw experience of repetition, up to and seemingly beyond the limits of human endurance. A Zen-like insistence on "pure" repetition would seem to make tiny Suzuki students the ideal performers of Glass's modular music, which, after all, depends more on mental discipline in the face of repetition than mastery of notation or traditional technique. But such repetitious training has also been the fundamental sticking point in Suzuki's American reception. The level of rote repetition in *Saino-Kyoiku* is not unusual within Japanese culture — especially, as we shall see, in the context of the Soto school of Zen — but it *was* felt as extreme by American parents and teachers. We have already seen resistance to the repetition involved in Suzuki's introductory *minari-kikan* period, and to his repetitious use of recordings. In general, American parents have consistently been impatient with what they perceive as the snail's pace of Suzuki instruction, where a conscientious teacher might work up to the first piece in Book I, the "Twinkle, Twinkle" Variations, for a full year; where students are asked to play the same short exercises hundreds, if not thousands, of times; and where

Example 17 Representative patterns generated by Philip Glass's additive process piece, *1 + 1* (1968).

pieces are kept in the repertoire long after their technical challenges have been exhausted.

Suzuki's standard response to all such complaints had the stern echo of the Zen Master: "Where are you hurrying?" On one level this rebuke makes sense: the American tendency is to evaluate both art and art education in terms of utilitarian goals, and thus prize efficiency and quick progress on the road to professional achievement. For Suzuki the *ongaku-do,* the path of music, wasn't supposed to lead to a high-paying job. The journey was the destination, the reward of practice not to *play* better, but to *be* a better person. ("I just want to make good citizens. By developing their musical sense and helping each other our children will bring a better world for tomorrow.")[40] But Americans' genuine discomfort with Suzuki repetition was not simply hard-nosed cost-benefit analysis, or a consumerist clamor for instant gratification. Paradoxically it showed just how unprecedented the practice of Talent Education was for even the most idealistic and musical families. Despite cultural misreading and awkward compromises, the Zen-like minimalism at the heart of Suzuki's *ongaku-do* was actually filtering through.

A phrase such as "Zen-like minimalism" flows easily onto the page — but this familiar simile risks the glibness of cross-cultural cliché, papering over fissures in both Japanese Zen and the American reception of it. If the goal is to pose Talent Education and its performances of Baroque music as an intermediate term between the other two, then Zen, Suzuki's relation to it, and the relation of American repetitive music to both must all be considered in at least some of their real historical complexity. It would be presumptuous, and far outside the scope of this book, to attempt a theological dissertation on the history and metaphysics of the various "meditative" (*Ch'an* in China; *Zen* in Japan) schools of Far

Eastern Buddhist thought. But to link Zen, Suzuki, Baroque music, and minimalism (as well as to understand why these terms have not previously been linked), we do need to establish what *kinds of experiences* were offered to Americans by Japanese teachers under the label "Zen"; in particular, we need to understand the position within those experiences of fundamental percepts like *practice* and *repetition*.[41]

It is a story of three Suzukis: we can place Shinichi Suzuki, inventor of *Saino-Kyoiku*, in the context of charismatic Western teachers from the two widely divergent schools of Japanese Zen, both, coincidentally, also named Suzuki. As early as the 1920s the sophisticated writings of Daisetsu (D. T.) Suzuki (1869–1966) introduced American bohemians to the violent antinomianism of the dominant Rinzai sect; almost four decades later Shunryu Suzuki (1905–71) influenced a younger West Coast generation with the gentle austerity of his lesser-known Soto practice.

What most Americans think of as "Zen" is Rinzai Zen, brilliantly translated for Western sensibilities by D. T. Suzuki. This first Suzuki analogized Rinzai Zen to existentialism: seized with a feeling that the world as perceived through the ego was meaningless and unreal, the Zen Buddhist strove for the purely intuitive "leap of faith" into ego-less *satori*, or enlightenment. Since the intellect, the seat of the ego, could not grasp *satori* directly, the practice of Rinzai Zen was a series of deliberate assaults on the rational mind. Zen masters acted irrationally, deliberately ignored sacred texts, fended off theological questions with nonsense, and often broke out into sudden violence if challenged. (This is the side of Rinzai that inspired the anarchic Beat Zen of "dharma bums" like Jack Kerouac and Gary Snyder.) D. T. Suzuki placed great emphasis on the Rinzai practice of the *koan*, a self-contradictory riddle ("What is the sound of one hand clapping?"; "What did your face look like before you were born?") that the student was asked to "answer" not by facile rationalization, but through prolonged, obsessive, and deliberately frustrating rumination. The experience of Rinzai was thus presented to Westerners as a dangerous existential struggle with the void; the breakthrough into *satori* would come at the moment of greatest psychological peril: "the main idea is to bring the mind to a state of concentration, to a state of the highest possible tension, so as to leave for the mind just two courses to pursue: either to break down and possibly go insane, or to go beyond the limits and open up an entirely new vista, which is satori."[42]

Once *satori* was reached, things would go on pretty much as before, except that with the screen of the ego out of the way, what Buddhists call the "suchness" of the material world could be perceived directly, in all its stunning clarity. In *Zen and Japanese Culture* (1938), Suzuki lauded the artlessness of Japanese Zen culture, striving not for self-expression, but always for an intense, poignant awareness of the present moment outside the self.[43] The life and works of John Cage, who studied informally with D. T. Suzuki in the 1930s, represent the translation of specifically Rinzai notions of practice, enlightenment, and culture into Western art music, and it is in the struggle with the impossibilities of his aleatory and indeterminate compositions, so obviously *koans* in musical notation, that most of us imagine the musical experience of Japanese Zen Buddhism to lie.

But there is a problem: the grim teleology of the Rinzai struggle toward enlightenment, its spasmodic unpredictability and violence, its ecstatic release into *satori,* would seem to have little to do with the regular, repetitive processes of 1960s minimalist music. Nor does a method that relies on driving its inductees to the brink of insanity seem like the best basis for Talent Education, a humane violin pedagogy involving very small children.

Rinzai Zen promises "sudden enlightenment" as a reward for intense mental struggle or for having a Zen Master break his staff over your head; there is almost no mention in D. T. Suzuki's writings of the quiet contemplation Westerners think of as "meditation." His Rinzai Zen is much more interested in the struggle with the *koan* than in the practice of *zazen,* the practice of sitting on a cushion and attempting to quiet and clear the mind of discursive thoughts. *Zazen* takes time; it is, to paraphrase Steve Reich and telegraph the direction of my argument, "enlightenment as a gradual process." Gradual enlightenment through sitting meditation is a practice that spans the globe, but no Buddhists are quite as single-mindedly focused on what they call "just sitting" *(shikan tazu)* as the Soto Zen school of Japan.

Americans who are not Buddhist practitioners have had relatively little exposure to Soto Zen; in fact, one of the first texts of American Soto Zen reception dates from 1970 and is hardly a book at all, rather a collection of the informal talks on practice given by the *roshi* (abbot) of the San Francisco Zen Center, Shunryu Suzuki, over the years since his arrival in the United States in 1958. This second Suzuki paints a totally different experiential picture of Japanese Buddhism. *Zen Mind, Beginner's Mind* never even mentions *satori;* there are no perplexing *koans,* no irascible Zen Masters, no analyses of poetry or painting.[44] There is . . . just sitting.

It would be a mistake to overemphasize the doctrinal differences between the Soto and Rinzai schools of Zen. (Indeed, most Soto teachers adamantly deny that Soto Zen is a "school" at all.) Both subscribe to the same view of the world, diagnose ego as suffering, and prescribe a remedy according to the famous Eight-fold Path of Buddhist doctrine. But Soto teaching places much less experiential emphasis on the "dramatic" struggle for sudden enlightenment. In his post-*zazen* talks, Shunryu Suzuki constantly warned against what he called "gaining ideas," that is, any idea that by Zen practice one can "acquire something" like enlightenment: "These forms are not a means of obtaining the right state of mind. To take this posture itself is the purpose of our practice. When you have this posture, you have the right state of mind, so there is no need to try to attain some special state" (26).

This nonteleological, resolutely nondramatic approach to practice ("Zen is not some kind of excitement, but concentration on our usual everyday routine" [57]) seems much more akin to minimalism and Talent Education than the pitched battles with the ego fought by Rinzai Masters and practitioners. Shunryu Suzuki, like Shinichi, advocated a gradual path, filled with repetition, by analogy with language acquisition: "After you have practiced for a while, you will realize that it is not possible to make rapid, extraordinary progress. Even though you try very hard, the progress you make is little by little. . . . It is like studying a foreign language; you cannot do it all of a sudden, but by repeating it over and over you will master it. This is the Soto way of practice" (47).

Indeed, although Shinichi Suzuki's English writings do quote approvingly from descriptions of Rinzai by D. T. Suzuki (perhaps because his books were already well known in the West), Talent Education's methods and attitudes seem much closer to those of Soto Zen. (It is not entirely clear in which lineage the originator of *Saino-Kyoiku* actually studied.)[45] *Zen Mind, Beginner's Mind* asserts flatly that "Zazen practice is the direct expression of our true nature" (23), by which Suzuki *roshi* meant our original, Buddha nature, the "big mind" at one with all things. Suzuki the violin pedagogue was interested in precisely the same quality, which he sought in classical music, and in the "beginner's mind" of young children: "Children in their simplicity seek what is true, what is good, what is beautiful, based on love. That, I believe, is 'the true nature of man' as described by Gautama Buddha. Mozart, whose music taught me the simple love and joy that overcome misery, must have believed that too."[46]

What obscures true nature is the ego, and both teachers prescribe single-pointed attention to precise formal aspects of practice (posture, breathing, hand position) to make that ego gradually disappear. In the *zen-do,* the meditation room, we are told, "Form is form. You must be true to your own way until at last you come to the point where you see it is necessary to forget all about yourself. . . . We must make some effort, but we must forget ourselves in the effort we make" (43, 37). On the wall of his violin studio, Shinichi Suzuki hung a hand-lettered poster that translated this insight into the language of the *ongaku-do:*

Do not play;
Let the bow play.

When a student complained that it was too hard to make a beautiful tone, Suzuki turned on him, reminding him of the real purpose of repetitive practice: "You always see this poster but you only read it. Who else makes your bow dance but you? Discard your 'I'm the one to play'–type ego, recognize your bow's own life, and serve it so as to make it easy for it to play the violin. Your self-centered approach produces unpleasant, scratchy tone, and the force of that ego fetters your own free action."[47] Shunryu Suzuki, a man of few words, once said almost the same thing: "You cannot practice true zazen, because *you* practice it" (114).

We have arrived, once again, at a familiar place. According to Steve Reich, the "I'm the one to play" type ego is precisely what minimalist process music seeks to eliminate: "Focusing in on the musical process makes possible that shift of attention away from *he* and *she* and *you* and *me* outwards towards *it.*" And one can imagine Robbins Landon's "I'm the one to listen"–type ego fading away under the gentle massage of minimalist repetition — or an overdose of Baroque concertos. *("Do not listen; Let the record changer listen.")* What, after all, is Zen practice but a 1,000-year-old method of what Western sociologists like Tia DeNora now analyze as mental "self-regulation"? In fact, Zen is quite familiar with the concept that through the construction of a carefully controlled minimalist ambience, one might become an "object of knowledge to one-self" in order to regulate oneself — and, eventually, to transcend one's self. Both Shunryu and Shinichi Suzuki were fond of quoting Dogen, Soto Zen's original patriarch: "To study Buddhism is to study ourselves. To study ourselves is to forget ourselves" (79).

How tightly can we tie all this together? Of the early minimalists, only Philip Glass is a Buddhist practitioner (not Zen, but Tibetan Vasjaryana); nor can one imagine Shinichi Suzuki, lover of Mozart and Tchaikovsky, much enjoying a repetitive, mechanical piece like Glass's *Strung Out* (1967) for amplified solo violin (Example 18). On the other hand, Glass's five-note circular figure, with its repeated string crossing, might make a

Example 18 Philip Glass, *Strung Out* (1967), opening figure.

etc.

nifty *tonalization* exercise for Talent Education students. Tonalizations are short musical fragments crafted to work a single technical issue; the Suzuki student is expected to practice them at length. Like the very different experience of Cage's *4'33"*, these humble musical exercises represent the direct translation of Zen practice into musical practice. But the model here is Soto, not Rinzai, not sudden enlightenment through a cryptic musical *koan,* but ego-free musical awareness through . . . *just playing:* "Suzuki's tonalizations are spare, using a minimum of material which is to be repeated many, many times. The priority is to apply the fullest attention possible to the actions taken and the tone resulting."[48]

My now redeemed cross-cultural cliché is worth restating: *Talent Education's tonalization practice is, literally, "Zen-like minimalism" in music.* The Zen in question is repetitive Soto practice, and the minimalism is repetitive musical process. Suzuki deliberately did not excuse himself from this kind of tonalization work; in later years he experimented on himself to find the human limits of repetition: "I tried an experiment to find out how my ability would grow at my age [then 59]. I placed the bow on a string, then produced beautiful tone with the well-balanced bow. I carefully played a stroke at a time after checking the balance of the bow each time. I did this exercise 100,000 times (it took me about 25 days). People recognized the leaping progress in the beauty and clarity of my tone in those 25 days."[49]

Nearly sixty, Suzuki had found a violin-based meditative practice of intimidating purity — and a perfect rejoinder to the impatient Talent Education students and teachers who rebelled against his inveterate prescription — *ichi-man* (10,000) repetitions — for overcoming any technical difficulty.

Suzuki himself characterized his 100,000-fold repetition of a single violin tone as an "experiment." He meant a *pedagogical* experiment, of course — but suppose one considered the 25-day "performance" as a piece of experimental music? If Suzuki could have been induced to perform his 1957 violin experiment in a lower Manhattan loft space, he would now be hailed as a pioneer of "hypnotic" musical minimalism, having beaten La Monte Young to the composition of *arabic number*

(any integer) by a full three years. (He would not have been the only vis-
itor from the Far East to feature a Western string instrument in a Zen-
like, avant-garde performance piece. Witness Nam June Paik's *One for
Violin Solo* (1962), a violent Rinzai *koan* in which the Fluxus regular
ever-so-slowly raised a violin over his head and then suddenly *[satori?]*
smashed it to smithereens.)[50]

Suzuki never performed repetitive music in America, but Talent
Education students did, endlessly, in barococo disguise. So did their
parents . . . but they were playing records, not violins. A new musical
experience was everywhere in 1960s America: at the mass concert in
the gymnasium, they called it Vivaldi — *but it was minimalism.* A few
years earlier, on the record changer in the living room, they had attacked it as Manfredini — *but it was already minimalism.* The actual arrival of a minimalist process music must be seen against this larger
backdrop; it was anything but an isolated countercultural event. In
social and historical context America's receptiveness to minimal music
in the 1970s and 1980s is largely the unintended consequence of a general postwar practice of repetitive listening and playing, loosely cen-
tered around the 1950s and 1960s revival of interest in late-Baroque
instrumental music.

Tracing these early trails between minimalism and the Baroque revival, we've taken up in turn two sides of the musical culture of repetition: repetitive consumption (listening to records) and repetitive production (learning to practice). The route has a satisfying symmetry: the path
of barococo listening passes through record changers and Vivaldi box
sets on its way to minimalism. The path of Suzuki practice passes
through Soto Zen and minimalist tonalizations on its way back to —
Antonio Vivaldi.

POSTLUDE: THE CONCERTO IN THE GRAY FLANNEL KIMONO

Recently I have been studying the works of the Japanese
poet Issa, and I understand the mind of Mozart even
more clearly. Haiku such as Issa wrote in his fifties are
pure Mozart.

Shinichi Suzuki, *Nurtured by Love* (1969)

It's worth pointing out as we close that this is not the way Vivaldi is supposed to work.[51] In a recent study Susan McClary chose another A-
minor Vivaldi concerto (Op. 3, no. 8) to exemplify the power of Western

tonal forms to dramatize the vicissitudes of the individual subject in a newly individualized society:

> Vivaldi's concertos make palpable one of the most cherished tenets of eighteenth-century thought: that individual will and social consensus are compatible — indeed, that the new progressive society requires the actions of imaginative, risk-taking agents, while those agents in turn rely on the approval of a supportive environment. It is largely tonality's cause-and-effect qualities that weave these potentially antagonistic forces together into a single coherent trajectory, so that we experience as virtually inevitable both the exuberance of the solos and the periodic arrivals at consensus. Even if it proves difficult (if not impossible) to implement in the real world, this is still one of our most cherished models of social interaction.[52]

The virtuoso solo part of a concerto speaks most eloquently in the voice of the inner-directed Western subject, the kind of risk-taking adventurer who ends up in non-Western regions (like Japan) playing the missionary — or the conquistador. Exuberant products of early-modern Europe, Vivaldi concertos epitomize the tonal language of the colonialist project, of small bands of adventurous risk-takers supported, at crucial cadences, by the imperial might of whole societies; in their native habitat, they represent a style of musicking that, as Christopher Small observes in his clear-eyed way, "has always been cultivated by holders of power, first in Europe and later in its colonies and outposts."[53]

Is Matsumoto just one of those colonial outposts, and the Suzuki Method no more than a strange and pathetic cargo cult of classical music? Suzuki himself, a rich Japanese factory owner's son who hero-worshiped Mozart, a Buddhist who converted to Catholicism to marry his German wife, might seem an unlikely postcolonialist hero. And yet, in a way that all the self-congratulatory harping on the "Eastern" roots of the minimalist aesthetic in contemporary Western art music can easily obscure, it is here, in the humble pedagogical repetitions of Talent Education, that we can actually hear the musical subaltern speak. As music, Vivaldi is Western to the core, a discourse on the delights and dangers of individual achievement and expression. But within the matrix of Suzuki's repetitive musicking, Western tonal form speaks in quite a different voice. Vivaldi's nervous *soli* disappear into the calm of an all-embracing cosmic *ripieno*, as the discourse of self-actualization becomes a discourse on group solidarity, on selflessness, on bodhisattva-like compassion ("When I listen to Mozart, he seems to envelop me in his great love"), on "the ephemerality of life and how infinitesimal existence must seem in relation to the universe."[54]

From the perspective of Attali's repetitive society, the Suzuki group concert looks like the ultimate liquidation of the subject, a gray-flannel musical conformity whose machine-like repetition heralds death. Suzuki would hardly have understood; in his view the group performance crushed the individual ego to set free what he apostrophized over and over as "the life force" that is "beyond human intellect." If Mozart speaks only in the language of power to Small, perhaps we would be better off listening to Shinichi Suzuki, who heard in the Clarinet Quintet, K. 581, a musical expression of profound equality within "the great soul of Buddhism." If in the West, Mozart and Vivaldi have been trapped in repetition, perhaps only the Zen-like repetition of *Saino-Kyoiku* can set them free.

We repeated ourselves into this culture.

We may — nurtured through love — be able to repeat ourselves out.

━━━

Man does not live in intellect.
Man lives in the wonderful life force.
Sound breathes life
Without form it lives

Shinichi Suzuki

PREFACE

1. See, for instance, the covers of Edward Strickland, *Minimalism: Origins* (Bloomington: Indiana University Press, 1993), gray with black letters; of James Meyer, *Minimalism: Art and Polemics in the Sixties* (New Haven: Yale University Press, 2001), black with white sans serif type and Donald Judd picture; of John Powson, *Minimum* (London, Phaidon, 1996), off-white cloth with title in reverse relief, sans serif, lowercase letters. Keith Potter's *Four Musical Minimalists* (Cambridge: Cambridge University Press, 2000) seems in this company quite flamboyant, with its white cover, black sans serif font, and *two* abstract graphic elements including a red (!) box.

2. See Strickland, *Minimalism*, p. 2.

3. Robert Morris, *Box with the Sound of Its Own Making*, 1961. See Meyer, *Minimalism*, p. 53.

4. Strickland, *Minimalism*, pp. 136–37, 141–45.

5. Milton Babbitt, "Who Cares if You Listen?" *High Fidelity* 8, no. 2 (February 1958): 38–40, 126–27. The composer's chosen title was less inflammatory but no less uncompromising: "The Composer as Specialist."

6. See Richard Crawford's magisterial *America's Musical Life: A History* (New York: W. W. Norton, 2001).

7. Strickland, *Minimalism*, p. 3.

8. "Mr. Hankey the Christmas Poo," *South Park*, Episode 110, first aired on 17 December 1997, my transcription.

9. For one account of the 1973 New York performance of *Four Organs*, see Steve Reich's interview with William Duckworth in Duckworth, *Talking Music: Conversations with John Cage, Philip Glass, Laurie Anderson, and Five Gener-*

ations of American Experimental Composers (New York: G. Schirmer, 1995), pp. 303–4.

INTRODUCTION

The first epigraph is from Jacques Attali, *Noise: The Political Economy of Music,* trans. Brian Massumi (Minneapolis: University of Minnesota Press, 1985), pp. 147–48.

1. The term *musicking* was coined to fill the lack of a generic verb in English by critic Christopher Small; see *Musicking: The Meanings of Performing and Listening* (Hanover, N.H.: University Press of New England, 1998). Small's term is particularly apropos here, since his broad definition of musicking covers listening — and even not-quite listening — as well as more traditionally "musical" activities like composing and performing.

2. Wim Mertens, *American Minimal Music,* trans. J. Hautekiet (New York: Broude, 1983), pp. 123–24. Adorno wrote: "[Stravinsky's] rhythmic procedures closely resemble the schema of catatonic conditions. In certain schizophrenics, the process by which the motor apparatus becomes independent leads to infinite repetition of gestures or words, following the decay of the ego" (Theodor Adorno, *The Philosophy of Modern Music,* trans. Anne G. Mitchell and Wesley V. Blomster [New York: Continuum, 1973], p. 178). It is worth noting that Adorno's later works, in particular "The Aging of the New Music (1955) and "Vers une musique informelle" (1961), show him as anything but a dogmatic partisan of high musical modernism. And yet — Adorno never engaged with minimal music directly, but it seems unlikely that he would have recognized the music of La Monte Young or Steve Reich as anything other than a sad, reactionary liquidation of the musical subject through complete reification of primitive musical material. Adorno's early 1960s ideal of "informal music" sounds like a negation of pulse pattern minimalism *avant le lettre:* "the spontaneous ear, conscious of itself, should resist not just tonal symmetry, but its most sublime derivatives — the predominance of an abstractly maintained pulse, the strong beat, and its negative retention in syncopation" (from "Vers une musique informelle," in Adorno, *Quasi una Fantasia: Essays on Modern Music,* trans. Rodney Livingstone [London: Verso, 1998], pp. 321–22). Though he did not live to read it, his dialectical reaction to Steve Reich's 1970 "Some Optimistic Predictions about the Future of Music" ("The pulse and the concept of a clear tonal center will reemerge as basic sources of the new music") can easily be imagined. See Steve Reich, *Writings on Music 1965–2000* (London: Oxford University Press, 2002), pp. 51–52.

3. Dick Higgins, "Boredom and Danger," *The Something Else Newsletter* 1, no. 9 (December 1968): 1–4, 6.

4. David Schwarz, "Postmodernism, the Subject, and the Real in John Adams's *Nixon in China,*" *Indiana Theory Review* 13, no. 2 (fall 1992): 134; Naomi Cumming, "The Horrors of Identification: Reich's *Different Trains,*" *Perspectives of New Music* 35, no. 1 (winter 1997): 129–52.

5. See Mertens, *American Minimal Music,* pp. 87–92.

6. Attali, *Noise,* p. 128.

7. Attali, *Noise,* p. 126, emphasis in original.

8. Attali, *Noise,* pp. 114–15.

9. Attali, *Noise,* pp. 141, 156–58.

10. "Use-time and exchange-time destroy one another. This explains the valorization of very short works, the only ones it is possible to use, and of complete sets, the only ones worth the effort of stockpiling." Attali, *Noise,* p. 101.

11. Lawrence Kramer, *Music as Cultural Practice, 1800–1900* (Berkeley: University of California Press, 1990), p. 10.

12. Thomas Frank, *The Conquest of Cool: Business Culture, Counterculture, and the Rise of Hip Consumerism* (Chicago: University of Chicago Press, 1997), p. 29.

13. See Vance Packard, *The Hidden Persuaders* (New York: McKay, 1957; reprinted with new introduction and epilogue, New York: Penguin Books, 1981), pp. 23–24.

14. See, for instance, Tom Johnson, "Music for Planet Earth," *The Village Voice,* 4 January 1973; Kyle Gann, *American Music in the Twentieth Century* (New York: G. Schirmer, 1997), p. 353.

15. Johnson coined the name in *The Village Voice,* 7 September 1972. By 1974 he had anointed the "hypnotic form" as one of six "new forms for new music": "Hypnotic pieces may be written for almost any instrumental ensemble, but they must always be rather long, extremely persistent, and highly repetitious. The tempo must be rather fast and must remain exactly the same throughout. The main concern is to lull the listener into a sequence of melodic or rhythmic patterns that shift very gradually as the music progresses. The form sprang up rather suddenly in America in the late 1960s, when Terry Riley's 'In C' became widely known, and several composers launched successful careers writing hypnotic pieces." See Tom Johnson, *The Voice of New Music (New York City 1972–82)* (Eindhoven: Apollohuis, 1989), pp. 44–45, 333–34.

16. For a general discussion in this vein, see David Nicholls, "Transethnicism and the American Experimental Tradition," *Musical Quarterly* 80, no. 4 (winter 1996): 569–94. Nicholls's concept of "transethnicism" — an attempt to absolve, on purely technical grounds, American experimental composers like Cowell, Cage, Harrison, and (presumably) Riley, Reich, and Glass of "Orientalism" — has been comprehensively critiqued by Cecilia Sun, whose study of the performing history of Terry Riley's *In C* provides a useful antidote to Occidental self-congratulation. See "Minimalism's Myths of Origin: Terry Riley's *In C,*" in Cecilia Sun, "Experiments in Musical Performance: Historiography, Politics, and the Post-Cageian Avant-Garde" (Ph.D. thesis, University of California, Los Angeles, 2004).

17. Shunryu Suzuki, *Zen Mind, Beginner's Mind* (New York: Weatherhill, 1970), p. 25.

18. Susan Sontag, "Against Interpretation" (1965), in *Against Interpretation and Other Essays* (New York: Farrar, Straus and Giroux, 1966), p. 7. A previous essay of the present author's devoted quite a bit of space to Sontag as guide to some related meta music-theoretical issues; see Robert Fink, "Elvis Everywhere:

Musicology and Popular Music Studies at the Twilight of the Canon," *American Music* 16, no. 2 (summer 1998): 159–67.

19. Sontag, "Against Interpretation," p. 11, ellipsis in original.

20. Reich, *Writings on Music*, p. 82.

21. Joan La Barbara, "Three by Reich," *High Fidelity/Musical America* 29, no. 6 (June 1980): MA 12.

22. Sontag, "Against Interpretation," pp. 12–13.

23. See Paul Epstein, "Pattern and Process in Steve Reich's *Piano Phase*," *Musical Quarterly* 72, no. 4 (1986): 494–502; Richard Cohn, "Transpositional Combination of Beat-Class Sets in Steve Reich's Phase-Shifting Music," *Perspectives of New Music* 30, no. 2 (1992): 146–77. The corresponding analytical discussions in Keith Potter's *Four Musical Minimalists* (Cambridge: Cambridge University Press, 2000), it must be said, represent a significant advance on these tentative, if pioneering, investigations.

24. See Jonathan Bernard, "The Minimalist Aesthetic in the Plastic Arts and in Music," *Perspectives of New Music* 31, no. 1 (1993): 86–132; and "Theory, Analysis, and the 'Problem' of Minimal Music," in Elisabeth Marvin and Richard Hermann, eds., *Concert Music, Rock and Jazz since 1945* (Rochester, N.Y.: University of Rochester Press, 1996), pp. 259–84.

25. See Edward Strickland, *Minimalism: Origins* (Bloomington: Indiana University Press, 1993), pp. 241–53, for a cogent overview of how musical minimalism got its name.

26. See Strickland, *Minimalism*, p. 10; Tom Johnson, 'The Original Minimalists,' *The Village Voice*, 27 July 1982.

27. Small, *Musicking*, p. 183.

CHAPTER 1: DO IT ('TIL YOU'RE SATISFIED)

Epigraph quoted in Kenny Berkowitz, "Minimal Impact," *Option* 77 (November–December 1997): 52–53.

1. All chart information from Joel Whitburn, *Joel Whitburn Presents Billboard Top 10 Charts 1958–1997* (Menomenee Falls, Wis.: Record Research, 1998).

2. "He seems to be regarded as the main representative of the new wave of classical American music. . . . Many other avant-garde genres are equally good, and it seems too bad that these are often over-shadowed by Reich's sleek, well-marketed product." Tom Johnson, "Steve Reich and 18 Other Musicians," *The Village Voice*, 10 May 1976.

3. Philip Glass, *North Star*, Virgin 91013-2 (1977); Mike Oldfield, *Platinum*, Caroline Records CAROL 1856-2 (1979). Both recordings have been rereleased on CD.

4. Steven Grant and Ira Robbins, "Polyrock" reference article on Trouser Press Web site (www.trouserpress.com).

5. Tom Lee, liner notes to Arthur Russell, *Another Thought*, Point Music CD 438 891-2 (1994). "Is It All over My Face" and the Francis Kervorkian remix of

"Go Bang" can be heard on *Jumpin': Original Full Length Hits from the Disco Underground,* Harmless Records, HURTCDL002 (1997).

6. Richard Sennett, "Twilight of the Tenured Composer," *Harper's* 269 (December 1984): 67.

7. Kristine McKenna, "Philip Glass: The Future Is Now," *Rolling Stone,* 8 March 1979: 19.

8. Robert Coe, "Philip Glass Breaks Through," *New York Times Magazine,* 25 October 1981: 69–70.

9. Quoted in Michael Walsh, "The Heart Is Back in the Game," *Time,* 20 September 1982: 61.

10. Arlene Croce, "Slowly Then the History of Them Comes Out," *The New Yorker,* 30 June 1980: 92, 95.

11. They made Summer laugh too: "Giorgio brought me these popcorn tracks he had recorded and I said, 'What the hell is this, Giorgio?' I finished it sort of as a joke." Interview in Mikal Gilmore, "Donna Summer: Is There Life after Disco?" *Rolling Stone,* 23 March 1978: 15. Actually, "I Feel Love" is technically closer to Steve Reich's early phase pieces: Moroder achieved a freaky "double-time" effect by panning the bass line hard right and left and then using tape delay to put it a half-beat out of phase with itself. The throbbing stereo effect was distinctively futuristic — but, as DJs soon found out, almost impossible to dance to.

12. "[Steve Reich's *Music for Eighteen Musicians* is] a radiant work which for me remains his masterpiece and the high point of ensemble music of the 1970s by composers identified as Minimalist, as *In C* was of the 1960s, and perhaps John Adams's *Fearful Symmetries* of the 1980s." Edward Strickland, *Minimalism: Origins* (Bloomington: Indiana University Press, 1993), p. 233. As for "Love to Love You Baby" and the 22 orgasms, stay tuned.

13. I have discussed at length the general implications of this leveling for both musicology and popular music studies; see "Elvis Everywhere: Musicology and Popular Music Studies at the Twilight of the Canon," *American Music* 16, no. 2 (summer 1998): 135–79. It is worth noting here that the leveling of hierarchies is not something for which musicology can take either credit or blame. My own work simply assumes it as a fact of postmodern mass cultural life — a fact that often makes the job of a cultural critic harder, not easier.

14. "Reich and Glass have lately written what is no more than a pop music for intellectuals, an easy-to-listen-to music free of the rage so marked in black-oriented music and the pop culture of the 1960s. But as far as serious music itself is concerned, the musical and ideological implications of the rise of this new music seem hardly comforting." Samuel Lipman, "From Avant-Garde to Pop" [*Commentary,* 1979], in *The House of Music* (Boston: Godine, 1984), p. 48.

15. Annalyn Swan, "The Spell of Philip Glass," *The New Republic,* 12 December 1983: 31.

16. The complaint that disco and its direct descendent, house music, are "not really black" has been a consistent refrain of African American partisans of funk and rap, often laced with virulent reverse racism and homophobia. As Simon Reynolds points out, "Discophobia wasn't limited to white rockers . . . many blacks despised it as a soulless mechanistic travesty of da funk. . . . Funkateer

critic Greg Tate coined the term 'DisCOINTELPRO' — a pun on the FBI's campaign to infiltrate black radical organizations like the Panthers — to denigrate disco as 'a form of record industry sabotage.'" See Simon Reynolds, *Generation Ecstasy: Into the World of Techno and Rave Culture* (Boston: Little, Brown, 1998), p. 24. Rickey Vincent was making the same accusations as late as 1995, calling disco "color-blind, brain-dead pop," whose ascendance was one of the "harsh realities of white ownership [of black radio]" which led to "nothing short of cultural suicide." See Rickey Vincent, *Funk: The Music, the Rhythm and the People of the ONE* (New York: St. Martin's Press, 1995), pp. 205–15. Trying to whitewash disco's image by comparing it to the music of Caucasians like Reich and Glass would play directly into this defensive (and offensive) trope. Lipman, no friend of black liberation, condescends to minimalism ("an easy-to-listen-to music free of the rage so marked in black-oriented music") in terms that, if applied to disco, could easily have come from the pen of Vincent or Tate.

17. "Capitalist cultural products are most likely to be contradictory at just those points — such as disco — where they are most commercial and professional, where the urge to profit is strongest. . . . The anarchy of capitalism throws up commodities [like disco] that an oppressed group can take up and use to cobble together its own culture." Richard Dyer, "In Defense of Disco" (*Gay Left* 8 [1979]), reprinted in Simon Frith and Andrew Goodwin, eds., *On Record: Rock, Pop, and the Written Word* (New York: Pantheon, 1990), p. 413.

18. Barbara Rose, "A B C Art," *Art in America* (October-November 1965), as reprinted in Gregory Battcock, ed., *Minimal Art: A Critical Anthology* (New York: Dutton, 1968), pp. 296–97.

19. Andrea True Connection, "More, More, More (Pt. 1)," Buddah LP 515 (1976). This paean to sexual and musical repetition reached no. 4 on the Billboard 100 during the week of 17 July 1976.

20. The above epigraph is from La Monte Young, ed., *An Anthology*, 2nd ed. (New York: H. Friedrich, ca. 1970), unpaginated.

21. Arthur Schopenhauer, *The World as Will and Representation* (New York: Dover, 1966), vol. 1, pp. 257–60; Charles Rosen, *The Classical Style* (New York: W. W. Norton, 1972), p. 120. Schenker wrote, "The fundamental line *(Urlinie)* signifies motion, striving towards a goal, and ultimately the completion of this course. In this sense we perceive our own life-impulse in the motion of the fundamental line, a full analogy to our inner life." Heinrich Schenker, *Free Composition (Der freie Satz): Volume III of New Musical Theories and Fantasies*, trans. and ed. Ernst Oster (New York: Longman, 1979), pp. 4–6.

22. Susan McClary, *Feminine Endings: Music, Gender, and Sexuality* (Minneapolis: University of Minnesota Press, 1991), pp. 112–13.

23. Leonard Meyer, *Music, the Arts, and Ideas* (Chicago: University of Chicago Press, 1967), p. 72.

24. Meyer, *Music, the Arts, and Ideas*, p. 83.

25. He later admitted, "Information was scanty, and I was aware of the feeling of breaking dangerous new ground in describing their work in the context of the 'Cage tradition.'" See Wim Mertens, *American Minimal Music*, trans. J. Hautekiet (New York: Broude, 1983), p. 7.

26. Michael Nyman, *Experimental Music: Cage and Beyond*, 2nd ed. (Cambridge: Cambridge University Press, 1999), pp. 4, 30.

27. Nyman, *Experimental Music*, pp. 4, 30.

28. Philip Glass, quoted in Mertens, *American Minimal Music*, p. 79.

29. "Since the beginning of the 17th century, Western music has been characterized by logical-causal development and by climax as the moment of teleological finality. Through contradictions that are dialectically integrated — through harmony, melody, rhythm, density and intensity, etc. — the work creates a physiological tension that grows towards a climax and then dissolves in relaxation. Repetitive music has no such obvious directionality: it does not progress along a straight, logical line but may shift suddenly from one synchrony to the next (Glass), may move through a process of gradual phase shifting (Reich), or may be completely lacking in directionality (Young). In addition, a repetitive work has no real beginning and no real end, but instead a series of random starting and finishing points. Nor is there a gradual building up of tension or evolution towards a climax." Mertens, *American Minimal Music*, p. 102.

30. Mertens, *American Minimal Music*, p. 124.

31. See Sontag, "Against Interpretation" (1965), in *Against Interpretation and Other Essays* (New York: Farrar, Straus and Giroux, 1966), pp. 3–14, and the extended discussion of its implications for popular music studies in Fink, "Elvis Everywhere," pp. 159–67.

32. John Rockwell, "Steve Reich and Philip Glass Find a New Way," *Rolling Stone*, 19 April 1979: 95.

33. Much sensationalized tripe has been written about this subject; for a good scholarly contextualization, see John Blofeld, *The Tantric Mysticism of Tibet* (New York: Dutton, 1970), pp. 226–28.

34. See McClary, "Getting Down off the Beanstalk," in *Feminine Endings*, pp. 122–23, 130–31. Given the extremely distorted reception (in both the popular and the scholarly press) that McClary's criticism has received over the last decade, the following unfortunately does *not* go without saying: McClary does not hold to essentialized notions of male and female sexuality; McClary does not argue that there is essential sexual content in any particular musical gesture; McClary's hermeneutics can in fact be grounded in historical evidence; McClary does not condemn male composers as if the sexually violent scenarios enacted on occasion by their music are somehow "real" and "their fault"; McClary does not condemn goal-directedness in either sex or tonal music out of hand, nor does she ask anyone to eschew either activity. Perhaps the current survey will put another nail in the coffin of what is an absurd conceit: that the sexual hermeneutic of tonal music is the recent and politicized work of a lone musicological gunwoman. For another exhaustive demonstration in the context of Beethoven reception, see the present author's "Beethoven Antihero: Sex, Violence, and the Aesthetics of Failure, or Listening to the Ninth Symphony as Postmodern Sublime," in Andrew Dell'Antonio, ed., *Beyond Structural Listening? Postmodern Modes of Hearing* (Berkeley: University of California Press, 2004), pp. 109–53.

35. Dyer, "In Defense of Disco," pp. 414–15.

36. McClary, *Feminine Endings*, p. 127.

37. Dyer, "In Defense of Disco," p. 415. Dyer is not naive; he is perfectly aware that there is no *essential* link between homosexuality and the kind of whole-body eroticism he values: "We are often even more cock-oriented than non-gays of either sex, and it depresses me that such phallic forms of disco as Village People should be so gay identified." Ironically, it may well be this very phallic thrust that made (and still makes!) the Village People so popular with often unsuspecting straight audiences.

38. Stephen Holden, "Disco: The Medium Is the Message," *High Fidelity* 28, no. 8 (August 1979): 105.

39. Stephen Holden, "Donna Summer's Sexy Cinderella [review]," *Rolling Stone*, 12 January 1978: 54-56.

40. Mertens, *American Minimal Music*, p. 124.

41. The primary texts here — Gilles Deleuze's *Difference and Repetition*, Deleuze and Guattari's *Anti-Oedipus*, Jean-François Lyotard's *Libidinal Economy* — are extraordinarily dense. Good introductory discussions can be found in Brian Massumi, *A User's Guide to Capitalism and Schizophrenia: Deviations from Deleuze and Guattari* (Cambridge, Mass.: MIT Press, 1992), and Eugene W. Holland, *Deleuze and Guattari's Anti-Oedipus: Introduction to Schizoanalysis* (London: Routledge, 1999).

42. See Renata Salecl, *(Per)versions of Love and Hate* (London: Verso, 1998) for a useful survey of the post-Lacanian territory.

43. A foundational text is Hélène Cixous, *Là* (Paris: Gallimard, 1976). An interesting overview appears in Kelly Ives, *Cixous, Irigaray, Kristeva: The Jouissance of French Feminism* (Kidderminster: Crescent Moon, 1996).

44. Slavoj Žižek, *Looking Awry: An Introduction to Jacques Lacan through Popular Culture* (Cambridge, Mass.: MIT Press, 1991), p. 5; Salecl, *(Per)versions of Love and Hate*, p. 63.

45. "From the Summer of Love rhetoric of early UK acid house evangelists to San Francisco's cyberdelic community, from the neo-paganism of Spiral Tribe to the transcendentalism of the Megalopolis/Goa Trance scene, rave has also been home to another 'politics of Ecstasy,' one much closer to the original intent behind Timothy Leary's phrase. Ecstasy has been embraced as one element of a bourgeois-bohemian version of rave, in which the music-drugs-technology nexus is fused with spirituality and vague hippie-punk-anarcho politics to form a nineties would-be counterculture." Reynolds, *Generation Ecstasy*, p. 239. One might add that there are plenty of Marxist ravers too.

46. Roland Barthes, *The Pleasure of the Text*, trans. Richard Miller (New York: Farrar, Straus and Giroux, 1975), p. 14. (Note that *jouissance* is translated in this edition as "bliss.")

47. Carolyn Krasnow, "Fear and Loathing in the 70s: Race, Sexuality, and Disco," *Stanford Humanities Review* 3, no. 2 (autumn 1993): 41, emphasis added.

48. Brian Chin, "A Tom Moulton Mix," liner notes for *The Disco Box*, Rhino CD 75595-4 (1999).

49. Chin, "A Tom Moulton Mix."

50. Brian Chin, "DJ Roundtable," liner notes for *The Disco Box*. The first

speaker is Boston-based DJ Danae Jacovidis; the second is San Francisco DJ Bob Viteritti.

51. Quoted in Mertens, *American Minimal Music,* p. 79.

52. Tim Page, "Music in 12 Parts" (1993), reprinted in Richard Kostelanetz, ed., *Writings on Glass* (New York: G. Schirmer, 1997), p. 100. Lest this be taken as ex post facto pleading, here is Art Lange in 1977: "The first section [of *Music in Twelve Parts*] began in 8/4, then alternated 8/4 and 6/4, then moved into a passage alternating one bar of 3/4 with one bar of 8/4 and one bar of 6/4. The result was a highly dramatic sensation of tension and release; of pushing forward then pulling back." See Art Lange, "The Ancient Avant-Garde Music of Philip Glass," reprinted in Kostelanetz, *Writings on Glass,* p. 89.

53. Michael Nyman, *Musical Times* 112, no. 4 (May 1971): 63–64.

54. Alan Rich, "Down to Essentials," *New York Magazine,* 6 November 1978: 97.

55. "Radio's hottest song right now is also the most lubricious: *Love to Love You Baby,* Donna Summer's marathon of 22 orgasms. Boston-born Donna wrote the lyrics herself. They are stunningly simple — mostly five words repeated 28 times. Donna's message is best conveyed in grunts and groans and languishing moans. Her goal is to make an album 'for people to take home and fantasize in their minds.' First she fantasized all alone in a dark studio, listening to the song's prerecorded track. 'I let go long enough to show all the things I've been told since childhood to keep secret.' She and her promoter, Neil Bogart, the president of Casablanca Records . . . are being hailed as the sex rock pioneers." "Sex Rock," *Time,* 29 December 1975: 39.

56. Most of these tropes and rumors can be found gathered in two magazine profiles from the day. Mikal Gilmore talked to the singer, her managers, and Casablanca's Bogart, watched her perform live, and surveyed the hysteria in "Donna Summer: Is There Life after Disco?" while Charles L. Sanders's piece in the October 1977 *Ebony* is a fascinating look at how the African American community was dealing with a black sexual icon who spoke German, might be transsexual, and dated only white men.

57. Pieter C. van den Toorn, *Music, Politics, and the Academy* (Berkeley: University of California Press, 1993), p. 43.

58. Quoted in Joseph Roddy, "Listening to Glass" (1981), in Kostelanetz, *Writings on Glass,* p. 172.

59. Holden, "Disco: The Medium Is the Message," 105; Tom Johnson, "Philip Glass in Twelve Parts," *The Village Voice,* 13 June 1974; Holden, "Donna Summer's Sexy Cinderella," p. 54.

60. Theodor W. Adorno, "The Radio Symphony. An Experiment in Theory," trans. Susan Gillespie, in Richard Leppert, ed., *Theodor W. Adorno: Essays on Music* (Berkeley: University of California, Los Angeles, 2002), pp. 251–70.

61. See Robert Fink, "Going Flat: Towards a Post-hierarchical Music Theory," in *Rethinking Music,* ed. Nicholas Cook and Mark Everist (New York: Oxford University Press, 1999), pp. 113–20.

62. This pattern of static *plateaus* followed by kinetic *linear ascents* is a basic theoretical model in Robert Fink, "Arrows of Desire: Long Range Linear Struc-

ture and the Transformation of Musical Energy" (Ph.D. diss., University of California, Berkeley, 1994), where it is used to discuss the teleology of music from Rossini and Beethoven to Reich, Glass, and Adams. For a shorter introduction to some of these ideas, see Fink, "Going Flat," pp. 113-21.

63. McClary, *Feminine Endings*, p. 123.

64. *Wired Magazine Presents Music Futurists*, WEA/Atlantic/Rhino BooooHZEK (1999).

65. Interview in William Duckworth, *Talking Music: Conversations with John Cage, Philip Glass, Laurie Anderson, and Five Generations of American Experimental Composers* (New York: G. Schirmer, 1995), pp. 310-11.

66. See Jonathan Bernard, "Theory, Analysis, and the 'Problem' of Minimal Music," in Elisabeth Marvin and Richard Hermann, eds., *Concert Music, Rock and Jazz since 1945* (Rochester, N.Y.: University of Rochester Press, 1996), pp. 275-78. Frank Oteri, writing in the liner notes to the Ensemble Modern's 1999 recording (RCA-Victor Red Seal 09026-68672-2) agrees: "Reich's chords are diatonic pitch groupings consisting of up to six different simultaneous tones, none of which imply functional progression."

67. Steve Reich interview with Jonathan Cott in the liner notes to *Steve Reich: Works 1965-1995* (Nonesuch 79451-2, 1997), p. 33. Reich goes on to describe the *Four Organs* chord in more detail: "You'll find the chord in Debussy and Thelonious Monk — the tonic on top and the dominant on the bottom." In *Music for Eighteen Musicians*, Reich voices the F♯minor-seventh chord just this way at the opening of Section VI — F♯ in the soprano at 597 and C♯ in the bass at 603.

68. See the analyses in Yara Sellin, "DJ: Performer, Cyborg, Dominatrix" (Ph.D. diss., University of California, Los Angeles, 2004).

69. From an interview conducted by Elliot Mintz in *Penthouse*, July 1979 (see www.donna-tribute.com/articles/70/penthous.html). Mintz was evidently disappointed to hear that the sex in "Love to Love You Baby" was simulated, for he pressed Summer on this point. She responded in terms that make it clear that she might well subscribe to Richard Dyer's more Lacanian reading of disco: "[Mintz]: You did all that heavy breathing, faking that orgasm, without thinking any sexual thoughts? [Summer]: I know it sounds funny. During the recording of the record, I had much more romantic thoughts than the record led you to believe. You know, there are ecstatic moments in life that are physical, that are like an orgasm. For a mother, I should think, there are moments — touching her child, realizing that this miracle is hers — that are ecstasy." Summer's evokes in this phallic context the presymbolic mother-child symbiosis — Lacan and post-Lacanians like Kristeva call this the realm of the Imaginary — and, in the Imaginary, the feeling of what sounds ("ecstasy") like female *jouissance*. Highly suggestive, to say the least.

70. Reich, *Writings about Music* (Halifax and New York: Nova Scotia College of Art and Design and New York University Press, 1974); reprinted in *Writings on Music*, p. 81.

71. See *Wired Magazine Presents Music Futurists* and *Machine Soul: An Odyssey into Electronic Dance Music* (Rhino R2-79788, 2000), which feature "I Feel Love" as the first and third track of their respective historical anthologies.

CHAPTER 2: "A COLORFUL INSTALLMENT . . ."

The first epigraph is from Daniel Boorstin, *The Image* (New York: Vintage, 1961), p. 211. The second is Elliott Carter as quoted in Frank Oteri, "In the First Person: Elliot Carter," on the *New Music Box* Web site (www.newmusicbox.org, March 2000). The editorial insertion of "politically" before "correct" is my attempt to clarify Carter's off-the-cuff comment.

1. Interview in Michael Walsh, "The Heart Is Back in the Game," *Time*, 20 September 1982: 60; interview in *High Fidelity* 23, no. 8 (August 1973): MA4.

2. Richard W. Pollay, "The Distorted Mirror: Reflections on the Unintended Consequences of Advertising," *Journal of Marketing* 50 (April 1986). Reprinted in Roxanne Hovland and Gary B. Wilcox, eds., *Advertising in Society: Classic and Contemporary Readings on Advertising's Role in Society* (Lincolnwood, Ill.: NTC Publishing Group, 1989), pp. 437–46. The chart in question appears on pp. 444–45.

3. Frans van Rossum and Sytze Smit, "Louis Andriessen: 'After Chopin and Mendelssohn We Landed in a Mudbath,'" *Keynotes* 28, no. 1 (March 1994): 12.

4. Charles Merrell Berg, "Philip Glass on Composing for Film and Other Forms: The Case of *Koyaanisqatsi*" (1990), in Richard Kostelanetz, ed., *Writings on Glass* (New York: G. Schirmer, 1997), p. 141.

5. Edward Strickland, *Minimalism: Origins* (Bloomington: Indiana University Press, 1993), pp. 1–2.

6. Strickland wrote about later developments within minimalism's popular reception: "It is difficult to say whether New Age music represents the Mantovani or the Sominex of baby-boomers. Its utterly specious claims to expand consciousness, while inducing *unconsciousness*, represent the last gasp of countercultural ideals for refugees to the same suburbs they once fled in youthful derision." *Minimalism*, p. 248.

7. Susan McClary, "Rap, Minimalism, and Structures of Time in Late Twentieth-Century Music," The 1998 Norman and Jane Geske Lecture in the History of the Arts (Lincoln: University of Nebraska–Lincoln College of Fine and Performing Arts, 1998), p. 24.

8. Pollay, "The Distorted Mirror," pp. 465–66. Pollay is no easier on his own colleagues, noting that academic marketing studies, perhaps due to "the immaturity of marketing and consumer behavior as autonomous academic disciplines," have produced "shamefully little" critical work — leaving open the question of whether business academics are "servants to marketing practice rather than scholars of it" (pp. 470–71).

9. Thomas Frank, *The Conquest of Cool: Business Culture, Counterculture, and the Rise of Hip Consumerism* (Chicago: University of Chicago Press, 1997), p. 6.

10. Glass interviewed in William Duckworth, *Talking Music: Conversations with John Cage, Philip Glass, Laurie Anderson, and Five Generations of American Experimental Composers* (New York: G. Schirmer, 1995), p. 337.

11. This is Glass's own rueful recollection. See Kostelanetz, *Writings on Glass*, pp. 20–28.

12. Frank, *Conquest of Cool*, pp. 26, 9.

13. The influence of non-Western musicians (Ravi Shankar on Glass, Ewe drumming on Reich) has been a bone of contention in the critical literature for decades. A particularly telling quote comes from Reich, who actually had the most multicultural contact: "The question often arises as to what influence my visit to Africa had on *Drumming?* The answer is *confirmation*" (Reich, *Writings on Music 1965–2000* [London: Oxford University Press, 2002], p. 58). Discussing *Piano Phase*, he says, "Looking back on the tape pieces that preceded *Piano Phase* I see that they were . . . the gateway to some instrumental music I would never have come to by listening to any other Western, *or for that matter, non-Western music*" (*Writings on Music,* p. 53, emphasis added). There are many places in his writing where Reich does cast non-Western music in a restorative, instructive role for Western musicians, but the influence is always at the technical level — new rhythms and structures — not the political. None of this exonerates Reich and his fellow minimalists from the twin charges of Orientalism and appropriation, of course — but we can assert that Reich and Glass were not, at least at first, *consciously* trying to inhabit some countercultural Eastern utopia. For a more acerbic take on Terry Riley, see Cecilia Sun, "Minimalism's Myths of Origin: Terry Riley's *In C*," in Sun, "Experiments in Musical Performance: Historiography, Politics, and the Post-Cageian Avant-Garde" (Ph.D. diss., University of California, Los Angeles, 2004).

14. Frank, *Conquest of Cool,* p. 29.

15. Strickland writes, "To date Minimal art from the 1960s is rather like dating British Romantic poetry from Tennyson." He sets the high-water mark of "real" minimal music as early as 1964, the year of Terry Riley's *In C* and La Monte Young's *Well-Tuned Piano.* See Strickland, *Minimalism,* pp. 4–10.

16. The coinage is that of *Village Voice* critic Tom Johnson. See "Philip Glass's New Parts" (6 April 1972), and "Changing the Meaning of 'Static'" (7 September 1972). Strickland provides an exemplary survey of the gradual victory of "minimal" over other critical labels for the music of Young, Riley, Reich, and Glass in *Minimalism,* pp. 241–47.

17. The epigraph above is from Suzi Gablik in John Russell and Suzi Gablik, *Pop Art Redefined* (New York: Praeger, 1969), p. 9.

18. Carl Andre, as quoted in Christopher Lasch, *The Minimal Self* (New York: W. W. Norton, 1984), p. 149. Andre's "Equivalent" series consisted of groups of firebricks, arranged in simple two-dimensional formations (1×32; 2×16; 4×8, etc.) on the floor of a gallery. Their purchase by the Tate Gallery in London was the occasion for one of the more notable art scandals of 1960s Britain.

19. Barbara Rose, "A B C Art," *Art in America* (October-November 1965), as reprinted in Gregory Battcock, ed., *Minimal Art: A Critical Anthology* (New York: Dutton, 1968), pp. 296–97.

20. John Russell in John Russell and Suzi Gablik, eds., *Pop Art Redefined* (New York: Praeger, 1969), p. 27.

21. Suzi Gablik in Russell and Gablik, *Pop Art Redefined,* pp. 18–20.

22. Gablik in Russell and Gablik, *Pop Art Redefined,* p. 20.

23. Michael Schudson, "Advertising as Capitalist Realism," in *Advertising, The Uneasy Persuasion: Its Dubious Impact on American Society* (New York:

Basic Books, 1984), reprinted in Hovland and Wilcox, *Advertising in Society*, pp. 74–77, emphasis added.

24. Thus I cannot disagree more strongly with Jonathan Bernard's argument that Glass's music for *Satyagraha* represents a deliberate and cynical attempt to use Pop musical progressions the way Warhol used Pop imagery: "A more cynical interpretation would hold that [Glass] invokes older Western and Eastern practice as a kind of smokescreen, that actually he had the true [banal, debased] quality of his material well in mind and deliberately exploited it, subjected it in fact to monstrous amplification and extension much as Warhol does with his (seemingly) endlessly repeated silkscreen images of such pop icons as Marilyn Monroe and Elvis Presley." The thrust of the present discussion is to uncover such criticism for the putdown that it surely is — Bernard's account all too soon returns to timeworn adjectives like "blatant" and "boring." One can hardly single out Glass as uniquely Pop if one understands the complex interpenetration of hard-edged Pop and Minimalism analyzed by Russell and Gablik. See Jonathan Bernard, "Theory, Analysis, and the 'Problem' of Minimal Music," in Elisabeth Marvin and Richard Hermann, eds., *Concert Music, Rock and Jazz since 1945* (Rochester, N.Y.: University of Rochester Press, 1996), pp. 280–81.

25. Tom Johnson, "Soundings from the West Coast," *The Village Voice*, 30 August 1973. Reprinted in Johnson, *The Voice of New Music (New York City 1972–82)* (Eindhoven: Apollohuis, 1989), p. 98. On La Monte Young's drug connections, see Legs McNeil and Gillian McClain, *Please Kill Me: The Uncensored Oral History of Punk* (New York: Grove Press, 1996), pp. 4–5. Thanks to Kate Bartel for bringing the latter to my attention.

26. Reich, during an interview with Jonathan Cott in the liner notes to Nonesuch 79101-2 (1985).

27. Helen Tworkov and Richard Coe, "First Lesson, Best Lesson," interview with Philip Glass, *Tricycle: The Buddhist Review* 2 (winter 1991), reprinted in Kostelanetz, *Writings on Glass*, pp. 316–27. Glass said, "In my opinion, the term 'trance music' is pejorative. I think that's true of any of those words that link supposed states of consciousness which are either mystical or religious or elevated. . . . Music has its own emotional content that doesn't have to relate to Zen, or Hindu mythology, or peyote. The fact that they all get mixed up in the culture doesn't have very much to do with me. . . . A lot of people hear music and I don't know what the hell they're listening to." Glass quoted in Linda Sanders, "A Classical Distinction," *Saturday Review* 9, no. 6 (May-June 1983): 10.

28. Samuel Lipman, "From Avant-Garde to Pop" [*Commentary*, 1979], in *The House of Music* (Boston: Godine, 1984), p. 41.

29. Vance Packard, *The Hidden Persuaders* (New York: McKay, 1957; reprinted with new introduction and epilogue, New York: Penguin Books, 1981), p. 93.

30. Pollay, "The Distorted Mirror," p. 452.

31. Herbert E. Krugman, "Electroencephalographic Aspects of Low Involvement: Implications for the McLuhan Hypothesis" (Cambridge, Mass.: Marketing Science Institute, 1970), p. 6.

32. Krugman, "Low Involvement," p. 15, emphasis in original.

33. Krugman, "Low Involvement," p. 16.

34. The epigraphs above are from Thorstein Veblen, *The Theory of the Leisure Class* (New York: Macmillan, 1899), reprint ed. (New York: Viking Press, 1934), p. 68; Jean Baudrillard, *Le Système des objets: la consommation des signes* (Paris: Denoel-Gonthier, 1968), translated and edited by James Benedict as *The System of Objects* (London: Verso, 1996), p. 191.

35. "If musicology took its subject matter as seriously as many pop critics take theirs, a central task would be explaining how mere pitches can be made to 'represent' gender or to manipulate desire." Susan McClary, *Feminine Endings: Music, Gender, and Sexuality* (Minneapolis: University of Minnesota Press, 1991), p. 54.

36. Michael Nyman, *Experimental Music: Cage and Beyond,* 2nd ed. (Cambridge: Cambridge University Press, 1999), pp. 4–8.

37. The closest approach would be La Monte Young's 1961 series of Compositions, composed in a single day early in the year, and then postdated to guarantee a predetermined rate of artistic productivity spread out equally through the next 12 months. The critique of industrial production is clear; still, Young's "pieces" were not in fact identical to each other—so the act had more of the Dadaist debunking of artistic "work" than the moralistic (in the Gablik sense) engagement à la Warhol with repetitive commodity culture.

38. Stephen Holden, "Donna Summer's Hot-to-Trot *Bad Girls,*" *Rolling Stone,* 12 July 1979: 72.

39. Lucid overviews of these distinctions are found in Slavoj Žižek, *The Plague of Fantasies* (London: Verso, 1997), pp. 30–39; and Renata Salecl, *(Per)versions of Love and Hate* (London: Verso, 1998), pp. 48–51.

40. Žižek, *Plague of Fantasies,* p. 32.

41. Lasch, *The Minimal Self,* pp. 195–96, 164.

42. Herbert Marcuse, *One-Dimensional Man* (Boston: Beacon Press, 1964), pp. 73–74.

43. Marcuse, *One-Dimensional Man,* p. 57.

44. David Riesman, *The Lonely Crowd: A Study of the Changing American Character,* abridged ed. (New Haven: Yale University Press, 1969), pp. 24–25.

45. See Ingrid Monson, *Saying Something: Jazz Improvisation and Interaction* (Chicago: University of Chicago Press, 1996), for a detailed analysis of the complex negotiations that go into this consensus.

46. Riesman himself seems to imply that ca. 1950 the most oppressed and segregated southern blacks (his shorthand: "delta Negroes") were one of the few remaining populations of tradition-directed characters in North America (*The Lonely Crowd,* pp. 32–34). One assumes that the urban black milieu of jazz performers and audiences would be dominated by those whose incipient inner-direction put them on the difficult path of migration.

47. Riesman, *The Lonely Crowd,* p. 25. See also Keith Potter, *Four Musical Minimalists* (Cambridge: Cambridge University Press, 2000), p. 112, where the same point about the performance practice of *In C* is made without my idiosyncratic cultural spin.

48. See Sun, "Minimalism's Myths of Origin: Terry Riley's *In C.*"

49. Douglas McGregor, *The Human Side of Enterprise* (New York: McGraw-Hill, 1960), pp. 33–49.

50. Thus when Christopher Small reads the modern symphony orchestra as "the very model of an industrial enterprise, permeated through and through with the industrial philosophy," the philosophy he quite devastatingly outlines is but one possible industrial philosophy, one McGregor would immediately have rejected as vintage Theory X: "[orchestral players] accept without question whatever is given them to play . . . leaving others . . . to take responsibility for the performance as a whole . . . the rank and file are rarely consulted about the nature of the product to be made . . . but are required simply to play the notes set before them, under the direction of as dynamic a managerial type as it is possible to engage. Time is money; they are generally unwilling to work extra time without extra pay." Small, *Musicking: The Meanings of Performing and Listening* (Hanover, N.H.: University Press of New England, 1998), pp. 68–69. In practical terms, one can hardly imagine a large symphony orchestra run according to Theory Y — even seeming counterexamples (the Berlin Philharmonic) only democratize certain personnel and organizational decisions, not the performance work itself.

51. Frank, *Conquest of Cool*, pp. 22–23.

52. Jean Baudrillard, *La Société de consommation, ses mythes, ses structures* (Paris: Denoel, 1970); in Mark Poster, ed., *Jean Baudrillard: Selected Writings* (Stanford: Stanford University Press, 1988), p. 35.

53. John Maynard Keynes, "Economic Possibilities for Our Grandchildren," in *The Nation and Athenaeum* (11 and 18 October 1930), reprinted in *Essays in Persuasion* (London: Macmillan, 1931), p. 365.

54. John Kenneth Galbraith, *The Affluent Society* (Boston: Houghton Mifflin, 1958), p. 131.

55. Galbraith, *The Affluent Society*, p. 127.

56. Packard, *The Hidden Persuaders*, pp. 23–24.

57. Packard, *The Hidden Persuaders*, p. 37.

58. Key is gloriously unhinged; witness this amazing passage late in his argument, where he implies that much of the seductive effect of classical music is in fact subliminal: "What, for example, is the difference between a very good violin and a Stradivarius? There is an enormous difference, any concert violinist will maintain, but one which defies conscious empirical description. Is it possible the Stradivarius violin emits subaudible tonalities which are perceived by audiences as vague undefinable [sic] feelings?" Wilson Bryan Key, *Subliminal Seduction: Ad Media's Manipulation of a Not So Innocent America* (New York: Penguin, 1973), p. 193.

59. Baudrillard, *Selected Writings*, p. 42.

60. Baudrillard, *The System of Objects*, p. 189.

61. McClary, *Feminine Endings*, p. 53.

62. Jean Baudrillard, "La genèse idéologique des besoins" (1969), in *Pour une critique de l'économie politique du signe* (Paris: Gallimard, 1972). Translated by Charles Levin "The Ideological Genesis of Needs" as *For a Critique of the Political Economy of the Sign* (St. Louis: Telos Press, 1981); the passage in question appears on page 75 of this edition.

63. Baudrillard, *Selected Writings*, p. 43.

64. Baudrillard, *The System of Objects*, p. 204.

65. Baudrillard, *Selected Writings*, p. 46.

66. Baudrillard, *Selected Writings*, p. 13.

67. Mark Poster, in his translator's introduction to Baudrillard, *Selected Writings*, p. 8.

68. It should go without saying that this postmodern, post-Marxist analysis of art and society leaves little room for the nostalgically self-righteous accusation that Minimalism equals "selling out." Baudrillard's response would be swift and merciless: in consumer society, if you can't sell it, it has no meaning.

69. The epigraph is my translation of the French text (Georges Perec, *Les Choses: une histoire des années soixante* (Paris: Julliard, 1965), p. x. All further references are to the English version: Georges Perec, *Things: A Story of the Sixties/A Man Asleep*, trans. David Bellos and Andrew Leak (Boston: Godine, 1990), p. 65.

70. Perec, *Things*, p. 9.

71. Perec, *Things*, p. 21. For Baudrillard's commentary, see *The System of Objects*, pp. 201–5.

72. Perec, *Things*, pp. 118–19.

73. Perec, *Things*, pp. 59–60, emphasis added.

74. Perec, *Things*, pp. 92–93, emphasis added. The entire passage spans pp. 88–95.

75. See Immanuel Kant, *Critique of Judgment*, SS. 28, "Nature as Might."

76. Perec, *Things*, p. 95.

77. Jean-François Lyotard, *The Postmodern Condition*, trans. Geoff Bennington and Brian Massumi (Minneapolis: University of Minnesota Press, 1992), p. 148.

78. See *The Wire*, January 1998, and the liner notes for Nonesuch 79101-2 (Reich, *The Desert Music*, 1985), 79144-2 (Adams, *The Chairman Dances*, 1987), and 79219-2 (Adams, *Chamber Symphony*, 1994).

79. Brian Eno, quoted on Philip Glass's music in Annalyn Swan, "What's in a Melody," *Time*, 19 June 1978: 62; Joan La Barbara, "Three by Reich," *High Fidelity/Musical America* 29, no. 6 (June 1980): MA13; A. Allenson, "Adaptive, Generative and Interactive Processes in Musical Systems" (1999), www.romandson.com; Alan Rich, "Over and Over and Over and . . ." *New York Magazine*, 25 May 1970: 54.

80. Liner notes for Nonesuch 79101-2 (Reich, *The Desert Music*, 1985).

81. A useful overview of developments in Reich's career can be found in K. Robert Schwarz's two-part article, "Steve Reich: Music as a Gradual Process," *Perspectives of New Music* 19 (1980–81): 373–92, and 20 (1981–82): 225–86.

82. Holograph score of Steve Reich, *Piano Phase* (1967) (London: Universal Edition, 1980).

83. Reich, *Writings on Music*, p. 21.

84. The holograph score is reproduced in Reich, *Writings on Music*, p. 28.

85. Reich first applied digital slow-motion sound to the anguished 1937 radio news commentary ("Oh, the humanity . . .") broadcast during the airship Hindenburg's final moments; see act 1, "Hindenburg," of his *Three Tales* (1998–2002).

86. Steve Reich, "An End to Electronics — Pulse Music, the Phase Shifting Pulse Gate, and Four Organs, 1968–70" (1972), in *Writings on Music*, p. 44.

87. Schwarz ("Steve Reich," pt. 2, p. 241) reports that *Music for Mallet Instruments* has been seen by many critics as a "breakthrough" piece.

88. Reich, *Writings on Music*, p. 76.

89. Jacques Attali, *Noise: The Political Economy of Music*, trans. Brian Massumi (Minneapolis: University of Minnesota Press, 1985), p. 112.

90. Reich, *Writings on Music*, p. 76.

91. Baudrillard, *The System of Objects*, p. 202.

92. Edward Strickland, *American Composers: Dialogues on Contemporary Music* (Bloomington: Indiana University Press, 1991), p. 46.

CHAPTER 3: THE MEDIA SUBLIME

The quote in the epigraph, thanks to its homespun wit and the old-timey gender politics of its punch line, has been a longtime staple of advertising histories and textbooks. But it is not easy to source. Perhaps the earliest modern citation of it is in James Playsted Wood, *The Story of Advertising* (New York: Ronald Press, 1958), p. 241. It is still being quoted in discussions of advertising media planning today; for instance, it opens the chapter called "The Uses of Repetition" in Leo Bogart, *Strategy in Advertising* (Lincolnwood, Ill.: NTC Business Books, 1996), p. 171.

1. This and many other curiosities of advertising's graphic evolution are collected in Frank Presbey, *The History and Development of Advertising* (New York: Greenwood Press, 1968); discussion and illustration of 1850s agate-type process pieces is on pp. 233–43.

2. Hermann Ebbinghaus, *A Contribution to Experimental Psychology*, trans. Henry Ruger and Clara Bussenius (New York: Teacher's College, Columbia University, 1913). A concise account of Ebbinghaus, as well as much subsequent research, is found in James Playsted Wood, *Advertising and the Soul's Belly: Repetition and Memory in Advertising* (Athens: University of Georgia Press, 1961), pp. 21–51. The following discussion is indebted to Wood's useful survey.

3. See Walter Dill Scott, *The Psychology of Advertising* (Boston: Small, Maynard, 1908); quoted in Wood, *Advertising and the Soul's Belly*, pp. 35–36.

4. Edward K. Strong, Jr., *The Psychology of Advertising and Selling* (New York: McGraw-Hill, 1925), p. 340.

5. David Ogilvy, *Ogilvy on Advertising* (New York: Random House, 1983), p. 208. Ogilvy was being disingenuous at best. Advertising agencies have traditionally made their money not by billing services at an hourly rate, but by assessing clients a fixed percentage of the gross advertising they purchase from print media, radio, and television on the client's behalf; the more ads bought, the more profit for the agency. Result: an endless barrage.

6. See the subchapter on Rosser Reeves in Stephen Fox, *The Mirror Makers: A History of American Advertising* (New York: William Morrow, 1984), pp. 187–94.

7. Thomas Frank, *The Conquest of Cool: Business Culture, Counterculture, and the Rise of Hip Consumerism* (Chicago: University of Chicago Press, 1997), p. 105.

8. The epigraph above is from Richard Sennett, "Twilight of the Tenured Composer," *Harper's* 269 (December 1984): 71.

9. William Boddy, *Fifties Television: The Industry and Its Critics* (Urbana: University of Illinois Press, 1990), p. 155. The following discussion draws from this useful source, as well as J. Fred MacDonald, *One Nation under Television: The Rise and Decline of Network TV* (New York: Random House, 1990), and Anthony Smith, ed., *Television: An International History* (Oxford: Oxford University Press, 1995).

10. Fox, *The Mirror Makers*, p. 211; quoted in Boddy, *Fifties Television*, p. 156.

11. "For television, time has an absolute existence independent of any imagery that may or may not be transmitted over its well-defended airwaves and cables. It is television's only solid, a tangible commodity that is precisely divisible into further and further subdivisible homogeneous units, the smallest quantum of which is measured by the smallest segment that could be purchased by a potential advertiser, which is itself defined by the minimum particle required to isolate a salable product from among a variable number of equivalent alternatives." David Antin, "Video: The Distinctive Features of the Medium," in Suzanne Delahunty, ed., *Video Art* (catalog of a 1975 exhibition at the Institute of Contemporary Art, University of Pennsylvania). Reprinted in *Video Art*, ed. Ira Schneider and Beryl Korot (New York: Harcourt, Brace, Jovanovich, 1976), p. 64. (Video artist Beryl Korot, interestingly enough, is married to, and a collaborator with, Steve Reich.) Sponsorship data taken from the Federal Communication Commission's Office of Network Study; see Boddy, *Fifties Television*, pp. 159-60.

12. Antin, "Video," pp. 65-66.

13. Antin, "Video," p. 64.

14. Antin, "Video," pp. 67, 64.

15. Antin is dealing with television ca. 1975, as witnessed by his observation that shots shorter than one second are "very rare and only used for special occasions" (p. 67). Post-MTV television has a quite different style — as does postminimalist music. Jerky, rhythmically jagged cutting in commercials and music videos disrupts the "flow" (see below); but, just as in 1980s hip-hop and 1990s Downtown totalism, these breaks have the paradoxical effect of making that flow even more powerfully visceral.

16. Raymond Williams, *Television: Technology and Cultural Form* (New York: Schocken, 1975), pp. 86, 93.

17. Characteristic are Michael Arlen, "Prufrock before the Television Set," and Todd Gitlin, "Prime Time Ideology: The Hegemonic Process in Television Entertainment," both in Horace Newcomb, ed., *Television: The Critical View*, 3rd ed. (New York: Oxford University Press, 1982), pp. 367-72, 426-54.

18. Dennis Porter, "Soap Time: Thoughts on a Commodity Art Form," *College English* 38, no. 8 (April 1977), quoted in Newcomb, *Television: The Critical View*, pp. 125, 131. The definitive treatment of soap opera as *jouissance* is Martha Nochimson, *No End to Her: Soap Opera and the Female Subject* (Berke-

ley: University of California Press, 1992), whose feminist viewpoint takes eloquent issue with Porter's masculine condescension. She valorizes the antiteleological strategies of female soaps on much the same terms that Susan McClary values minimalism: "Consisting of endless installments, soap opera imagines closure as a threat and in response involuntarily constructs an aesthetic that resists repression. Thus the possibility of imagining HER desire is allowed. . . . Soap opera provides a permanent hiatus from the tyranny of the language of logic and reason — and patriarchy" (159; orthography in original).

19. See Jerry Mander, *Four Arguments for the Elimination of Television* (San Francisco: Quill Press, 1978), pp. 194, 169, emphasis added.

20. Michael Novak, "Television Shapes the Soul" in Leonard L. Sellars and Wilbur C. Rivers, eds., *Mass Media Issues* (New York: Prentice Hall, 1977). Reprinted in Newcomb, *Television: The Critical View*, pp. 336, 338.

21. Sennett, "Twilight of the Tenured Composer," p. 71.

22. Susan McClary, *Feminine Endings: Music, Gender, and Sexuality* (Minneapolis: University of Minnesota Press, 1991), p. 123.

23. Sennett, "Twilight of the Tenured Composer," p. 72.

24. Jim Callaway, executive vice president of Lois Holland Callaway, as quoted in *Media-Scope* (October 1969): 88.

25. Definitions taken from Arnold Barban, Steven Cristol, and Frank Kopec, *Essentials of Media Planning*, 3rd ed. (Lincolnwood, Ill.: NTC Business Books, 1993); and Jack Sissors and Lincoln Bumba, *Advertising Media Planning* (Lincolnwood, Ill.: NTC Business Books, 1996). "M" is, in the manner of Roman numerals, advertising shorthand for 1,000.

26. Hubert A. Zielske, "The Remembering and Forgetting of Advertising," *Journal of Marketing* 13, no. 1 (January 1959): 239–43.

27. Herbert E. Krugman, "Why Three Repetitions May Be Enough," *Journal of Advertising Research* 12, no. 1 (December 1972/January 1973): 47–51; Mike Naples, *Effective Frequency* (New York: Association of National Advertisers, 1979). This study was reissued and updated by Colin McDonald for the Advertising Research Foundation in 1995. See also Bogart, *Strategy in Advertising,* pp. 171–96. For another summary with an exhaustive bibliography, see George E. Belch et al., "Effects of Advertising Communications: Review of Research," *Research in Marketing* 9 (1987): 84–87. A section on repetition, learning, and influence is standard in almost all textbooks of consumer behavior, any of which will provide a concise overview of the basic research on the advertising response function and the threshold effect. See Kenneth E. Runyon and David W. Stewart, *Consumer Behavior and the Practice of Marketing* (Columbus, Ohio: Merrill, 1987), pp. 304–34; and Peter Chisnall, *Marketing: A Behavioural Analysis* (London: McGraw-Hill, 1975), pp. 200–209.

28. Bogart, *Strategy in Advertising,* p. 183.

29. See Dominique M. Hanssens, Leonard J. Parsons, and Randall L. Schultz, *Market Response Models: Econometric and Time Series Analysis,* International Series in Quantitative Marketing 2 (Boston: Kluwer, 1989), pp. 178–83.

30. Don Peppers and Martha Rogers, *The One to One Future: Building Relationships One Customer at a Time* (New York: Doubleday, 1993).

31. Barbara Rose, "A B C Art," *Art in America* (October-November 1965),

as reprinted in Gregory Battcock, ed., *Minimal Art: A Critical Anthology* (New York: Dutton, 1968), p. 296. Marshall McLuhan, *Understanding Media: The Extensions of Man* (New York: McGraw-Hill, 1964), pp. 64–66.

32. McLuhan, *Understanding Media*, p. 65.

33. This terminological discussion follows Bogart, *Strategy in Advertising*, pp. 176–78.

34. Roger Barton, *Media in Advertising* (New York: McGraw-Hill, 1964), p. 423.

35. These plans are reproduced and discussed in Barban, Cristal, and Kopec, *Essentials of Media Planning*, pp. 138–39.

36. Reich makes this claim in William Duckworth, *Talking Music: Conversations with John Cage, Philip Glass, Laurie Anderson, and Five Generations of American Experimental Composers* (New York: G. Schirmer, 1995), p. 296.

37. Steve Reich, *Writings on Music 1965–2000* (London: Oxford University Press, 2002), p. 98.

38. Recorded performances of *In C* are surveyed in Sun, "Minimalism's Myths of Origin." Her extended discussion provides more insights into the piece's structure than the more traditional analytical approach taken by Keith Potter in *Four Musical Minimalists* (Cambridge: Cambridge University Press, 2000), pp. 112–15.

39. See Robert Fink, "Arrows of Desire: Long Range Linear Structure and the Transformation of Musical Energy" (Ph.D. diss., University of California, Berkeley, 1994), for a detailed linear analysis of Reich's 1984 *The Desert Music*, as well as discussions of long-range linear structure in Philip Glass's *Akhnaten* (1984) and John Adams's *Harmonielehre* (1985).

40. See the discussion of the 1946 *Symphony* in Robert Fink, "Going Flat: Towards a Post-hierarchical Music Theory," in *Rethinking Music*, ed. Nicholas Cook and Mark Everist (New York: Oxford University Press, 1999), pp. 113–20.

41. See Jonathan Cross, *Stravinsky's Legacy* (Oxford: Oxford University Press, 1996), pp. 172–74, 179–89. Andriessen's debt was always out in the open, as the composer's own monograph on Stravinsky makes abundantly clear. See Louis Andriessen and Elmer Schoenberger, *The Apollonian Clockwork on Stravinsky*, trans. Jeff Hamburg (Oxford: Oxford University Press, 1989).

42. Herbert E. Krugman, "The Impact of Television Advertising: Learning without Involvement," *Public Opinion Quarterly* 29, no. 3 (fall 1965): 349–56.

43. Krugman, "Impact of Television Advertising," p. 354.

44. Quoted in Michael Walsh, "The Heart Is Back in the Game," *Time*, 20 September 1982: 60.

45. Krugman, "Impact of Television Advertising," p. 355.

46. Claire Polin, "Why Minimalism Now?" in Christopher Norris ed., *Music and the Politics of Culture* (London: Lawrence and Wishart, 1989), pp. 226–39. Polin's rather anemic defense of minimalism as a cultural strategy leaves her vulnerable to Christopher Norris's recontextualizing introduction, where her position is given rather short shrift so that minimalism can be viewed as Adorno's worst nightmare, a "facile escape-route from the problems and complexities of authentic musical experience, into a realm of naïve, uncritical pleasure that

merely reproduces the dominant patterns of present day cultural consumption" (16). One can only ward off this kind of puritanical put-down by taking critical responsibility for the real connections between minimalism and the culture of "industrialized" consumption.

47. Jean Baudrillard, *The System of Objects*, trans. and ed. James Benedict (London: Verso, 1996), pp. 186–89.

48. See Robert Fink, "Going Flat," pp. 108–13, 113–20; and "Beethoven Antihero: Sex, Violence, and the Aesthetics of Failure, or Listening to the Ninth Symphony as Postmodern Sublime," in Andrew Dell'Antonio, ed., *Beyond Structural Listening? Postmodern Modes of Hearing* (Berkeley: University of California Press, 2004), pp. 109–53.

49. The epigraph above is from George W. S. Trow, *Within the Context of No Context* (New York: Atlantic Monthly Press, 1997), p. 43.

50. "Four years ago, for example, we thought *Koyaanisqatsi* was a very political film. Now, it doesn't look that way to me at all." Glass interviewed (1987) in Richard Kostelanetz, ed., *Writings on Glass* (New York: G. Schirmer, 1997), p. 142.

51. Quoted in review of *Koyaanisqatsi* by Merrill Shindler, *Los Angeles Magazine*, April 1983: 96.

52. Charles Sopkin, *Seven Glorious Days, Seven Fun-Filled Nights: One Man's Struggle to Survive a Week Watching Commercial Television in America* (New York: Simon and Schuster, 1968).

53. Jack Lechner, *Can't Take My Eyes Off of You: One Man, Seven Days, Twelve Televisions* (New York: Crown Books, 2000).

54. Bill McKibben, *The Age of Missing Information* (New York: Random House, 1992), pp. 9–10.

55. McKibben, *The Age of Missing Information*, pp. 14, 21.

56. Kostelanetz, *Writings on Glass*, p. 142.

57. Reich, *Writings on Music*, pp. 9–10.

CHAPTER 4: "A POX ON MANFREDINI"

The first epigraph is from Samuel Lipman, "From Avant-Garde to Pop" [*Commentary*, 1979], in *The House of Music* (Boston: Godine, 1984), p. 46.

1. The piece appears on *P. D. Q. Bach: 1712 Overture and Other Musical Assaults*, Telarc 80210 (1989). The liner notes cannot resist a similar poke at the slow pace of Robert Wilson's stagings: "The plot is not as complicated as that of most operas: Einstein feels a sneeze coming on, and takes his handkerchief from his pocket. In Act II, he realizes that he is not going to sneeze after all, and he puts his handkerchief back in his pocket in Act III."

2. Andrew Porter, "Gospel of Peace" [review of *Satyagraha*], *The New Yorker*, 17 August 1981: 102. Michael Walsh used the same trope a year later in *Time*: "The movement [minimalism] actually has old and honorable antecedents. In the first of the 48 preludes and fugues that make up *The Well-Tempered Clavier*, Bach unfolded a serene meditation in the key of C over a placid,

unchanging rhythmic pattern." See Walsh, "The Heart Is Back in the Game," *Time*, 20 September 1982: 61.

3. "I was someone who had come from loving jazz, Bach, and Stravinsky. That's really why I became a composer. It was that kind of music which brought me to tears, and nothing else. Still is." Steve Reich interview in William Duckworth, *Talking Music: Conversations with John Cage, Philip Glass, Laurie Anderson, and Five Generations of American Experimental Composers* (New York: G. Schirmer, 1995), p. 300. For Reich on his tastes at 14, see Annalyn Swan, "The Rise of Steve Reich," *Newsweek*, 29 March 1982: 56.

4. Tom Johnson, "Philip Glass's New Parts," *Village Voice*, 6 April 1972: 42; Allen Shawn, "Music: Contemporary American Composers," *The Atlantic* 274, no. 4 (April 1981): 117.

5. Joseph McClellan, "Pachelbel's Simple Success," *The Washington Post*, 2 December 1984.

6. The concerts, which counterpoised music of Arvo Pärt, Steve Reich, Philip Glass, and John Adams with that of Bach and Handel, took place on 20–22 January 1997; *Perceptible Processes: Minimalism and the Baroque*, edited by Claudia Swan, was published in New York by Eos, that year. Scheffer's quote is on p. iv.

7. Scheffer, Foreword to *Perceptible Processes*, p. iv.

8. Ben Yarmolinsky, "Minimalism and the Baroque," in *Perceptible Processes*, pp. 61–72.

9. David Paul, "Steve Reich," *Seconds* 47 (1998).

10. For an exceptionally trenchant survey of this kind of Bach reception see Theodor W. Adorno, "Bach Defended against His Devotees," in *Prisms*, trans. William Weber (Cambridge: Cambridge University Press, 1981), pp. 133–46.

11. Quoted in Swan, *Perceptible Processes*, p. 81. Adams had reason to worry. Justin Davidson, reviewing the Eos concert for *Newsday*, found *Shaker Loops* "vaguely reminiscent of a concerto grosso, stretched out and stripped of the essential baroque element of drama" ("Minimalists Take Bach to the Future," *New York Newsday*, 25 January 1997).

12. Peter G. Davis, "Minorities, Minimalism, and Melodrama," *New York Magazine*, 11 October 1982: 90.

13. Harold C. Schonberg, "Plumbing the Shallows of Minimalism," *New York Times*, 21 February 1985.

14. Joshua Kosman, "Philharmonia's Latest Discovery: Ingenious Work Stands Out at Concert," *San Francisco Chronicle*, 16 October 2000.

15. The first epigraph is from Lipman, "From Avant-Garde to Pop," in *The House of Music: Art in an Era of Institutions* (Boston: Godine, 1984), pp. 45–46. The second is advertising copy from a generic Columbia record sleeve of the late 1960s.

16. David Morton, *Off the Record: The Technology and Culture of Sound Recording in America* (New Brunswick, N.J.: Rutgers University Press, 2000), pp. 68–72. "Live" is in scare quotes because, as Morton points out, radio networks had been surreptitiously using transcription discs and magnetic tapes since the 1930s to time-shift supposedly live programming and save money.

17. Edward Wallerstein, "Creating the LP Record," *High Fidelity* 26, no. 4 (April 1976): 56–61.

18. Morton, *Off the Record*, p. 38.

19. Craig Pittman, "Technology's Orphans Series: Discovery," *St. Petersburg Times,* 16 March 1993.

20. Roland Gelatt, "Pangs of Progress," *High Fidelity* 8, no. 1 (January 1958): 40.

21. Joseph Lanza, *Elevator Music: A Surreal History of Muzak, Easy-Listening, and Other Moodsong* (New York: Picador, 1994).

22. Ferris Benda, Liner notes for The Melachrino Strings, *Music for Relaxation* (Moods in Music), a "New Orthophonic" High-Fidelity Recording, RCA-Victor LPM-1001 (1958), emphasis added.

23. Tom O'Regan has linked this new repetitive possibility to ever-shortening cycles of popular taste: "the durable nature of the new records permitted both the radio station and the consumer to play the record a potentially infinite number of times. This enabled a greater recognition value to become associated with a particular record as sustained re-playings over shorter and shorter time intervals developed. As a consequence, the technology that seemed at one level to promise the kind of perdurance previously associated with books was integral to the exhaustion of records over a shorter period of time." See "Radio Daze: Some Historical and Technical Aspects of Radio," *Continuum: The Australian Journal of Media and Culture* 6, no. 1 (1992): 29–30. Playing a shellac recording as little as two times in a row on an old turntable using a heavy-tracking steel needle can be enough to ruin it — the repeated friction generates enough heat to weaken the groove walls. Collectors of 78 rpm records advise playing a given record no more than once every 24 hours.

24. Joseph Braunstein, liner notes for Hoffman, *Giuliani Mandolin Quartets,* Turnabout Stereo TV 34016S.

25. Jacques Barzun, "The Art, and Pleasure, of Listening," notes to *The Story of Great Music: The Baroque Era,* Time-Life Records TL-1/144-TL4/144.

26. John Cage, *Silence* (Cambridge, Mass.: MIT Press, 1966), p. 93.

27. See Roland Gelatt, *The Fabulous Phonograph* (Philadelphia: Lippincott, 1954), pp. 179–84, 200–201. Incidentally, this makes most arguments about tempos speeding up to "fit" works onto four-minute 78 rpm sides suspect before about 1925.

28. David Hamilton, "Some Thoughts on Listening to Records," in H. Wiley Hitchcock, ed., *The Phonograph and Our Musical Life: Proceedings of a Centennial Conference,* I.S.A.M. Monographs 14 (New York: Institute for Studies in American Music, ca. 1980), pp. 66–67.

29. See Richard Taruskin, "The Pastness of the Present and the Presence of the Past," in Nicholas Kenyon, ed., *Authenticity and Early Music* (Oxford: Oxford University Press, 1988), pp. 137–210.

30. Quoted in Paul, "Steve Reich." In this context it is worth noting that Steve Reich's first appearance on a symphony program was when Michael Tilson Thomas yoked *Four Organs* to other pieces that used "multiples": Bartók's *Music for Strings, Percussion, and Celesta,* the Liszt *Hexameron* (six pianos), and — shades of the barococo! — a J. C. Bach *Sinfonia-Overture* for two orches-

tras (see Edward Strickland, *Minimalism: Origins* [Bloomington: Indiana University Press, 1993], pp. 221–22).

31. These comments are taken from Canby's annotations of Nonesuch H71017, H71042, and H71079.

32. Nathan Broder, "Music for the Age of Calorie Counters," *High Fidelity* 10, no. 8 (August 1960): 29.

33. Abraham Veinus, notes to *L'estro harmonico*, Vanguard SRV 143.

34. R. D. Darrell, notes to Nonesuch H71066; Canby, notes to Nonesuch H71017, emphasis added.

35. Darrell, notes to Nonesuch H71066.

36. Canby, notes to Nonesuch H71017; Darrell, notes to Nonesuch H71066.

37. Jacques Barzun, *God's Country and Mine: A Declaration of Love Spiced with a Few Harsh Words* (Boston: Little, Brown, 1954), quoted in Roland Gelatt, *The Fabulous Phonograph: From Tin Foil to High Fidelity* (Philadelphia: Lippincott, 1955), pp. 301–2.

38. C. G. Burke, "Repertory Unlimited," *High Fidelity* 1, no. 1 (summer 1951): 25–28.

39. Gelatt, "The Pangs of Progress," pp. 39–41.

40. H. C. Robbins Landon, "A Pox on Manfredini," *High Fidelity* 11, no. 6 (June 1961): 38–39, 86–87; Paul Henry Lang, "A Second Look at Manfredini," *High Fidelity* 12, no. 5 (April 1963): 57–59; Milton Babbitt, "Who Cares if You Listen?" *High Fidelity* 8, no. 2 (February 1958): 38–40, 126.

41. Robbins Landon, "A Pox on Manfredini," pp. 38–39.

42. William Livingstone, "Music for Yuppies," *Stereo Review* 49, no. 6 (June 1984): 54–56, 100. Livingstone takes the lead of *The Yuppie Handbook* (1984), in which the prototypical Young Urban Professionals start their day with Pachelbel on the clock-radio/cassette — but adds his own fillip: "[the Jean-François Paillard version] now belongs on a walnut-veneered shelf. It is far too bloated for Yuppies, who are devoted to less caloric *nouvelle cuisine* and the pursuit of physical perfection through aerobic exercise. [We] recommend the leaner performance — on original instruments, of course — by Christopher Hogwood and the Academy of Ancient Music." Music for the Age of Calorie Counters, indeed!

43. Samuel Lipman, *"Einstein's Long March to Brooklyn"* [*The New Criterion*, February 1985], in *Arguing for Music, Arguing for Culture* (Boston: Godine, 1990), pp. 178–80.

44. "A Pox on Manfredini," passim.

45. Heinrich Schenker, *Free Composition (Der freie Satz): Volume III of New Musical Theories and Fantasies*, trans. and ed. Ernst Oster (New York: Longman, 1979), p. 3.

46. See Robert Fink, "Going Flat: Towards a Post-hierarchical Music Theory," in *Rethinking Music*, ed. Nicholas Cook and Mark Everist (New York: Oxford University Press, 1999), pp. 132–37.

47. Andrew Porter, "Patterns," *The New Yorker* (6 November 1978): 187. Porter consoles himself with the reflection that "Beethoven and Reich seem to have worked at some of the same 'problems,'" and concludes positively: "There is substance beneath" (188). Annalyn Swan, "The Spell of Philip Glass," *The New Republic* (12 December 1983): 31.

48. Gelatt, *The Fabulous Phonograph*, p. 301.
49. Burke, "Repertory Unlimited," p. 25.
50. Gelatt, "Pangs of Progress," p. 40.
51. Lang, "Another Look at Manfredini," pp. 58, 59.
52. Igor Kipnis, "Baroque at Flood Tide," *HiFi-Stereo Review* 15 (December 1965): 110–11.

53. As I have pointed out elsewhere, these anxieties also resonate with a contemporaneous set of anxieties — fear of the masses, fear of pleasure, fear of the loss of self — painstakingly documented within Weimar culture by Klaus Theweleit, whose two-volume compendium of *Male Fantasies* exhaustively catalogs the violent imagery and rhetoric of *"Freikorps* culture," the extreme, often paramilitary right wing of German society after the First World War. (Klaus Theweleit, *Male Fantasies*, trans. Erica Carter and Chris Turner, has been published in two volumes [vol. 1: *Women, Floods, Bodies, History;* vol. 2: *Male Bodies: Psychoanalyzing the White Terror*] by the University of Minnesota Press in 1987 and 1989. These are a translation of *Männerphantasien*, 2 vols., published by Verlag Roter Stern in 1977 and 1978.) Theweleit usefully provides a concordance of the imagery that these "soldier-males" used to describe their psychic and political struggles. An entire chapter is devoted to the master metaphor: "Floods, Bodies, History." In *Freikorper* literature threats to the ego are repeatedly analogized to liquid (water, blood, mire) in violent motion: "In the east, coming from the Baltic, the Red wave surged onward"; "shame and betrayal, filth and misery rose higher around us, we could practically have drowned in it"; "the Red flood brought all the worst instincts to the surface." (See Theweleit, pp. 229–49. I pick these examples at random. Theweleit provides literally thousands of such citations.) Theweleit, following Deleuze and Guattari, reads this pervasive flood imagery as indexing the breakdown of both internal and external boundaries: the outer collapse of social institutions, setting free the "Red Flood," is mirrored by an inner collapse of ego structure, setting free intense libidinal energies, fugue states, the self-annihilating "streaming flows" of desiring-production familiar to any reader of the *Anti-Oedipus.* "Drowning" in this flood (the swamping of the ego by inner and outer flows) is a terrifying possibility. At the same time, such drowning is intensely seductive: overwhelmed by the mass, one could just let go. As Theweleit points out, soldier-males saw themselves standing rigid against the rising tide: "The defensive passages are consistently organized around the sharp contrast between summit and valley, height and depth, towering and streaming. Down below: wetness, motion, swallowing up. Up on the height: dryness, immobility, security" (p. 249). Of course, I am aware of the immense gulf in *gravitas* between the physical violence of Weimar protofascism and the rhetorical violence of the barococo backlash; still, the intensity of Robbins Landon's homophobic disgust, with its Spenglerian intimations of cultural collapse, might argue that he, like Theweleit's soldier-males, felt an answering torrent of illicit pleasure arising within: "To collide with a red flood means death; the solid dissolves (whether the flood comes from within or without). Within this process the desire for collision seems to be as strong as the fear of it" (p. 234). For my discussion of Schenker, Theweleit, and *Freikorps* culture, see Fink, "Going Flat," pp. 133–36.

54. Lawrence Shames, "Listen to John Adams," *Esquire* 102 (December 1984): 160.

55. Swan, "The Spell of Philip Glass," pp. 28, 31.

56. Walsh, "The Heart Is Back in the Game," p. 62.

57. Tim Page, "Framing the River: A Minimalist Primer," *High Fidelity/Musical America* 31, no. 11 (November 1981): 65.

58. Reich, "Music as a Gradual Process," in *Writings about Music* (Halifax and New York: Nova Scotia College of Art and Design and New York University Press, 1974); reprinted in *Writings on Music 1965–2000* (London: Oxford University Press, 2002), p. 34.

59. Robbins Landon, "A Pox on Manfredini," p. 87.

60. The epigraph above is from Richard Sennett, "The Twilight of the Tenured Composer," *Harper's* 269 (December 1984): 72.

61. Hitchcock, *The Phonograph and Our Musical Life*, p. 16.

62. Schonberg, "Plumbing the Shallows of Minimalism"; Bayan Northcott, "Radio Roundup," *The Independent*, 11 August 1995; Lipman, "Avant-garde to Pop"; Robbins Landon, "A Pox on Manfredini."

63. Robbins Landon, "A Pox on Manfredini," p. 38.

64. Jacques Attali, *Noise: The Political Economy of Music*, trans. Brian Massumi (Minneapolis: University of Minnesota Press, 1985), pp. 111–12. Attali's four models of music in society — sacrificing, representing, repeating, and composing — are laid out concisely on pp. 4–5.

65. Robbins Landon, "A Pox on Manfredini," p. 39.

66. Andrew Porter, "Many-Colored Glass," *The New Yorker* (13 December 1976): 166.

67. Brian Eno, liner notes to *Music for Airports: Ambient 1*, AMB 001 (1978).

68. Brian Eno, liner notes to *Discreet Music*, EEG CD 23 (1975).

69. The article is reprinted in [Sir Edward Montague] Compton Mackenzie, *My Record of Music* (New York: Putnam, 1955), pp. 100–113. Cobbett was an early patron of Mackenzie's "National Gramophonic Society," which sold recordings of complete chamber works by subscription through the 1920s and 1930s. A fascinatingly eccentric millionaire, Cobbett maintained a private string quartet, which Mackenzie professed not to envy by virtue of his beloved gramophone.

70. Mackenzie, *My Record of Music*, pp. 106–7.

71. Mackenzie, *My Record of Music*, p. 34.

72. Tia DeNora, *Music in Everyday Life* (Cambridge: Cambridge University Press, 2000), p. 59.

73. DeNora, *Music in Everyday Life*, p. 59.

74. DeNora, *Music in Everyday Life*, p. 41.

75. Johnson, "Philip Glass's New Parts."

76. Susan McClary, *Feminine Endings: Music, Gender, and Sexuality* (Minneapolis: University of Minnesota Press, 1991), p. 118–19.

77. Porter, "Many-Colored Glass," p. 166.

78. Elisabeth LeGuin, "Uneasy Listening," *repercussions* 3, no. 1 (spring 1994): 6.

79. Christopher Lasch, *The Minimal Self* (New York: W. W. Norton, 1984), p. 152.

80. Annahid Kassabian, "UBISUB: Ubiquitous Listening and Networked Subjectivity," *ECHO* 3, no. 2 (fall 2001), www.humnet.ucla.edu/echo; DeNora, *Music in Everyday Life*, pp. 149–50.

81. DeNora, *Music in Everyday Life*, p. 148.

82. Steve Reich, "Music as a Gradual Process," in *Writings* (1974); reprinted in *Writings on Music*, p. 36.

83. Theodor W. Adorno, *Sound Figures* (Stanford: Stanford University Press, 1999), p. 14; quoted in DeNora, *Everyday Life*, p. 149.

84. Lanza, *Elevator Music*, p. 5.

CHAPTER 5: "I DID THIS EXERCISE 100,000 TIMES"

The first epigraph is from Shinichi Suzuki, "Inner Strength," *Talent Education Journal* 13 (1983): 22. The second epigraph is from Shunryu Suzuki, *Zen Mind, Beginner's Mind* (New York: Weatherhill, 1970), p. 72.

1. See Andrew Porter, "Violent Vivaldi," *The New Yorker,* 19–26 February 2001, for a trenchant comparison of Giardino's Vivaldi with that of Neville Marriner and his Academy of St. Martin's-in-the-Fields; Porter finds Marriner's barococo "smooth, pleasant, and slightly nauseating" (226).

2. Roland Gelatt, *The Fabulous Phonograph* (Philadelphia: Lippincott, 1954), p. 301.

3. Timothy Day, *A Century of Recorded Music: Listening to Musical History,* (New Haven: Yale University Press, 2000), p. 97.

4. Quoted in Roland Gelatt, "Pangs of Progress," *High Fidelity* 8, no. 1 (January 1958): 41.

5. Gelatt, "Pangs of Progress," p. 40.

6. See Frederic Dorian, *The History of Music in Performance* (New York: W. W. Norton, 1942), pp. 336–43.

7. "The owner of the then newly founded L'Oiseau-Lyre record label came to their first concert in the Church of St. Martin-in-the-Fields. He signed the new ensemble on the spot. 'We immediately recorded all those Italian ice-cream merchants — Manfredini, Corelli, and so on,' Marriner recalls. 'So in one leap we had gone from being a friendly society to something almost professional.' " Anthony Kirby, "Sir Neville Marriner: Beyond the Academy," *La Scena Musicale* 5, no. 9 (1 June 2000) (Web site).

8. Day, *Recorded Music*, p. 28.

9. See Richard Taruskin, "The Pastness of the Present and the Presence of the Past," in Nicholas Kenyon, ed., *Authenticity and Early Music* (Oxford: Oxford University Press, 1988), pp. 137–210.

10. The epigraph above is as quoted in Eric Madsen, "The Genesis of Suzuki: An Investigation into the Roots of Talent Education" (M.A. thesis, McGill University, 1990), pp. 116–17.

11. The following discussion is based on: Shinichi Suzuki, *Nurtured by Love*

(Smithtown, N.Y.: Exposition Press, 1969); Clifford A. Cook, *Suzuki Education in Action* (Smithtown, N.Y.: Exposition Press, 1970); Evelyn Hermann, *Shinichi Suzuki: The Man and His Philosophy* (Athens, Ohio: Senzay, 1981); and Madsen, "The Genesis of Suzuki." More general insights into Suzuki and Japanese ways of learning can be found in Thomas P. Rohlen and Gerald K. LeTendre, eds., *Teaching and Learning in Japan* (Cambridge: Cambridge University Press, 1996).

12. Suzuki, *Nurtured by Love*, pp. 78–79.

13. From Suzuki's 1963 address to the International Society for Music Education; in Hermann, *Shinichi Suzuki*, p. 136.

14. Madsen, "Genesis of Suzuki," p. 97.

15. Suzuki, *Nurtured by Love*, p. 107.

16. Rohlen and LeTendre, *Teaching and Learning in Japan*, p. 373.

17. Cook, *Suzuki Education*, pp. 42–43.

18. Cook, *Suzuki Education*, p. 75.

19. Madsen, "Genesis of Suzuki," pp. 84–85.

20. Tony Conrad, liner notes to *Early Minimalism, Volume One*, "Table of the Elements 33" (1997), pp. 16, 21; Philip Glass, *Music by Philip Glass* (New York: Harper & Row, 1987), p. 43.

21. "In its transplantation to the United States, the Suzuki Method has so completely lost its original spiritual aspects and character-molding techniques that few American teachers or parents are even aware of their existence. The method focuses on the concrete task of teaching a child to play an instrument." Lois Peak, "The Suzuki Method of Music Instruction," in Rohlen and LeTendre, *Teaching and Learning in Japan*, p. 365.

22. The term is analogous to other, more traditional "ways" of Japanese culture: *kyu-do* (archery), *cha-do* (tea ceremony), *ken-do* (swordsmanship). See Madsen, "The Genesis of Suzuki," p. 135.

23. "Invasion from the Orient," *Time* 90, no. 18 (3 November 1967): 32. To be fair, this quote seems a paraphrase of rationalizations attributed to the expatriate Japanese Talent Educator Suzuko Hillyer by Clifford Cook (*Suzuki Education*, pp. 91–92).

24. D. Chapman, "Every Child a Prodigy," *Look*, 28 November 1967: M26–28.

25. "Fiddling Legions," *Newsweek*, 23 March 1964: 73.

26. Peak, "The Suzuki Method," p. 352. Japanese Suzuki teachers often refer to the process without embarrassment as "indoctrination."

27. Richard Coff, "Suzuki Violin versus Traditional Violin: A Suzuki Teacher's View," www.suzuki-violin.com/suzuki_violin_vstraditionalviolin.htm; Madsen, "The Genesis of Suzuki," p. 62.

28. Cook, *Suzuki Education*, p. 67; Coff, "Suzuki Violin." In Japan the nascent tape recorder was indeed crucial in creating a truly ubiquitous music: "Many of the mothers in Matsumoto taped the records onto long-playing tapes so that the child could hear the same record over and over without turning the record over. Japanese houses are small, so when the mother plays a tape or record for the child, he can hear it no matter where he is in the house." William Starr, *The Suzuki Violinist* (Knoxville, Tenn.: Kingston Ellis Press, 1976), p. 24.

29. Peak, "The Suzuki Method," pp. 358–62.

30. Suzuki clearly thought this way. "Forty years ago, I accepted two young children as my violin students for experiment. They were nurtured by listening to Kreisler and Thibaud on records at home every day. One boy, who was four years old at that time, is now a professor at Curtis School of Music . . . the other boy, who was three, is now concertmaster of the Berlin Radio Symphony. *It might be said that Kreisler and Thibaud were really their teachers, and I myself was just an assistant.*" Quoted in Hermann, *Shinichi Suzuki*, p. 236, emphasis added.

31. Klaus Theweleit, *Male Fantasies*, trans. Erica Carter and Chris Turner (Minneapolis: University of Minnesota Press, 1987), vol. 1, p. 211.

32. Steve Reich, *Writings on Music 1965–2000* (London: Oxford University Press, 2002), pp. 22–24, emphasis added.

33. Starr, *The Suzuki Violinist*, p. 108.

34. Hermann, *Shinichi Suzuki*, pp. 101–2.

35. Cook, *Suzuki Education*, p. 73. He goes on: "In working to jack up the tempo, [Hiroko] often said the children play fast in Japan. (I have noticed that a Japanese child frequently tends to go faster in a hard spot, instead of slacking off in such a place.)" (p. 81).

36. The vaudevillian ne plus ultra: "On a mock recital program, the Fiocco 'Allegro' and Gossec 'Gavotte' were played by Eiko Numanami, violin. Eiko Suzuki bowed, and Kazuko Numanami fingered. The second piece they played while fluttering Japanese fans in their free hands. This brought them a standing ovation." Cook, *Suzuki Education*, p. 87.

37. Even the most sympathetic Western observers related to Suzuki's Japanese students as if they were products of the Japanese electronics industry: "I often thought that [Eiko's] playing worked on the transistor principle — it came on right away — not like a tube that must warm up before it gives a picture." Cook, *Suzuki Education*, p. 85.

38. The epigraph above is from Suzuki, *Zen Mind, Beginner's Mind*, p. 35.

39. Cook, *Suzuki Education*, p. 73.

40. Quoted in Cook, *Suzuki Education*, p. 76.

41. A useful overview of Buddhist transmission in twentieth-century America is found in Rick Fields, *How the Swans Came to the Lake: A Narrative History of Buddhism in America* (Boston: Shambhala, 1992).

42. D. T. Suzuki, *Living by Zen* (London: Rider, 1950), p. 165.

43. D. T. Suzuki, *Zen and Japanese Culture* (first published as *Zen Buddhism and Its Influence on Japanese Culture*, 1938), 2nd ed. (New York: Pantheon, 1959; reprinted, Princeton: Princeton University Press, 1970).

44. Suzuki, *Zen Mind, Beginner's Mind*.

45. Shinichi Suzuki refers several times in *Nurtured by Love* (pp. 34, 74) to himself as a student of Dogen, the mythic monastic originator of the Soto lineage. According to Hermann, Suzuki studied with his mother's uncle, Fuzan Asano, who was a professor at Senshu University and later the head priest of Chuzenji Temple. Hermann, *Shinichi Suzuki*, p. 15.

46. Suzuki, *Nurtured by Love*, p. 95. We should note here that Suzuki appears to have had a Rinzai-style moment of sudden enlightenment while listening to the Klingler quartet's performance of the Mozart Clarinet Quintet in

1920s Berlin: "An indescribable, sublime, ecstatic joy had taken hold of my soul. I had been given a glimpse of Mozart's high spiritual world. Through sound, for the first time in my life I had been able to feel the highest pulsating beauty of the human spirit. . . . I, a human being, had gone beyond the limits of this physical body" (pp. 92–93). The forgoing is undoubtedly why the entire thrust of Suzuki's 10 books of instruction is toward the performance of Mozart violin concertos.

47. Shinichi Suzuki, "Ability Is Not Inborn," *Talent Education Journal* 27 (winter 1987): 42.

48. Madsen, "The Genesis of Suzuki," p. 105.

49. Shinichi Suzuki, "Ability Development in Music," *Talent Education Journal* 34 (summer 1989): 41.

50. This performance is referenced and contextualized in an excellent overview by David W. Bernstein, "John Cage and the 'Project of Modernity': A Transformation of the Twentieth-Century Avant-Garde," in the online journal *Corner* 3 (fall 1999–spring 2000), www.cornermag.org/corner03/index.htm.

51. The epigraph above is from Suzuki, *Nurtured by Love*, p. 93.

52. Susan McClary, *Conventional Wisdom: The Content of Musical Form* (Berkeley: University of California Press, 2000), pp. 81–82.

53. Christopher Small, *Musicking: The Meanings of Performing and Listening* (Hanover, N.H.: University Press of New England, 1998), p. 220.

54. Suzuki, *Nurtured by Love*, pp. 92–96. These and the Suzuki quotations that follow can be found on these pages.

Illustrations

FIGURES

MUSIC EXAMPLES

Index

Text: 10/13 Sabon
Display: Franklin Gothic
Compositor: BookMatters, Berkeley
Indexer: Kevin Millham
Printer and Binder: Thomson-Shore, Inc.